CHRISTMAS ON THE FARM

A Collection of Favorite Recipes,
Stories, Gift Ideas, and Decorating Tips
from *The Farmer's Wife*

EDITED BY LELA NARGI

First published in 2011 by Voyageur Press, an imprint of MBI Publishing Company, 400 First Avenue North, Suite 400, Minneapolis, MN 55401 USA

Voyageur Press titles are also available at discounts in bulk quantity for industrial or sales-promotional use. For details write to Special Sales Manager at MBI Publishing Company, 400 First Avenue North, Suite 400, Minneapolis, MN 55401 USA.

To find out more about our books, visit us online at www.voyageurpress.com.

ISBN-13: 978-0-7603-4638-9

Editor: Melinda Keefe
Design Manager: Katie Sonmor
Designed by: Helena Shimizu
Cover designed by: Mighty Media

Cover image: © *H. Armstrong Roberts/ClassicStock*

On the endpapers (from left to right):
© *Constance Bannister/Constance Bannister Corp./Getty Images*
© *D. Corson/ClassicStock/Alamy*
© *Nina Leen/Time & Life Pictures/Getty Images*
© *Evans/Hulton Archive/Getty Images*
© *H. Armstrong Roberts/ClassicStock/Alamy*
© *H. Armstrong Roberts/ClassicStock*
© *H. Armstrong Roberts/ClassicStock/Alamy*

CONTENTS

Introduction **5**

Cooking the Big Dinner **9**

To Start **11**

Main Courses **23**

Side Dishes **36**

Desserts **57**

Making Festive Gifts and Decorations **81**

Candy, Cookies, and Cakes **83**

Other Gifts **117**

Decorations **151**

After-Dinner Holiday Entertainment **167**

A Few Games to Enliven the Party **168**

Stories of and for Christmas **174**

Index **219**

INTRODUCTION

What Is Christmas?
By Edith C. Wherry • December 1936

A tickled feeling,
A delighted squealing,
Surprises, gifts and a Christmas greeting:
A lot of jokes
And jolly folks
Good dinners and families meeting.
A tree, a bell,
And a spicy smell,
A knobby bundle and a silver string;
A secret or two,
A sky, deep blue,
And beautiful carols to sing.

The *Farmer's Wife* was a monthly magazine published in Minnesota between the years 1893 and 1939. In an era long before the Internet and high-speed travel connected us all, the magazine aimed to offer community among hard-working rural women, to provide a forum for their questions and concerns, and to assist them in the day-to-day goings-on about the farm—everything from raising chickens and slaughtering hogs, to managing scant funds and dressing the children, to keeping house and running the kitchen.

Christmas was the be-all, end-all celebration on the farm—more than Easter, New Year's, or even Thanksgiving. This quintessential holiday of giving and togetherness gave rise to pages and pages on the topic in every December issue of the magazine. And these pages weren't just about food—although recipes for all the various components of dinners and parties and holiday gift baskets certainly abounded.

The magazine's experts expounded on the best and latest ways to decorate home, tree, and parcels. Its monthly columnists devoted themselves to the matters of home-made gifts for family and friends, and games to be played to festively capture the spirit of the season. Its readers wrote in with tales of Christmases in other lands, in times gone by. Its editors rhapsodized, in and out of two wars, on the value of peace and of compassion.

In short, *The Farmer's Wife* presented its own opinion—both grand and humble, broad and minute, and always, always bearing in mind the idea of community among its readers—about the ways in which Christmas *should* be celebrated.

You'll find in this book a smattering of that opinion. Here are recipes to see you through the entire Christmas season; gift ideas guaranteed to get your creative juices flowing; tips for decking your halls and ringing in the day; and even a few stories to inspire and delight both the young and the young at heart.

Let's kick off the festivities with these words from the December 1920 issue of the magazine:

To those who live in the land of snow and Christmas trees, the twenty-fifth of December blends all its associations with the gleam of snow on hills and fields and woods, the fragrance of fir and pine, the leaping light of Christmas hearthfires. But Christmas is a world-wide day and the environment determined by climate is but an external.

They tell us, too, that "Christmas on the farm" is the only ideal Christmas. That were a hard saying on the city dwellers! *The Farmer's Wife* carries its Christmas message into all zones, from Florida to the frozen North, and from its own home in the corn-belt to the edges of the continent where the oceans roar out their accompaniment to the carols of the good, glad day. Our message is first, last, and at all times to farm women. It is a message of love and faith and cheer as befits a Christmas message: of love, because love is always the winner; of faith, because without that staunch quality, nothing would ever be accomplished; of cheer, because when we have love and faith, the flame of cheer follows as a matter of course—as light follows the burning torch.

The farm is a good setting for Christmas and the atmosphere of the home at Christmas time rests mainly in the hands of womenfolk. So here's to you all, from *The Farmer's Wife*: May you have more than a stockingful—may you have hearts full of Christmas love and Christmas faith and Christmas cheer.

—Lela Nargi

MARION T. JUSTICE

COOKING THE BIG DINNER

So frugal during the workaday week, the farmer's wife pulled out all the stops when it came to cooking the big holiday meal. From simply roasted game birds to elaborate desserts, there are recipes in this chapter to cover every sort of festive dinner—start to finish.

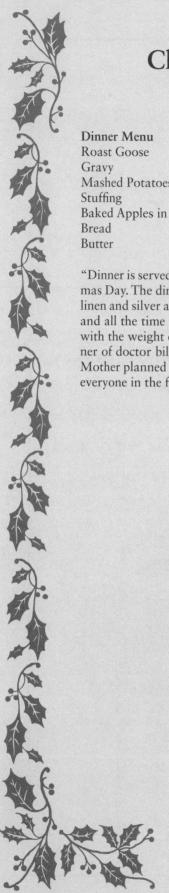

Christmas Dinner Is Served

By Gertrude Brown • December 1929

Dinner Menu

Roast Goose
Gravy
Mashed Potatoes
Stuffing
Baked Apples in Cranberry Jelly
Bread
Butter

Preserves
Baked Hubbard Squash
Mixed Vegetable Salad
Fig Pudding
Lemon Cream Sauce
Milk
Coffee

"Dinner is served." There is magic in the drawing power of those words on Christmas Day. The dinner has a company air even in the absence of company. The best linen and silver are used, the choicest foods prepared, the most courtesy practiced, and all the time wanted allowed for eating and visiting. The table doesn't groan with the weight of the food. Indeed not! Such a load would only be the forerunner of doctor bills or discomfort for a worn-out mother or overstuffed children. Mother planned well in advance to make this day a pleasant, jolly one for all, and everyone in the family cooperated in working out her plans.

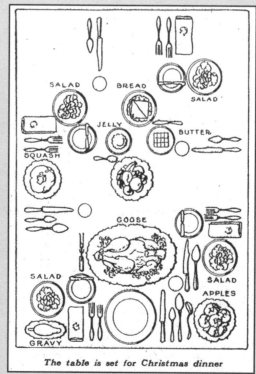

The table is set for Christmas dinner

To Start

DRINKS

❄ FRUIT PUNCH
January 1913

1 qt. water
1 c. sugar
grated rinds of 2 lemons and 2 oranges
6 bananas
4 c. pineapple
juice of 12 lemons and 6 oranges
additional 4 qt. water

Cook all together for 5 minutes. While hot add 6 bananas and 4 c. pineapple cut small. When cold and ready to serve add the juice of 12 lemons and 6 oranges with 4 qt. water. This makes 2 gallons and will serve 30 people.

❄ MULLED GRAPE JUICE
January 1914

Soak for 15 minutes the grated rind of 1 orange in the juice of 1 lemon, adding 1 c. boiling water and 1 tbsp. sugar. Place the ingredients in a heavy saucepan, adding 1 qt. grape juice, 4 whole cloves and 1 pinch powdered cinnamon. Bring slowly to a boil, simmer for 15 minutes. Prepare a meringue by boiling together 1 c. sugar and 2 tbsp. water until it threads, then pour this gradually upon the stiffly beaten whites of 2 eggs. Add the boiling grape liquor, dust lightly with grated nutmeg, and serve at once.

❄ CRANBERRY COCKTAIL
1934

½ c. sugar
1 c. pineapple juice
1 c. cranberries, cut in half
½ c. diced pineapple
1 c. raisins

Pour sugar and juice over fruit and let stand in refrigerator 4 hours or overnight.

❄ CRANBERRY GINGERALE COCKTAIL
November 1937

1 qt. cranberries   ⅔ c. sugar
4 c. water   gingerale, chilled

Cook cranberries and water till berries burst, about 5 minutes. Strain through sieve, add sugar, and cook 2 minutes. Chill. Fill small serving glasses ⅓ full of cranberry syrup, add chilled gingerale to make ⅔ full. Stir, then drop in whole candied cranberry to serve.

❄ EGG NOG
1934

2 egg yolks   2 drops vanilla
⅔ c. milk, chilled   nutmeg
1 tsp. sugar

Beat yolks; add chilled milk, sugar, and vanilla. Mix together well. Whipped cream may be added for variety, and 1 tsp. cocoa syrup or honey may be used for sweetening rather than sugar. Grate a little nutmeg over top.

❄ MRS. HEY'S COCOA
October 1938

1 c. cocoa   1 gallon milk
1 c. sugar

Mix cocoa and sugar and combine with enough cold milk to make a stiff paste. Add scalded milk and beat till frothy.

TO ACCOMPANY DRINKS

❄ CANDIED NUTS
January 1913

Boil 1 c. sugar with ½ c. water until it spins a thread. Have ready 1 qt. shelled nuts of any variety, pour into the syrup and stir until each one is crystallized with the sugar. Remove from the fire, stir a few more times, and serve.

❄ BAKED MUSHROOMS
1934

Wash mushrooms and remove stems. Slice caps if very large. Sprinkle with flour. Put in baking dish, add cream, salt and pepper to taste. Cover and bake at 350°F for 30 minutes till tender, uncovering for the last 5 minutes. Serve on toast.

❄ RELISH PLATE
November 1934

Arrange on one large plate three radiating bands of crisp carrot strips and celery, all of the same length. In the sections formed by these radiating vegetables put three different relishes, such as whole or chunk pickles, olives, dates, or prunes stuffed with cheese.

❄ CHEESE AND CRACKER TRAY
November 1934

A large plate or medium-sized tray is best to display an assortment of crackers and cheese. Heat crackers in the oven till crisp through, and until very lightly toasted, if desired. Arrange crackers around the edge of the plate and in the center one or more kinds of cheese of soft enough consistency to cut and spread easily. Prepared and packaged cheese may be used, unwrapping them and leaving them in their brick shape. Or season and soften cottage and American cheese—add cream, salt, and lemon juice to cottage cheese and mix well; may be rubbed through a sieve till smooth. Accompany tray with knife for cutting and serving cheese. Also on tray may be stuffed dates or prunes or Sultana raisins, or fresh fruit, or cherry or berry preserves may be passed.

❄ HORS D'OEUVRES
November 1937

Call them appetizers if you shy at the French-sounding "or doeuv," for their purpose is to serve as a tidbit or tasty bite of food along with a refreshing beverage. They must be just a mouthful, taken with the fingers, so some kinds are impaled on a toothpick or colored wooden skewer and stuck into a bright apple or grapefruit. The open-faced sandwich kind or canapé, pronounced can-a-pay, are arranged on a large plate to pass with the beverage. Or two or three may be on individual plates at the dinner able to serve as a first course.

Here are some easily prepared kinds:

Hot: large potato chips or small crackers spread with a bit of snappy cheese, with a dab of peanut butter, or one of the fillings listed below. Heat in the oven or under the broiler till crispy.

Cold: these may be toasted and hot if desired. Thin slices of white, rye, or dark bread or small cracker spread with filling and used open-faced or as a thin finger sandwich. If open-faced, canapé style, cut in rounds, strips, or triangles and garnish with slice of olive, sprig of parsley, decorative bit of pimiento, egg yolk, etc. Good fillings are:

- Ground black walnuts mixed with mayonnaise
- Grated or spreading cheese mixed with a little horseradish
- Hard-cooked egg yolk mixed with melted butter and mustard. Top with strip of sardine, anchovy paste, or chopped dill pickle
- Peanut butter and bacon bits topped with dill pickle
- Ground chicken liver mixed with crisp bacon bits, onion juice, celery salt, and Worcestershire sauce to season highly

❄ CHEESE PUFF
July 1922

1 tbsp. butter
2 tbsp. flour
6 tbsp. grated cheddar cheese

1 c. milk
5 eggs, separated
salt and pepper

Melt butter, add flour, and stir to blend. Add milk and stir well. Cook in double boiler for 5 minutes, stirring. There must be no lumps. Remove from stove; add cheese and beaten egg yolks, then pepper and salt to taste. Fold in the stiffly beaten egg whites. Pour into buttered baking dish and bake at 325°F for ½ an hour.

❄ PINWHEEL CHEESE BISCUITS
October 1926

3 c. flour
½ tsp. salt
5 tsp. baking powder
4 tbsp. butter
¾ to 1 c. milk
1 c. grated cheddar cheese
paprika

Sift together flour, salt, and baking powder; rub in butter and add enough milk to make a dough soft enough to roll. Roll into oblong ½ inch thick and sprinkle with cheese and paprika. Roll like jelly roll and cut into 1-inch pieces. Place close together in buttered pie pan with cut side up. Bake at 450°F about 15 minutes, till brown. Serve hot.

❄ PIGS IN BLANKETS
April 1919

Pigs in Blankets sounds mysterious but is nothing more than an oyster wrapped up in a long strip of nice bacon cut thin, and fastened with toothpicks to hold it together. Put them in a hot fry pan without any fat, since the bacon is fat, and brown all over evenly. This will not take more than 10 minutes. Be careful not to let them get too hot and burn. Oysters are so delicate that they do not require a very long time or a hot fire for cooking.

❄ FRIED OYSTERS
January 1914

Drain liquor off 1 qt. of plump oysters. Roll oysters in beaten egg, then in cracker crumbs, and fry in hot butter. Salt and pepper to taste. Garnish with parsley and sliced lemon.

❄ SCALLOPED OYSTERS
November 1916

2 cups cracker crumbs
½ c. melted butter
1 pt. oysters
1 tsp. salt
pepper to taste
¼ c. oyster liquor
⅛ c. milk

Mix the cracker crumbs and butter. Butter a deep glass or earthen baking dish; put a layer of crumbs on the bottom, then a layer of oysters, seasoned with salt and pepper, and pour over half the oyster liquor and part of the milk. Put on another layer of crumbs, then the rest of the oysters and the remaining liquor and milk. Cover the top with crumbs and bake ½ an hour at 350°F. Never use more than two layers of oysters as they do not require much heat and they cook more evenly. This dish may be prepared several hours before time for baking—if kept in a cool place until ready to bake.

❄ OYSTERS SCALLOPED WITH CORN
October 1938

1 pt. oysters (standards or medium selects)
2 pimientos, chopped
1½ c. corn kernels
2 c. crushed crackers
½ c. butter, melted
½ c. liquid—use oyster liquor and add milk to make ½ c.
¼ tsp. salt
pepper

Drain and look over oysters, removing any bits of shell. Combine pimientos, corn, and crumbs with butter. In a greased baking dish, put in half of oysters, then a layer of crumbs. Repeat, reserving enough crumbs for the top. Pour on liquid to which salt and pepper has been added, then top with crumbs. Bake at 400°F for 30 minutes, till puffed and brown on top.

TABLE TALK

Inexpensive Recipes for Yuletide Dishes

By Mrs. Sarah Cooke • December 1914

Christmas soup should be a light one. If chicken is selected, the stock may be prepared the day before, an old fowl being as good as a tender one for the purpose. The breast meat may be used separately, if desired, balance of fowl being cut in small bits and broken into short pieces. One quart of water and one teaspoonful of salt should be allowed for each pound of meat. Two chopped onions and ¾ cup of chopped celery, with any other desired flavoring, may also be added. Let stand until the juice slightly discolors the water, then bring slowly to a boil, skimming the scum as it rises. A cup of cold water thrown in when the stock is boiling will cause the scum to rise more freely. It should boil steadily for about an hour to each pound of meat and bone. The water should boil away until there is about one-third the original amount. Strain and cool; it will become a clear jelly.

Christmas morning heat a quart of milk and slightly thicken it with a heaping tablespoonful of cornstarch or flour. Add 1 tablespoon of butter, a saltspoonful each of white pepper and mace, and the jellied soup stock. Let come to a boil. Two or three beaten eggs, stirred into the soup just before it is turned into the tureen and not boiled, makes a richer soup; but it will be excellent even without the eggs.

SOUP

❄ COCKIE LEEKIE SOUP
December 1914

Our English cousins consider cockie leekie the proper Christmas soup. When they have not fowl for this they substitute beef.

To 2 or 3 lbs. meat, allow 8–10 leeks (white parts only, slit first in half then well washed between layers). The meat and half the leeks are cut into 1-inch pieces, covered with cold water, and simmered 1 hour. The remainder of the leeks, in larger pieces, are then added and the soup gently boiled 3 or 4 hours. The first leeks entirely break up, but the others retain some shape. The broth is carefully skimmed and seasoned to taste with salt and pepper. It is very nourishing and economical.

❄ TOMATO BISQUE
January 1935

1 pt. canned tomatoes
2 tbsp. diced onion
1 bay leaf
1 peppercorn
¼ tsp. baking soda
3 tbsp. butter
1 tsp. sugar
3 c. milk, scalded with
  1 c. cream
1 tsp. salt

Cook tomatoes for 10 minutes with seasonings. Strain, puree in blender, add baking soda, butter, and sugar. Keep hot. To milk and cream add salt. Pour tomatoes into milk mixture. Serve at once.

May Your Christmas be a Happy One And may the New Year bring You Contentment and Prosperity in overflowing measure.

❄ HOLIDAY SOUP
November 1938

2 tbsp. butter
1 onion, minced
1 pt. diced cooked pumpkin or squash
1½ qt. seasoned meat broth
½ tsp. sugar
1 tsp. salt
½ tsp. pepper
3 whole cloves
½ tsp. ginger
½ tsp. celery seed
1 tbsp. flour
1 c. whipping cream
salt to taste

Melt butter, cook onion in it; add squash or pumpkin, diced quite small. Stir carefully to keep cubes unbroken. Meanwhile heat broth with seasonings to boiling. Add vegetables. Thicken slightly with flour rubbed with a little water. Serve hot with a dab of slightly salted whipped cream on each serving.

❄ JULIENNE SOUP
November 1919

Into 3 qt. water place ½ c. each diced carrots and turnips, finely chopped onion and celery, 1 bay leaf, and 1 tbsp. finely chopped parsley. Bring to the boiling point, then add 2 beef bouillon cubes, 2 tsp. Worcestershire sauce, and 1 tsp. salt, or to taste. Allow to simmer ½ an hour; strain and serve. Instead of beef bouillon and water, 3 qt. of strong clear beef broth made from good shank portions may be used.

❄ SOUP
November 1925

A clear broth or consommé is probably all that will be desired, although a clear tomato soup is a good appetizer.

Make as follows: To 1 qt. meat broth or soup stock, add 28 oz. can of tomato puree. Blend 2 tbsp. butter with 3 tbsp. flour and add gradually to the simmering soup. Any seasonings may be added such as clove, bay leaf, or onion. The soup should be strained before serving. Wafers or croutons are nice to serve with the soup. For the latter, cut bread into small squares and brown in the oven.

❋ CHICKEN BROTH WITH RICE
Ladies' Home Journal, December 1917

2 c. chicken stock
½ c. rice, cooked
1 tbsp. chopped celery leaves
¼ tsp. grated nutmeg
paprika

Heat the chicken stock over a low flame. Add to the stock the rice. Then add seasonings to taste and serve.

❋ ASPARAGUS-BARLEY SOUP
March 1939

1 beef soup bone
3½ qt. water
⅓ c. fine barley
1 tbsp. salt
celery leaves
1½ c. asparagus tips
2 eggs, beaten

Simmer soup bone with water, barley, salt, and a few celery leaves for 2 hours. Remove bone; skim off excess fat. Add asparagus tips. Stir in eggs with a wire whisk, taking care not to break asparagus. Serve at once.

❋ WHITE SOUP
Ladies' Home Journal, December 1917

Put 4 large peeled and sliced potatoes and 1 sliced onion into a saucepan; cover with water and boil till tender. Rub through a sieve or puree. Melt 1 tbsp. butter and stir in 1 tbsp. flour; add potato cooking water and ½ c. cream. Season with salt and pepper and serve with croutons.

❋ SPINACH SOUP
May 1930
Contributed by Mrs. G. C. M., New York

Rub through a sieve 2 c. chopped cooked spinach. Add 1 qt. milk. A little onion may be scalded in the milk before it is added to the spinach. Salt and pepper to taste and add 3 to 4 tbsp. butter.

TABLE TALK

Anna Barrows • December 1915

Many of our holiday and festival occasions have come down to us from remote ancestors. The boar's head that graced the Christmas boards of long ago is now replaced by the little pig of six or eight weeks, trussed, stuffed, and served with an apples in its mouth. Instead of the baron—a double sirloin of beef—which still continues to appear on the table of British royalty at holiday time, we serve a crown of pork or lamb. The goose has figured prominently in Yule menus for centuries.

It is not infrequent on our modern farms that a family must depend for a winter principally upon mutton or pork. It therefore falls upon the farmer and his wife to understand the best methods of preserving their meat supply as well as to study how to give an appetizing variety in ways of cooking and serving.

If you choose for your Christmas roast meat, lamb, or pork, either one may be served as a "crown." This style is too elaborate for frequent use but is effective on the holiday table.

If your central dish is to be goose, choose a gosling or "green" goose. You will know it—it cannot be from your own flock—by its yellowish feet and bill, tender windpipe, and pliable feet.

These menus are meant merely as a suggestive guide for the woman who has been "getting dinner" week in and month out and will welcome some ideas from "outside."

Main Courses

❄ CHRISTMAS DAY
December 1926

Tomato Bouillon
Roast Goose with Dressing
Mashed Potatoes
Beets

Baked Squash
Cranberry Jelly
Fruit Salad
Date Tort

As every farm does not "grow" geese, but all grow chickens, here is an alternative menu:

Chicken Pie
Candied Sweet Potatoes
String Beans

Apple Jelly
Cream Slaw
Jellied Prunes

❄ ROAST GOOSE
November 1913

Sauté 4 sliced onions in oil till tender then mix with 4 c. boiled or roasted chestnuts, roughly chopped. Add 1 tbsp. butter, salt to taste, ground black pepper, 1 tsp. prepared Dijon mustard, and 1 well-beaten egg. With this mixture, stuff the body of a 10-lb. goose. Truss with string. Prick the skin all over with a sharp knife. Cover the bird with buttered wax paper and roast ½ hour at 425°F, then 1½–2½ hours at 350°F. Be sure to baste frequently with boiling water. Allow to rest 15 minutes before carving. Serve with a border of stuffed tomatoes.

❄ ROAST DUCK
January 1930

If a mildly flavored duck is desired, stuff the fowl with cored and quartered apples to absorb some of the duck flavor. Remove the apples before serving the duck. A stuffing of 2 tbsp. chopped onion to every 1 c. chopped celery (leaves and green stalks that are not desirable for the table) imparts a delicious flavor to the duck. The seasoning should also be removed just before serving.

   After the duck has been trussed, season with salt and pepper and sprinkle with flour. Roast from 20 to 25 minutes per pound at 375°F.

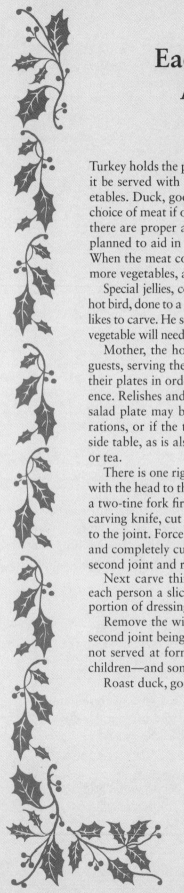

Each Bird Calls for Special Accompanying Dishes

By Anna Coyle • November 1921

Turkey holds the place of honor on [holiday] tables. Custom has established that it be served with cranberry sauce and other special sauces, dressings, and vegetables. Duck, goose, chicken, guinea hen, and squab offer pleasing variety for choice of meat if one wishes to stray from beaten paths. With each of these birds there are proper accompanying dishes. The chart given here has been carefully planned to aid in the selection of just the right dish to go with the chosen bird. When the meat course is decided on, select one sauce, dressing, garnish, one or more vegetables, a salad, and a dessert from the groups opposite.

Special jellies, conserves, and pickles add piquancy to the menu. The steaming-hot bird, done to a golden brown, is placed before Father if he is one of the men who likes to carve. He serves each plate to meat, dressing, sauce, and a vegetable. A juicy vegetable will need its own separate side dish.

Mother, the hostess of the occasion, is served first, then guests if there are guests, serving the ladies first, and last but most important the children receive their plates in order of their ages, the boys always gladly giving the girls preference. Relishes and other dishes are passed around. The salad when served on a salad plate may be placed at the beginning of the meal as a part of the decorations, or if the table is too crowded it may be conveniently served from the side table, as is also dessert. Mother from her end of the table pours the coffee or tea.

There is one right way to carve the turkey. Place it on a platter upon its back, with the head to the left, the turkey resting diagonally to the carver's body. Insert a two-tine fork firmly across the breast bone and hold the bird steady. With the carving knife, cut down the side farthest from the carver to serve the leg down to the joint. Force the leg over sharply from the turkey so as to expose the joint and completely cut off the drumstick and second joint. Separate drumstick and second joint and remove the bone from the second joint.

Next carve thin slices from the breast, parallel with the breastbone. Serve each person a slice of light and a slice of dark meat with a sprig of garnish; a portion of dressing and a spoonful of gravy on the side of the plate.

Remove the wing in the same manner as the leg and divide at the joint, the second joint being served as one portion. The tip of the wing and drumstick are not served at formal dinings but at the home dinner cannot be denied to the children—and some of the grownups.

Roast duck, goose, and chicken are carved in like manner.

The Correct Dish to Serve with the Holiday Bird

Bird	Sauce	Stuffing	Garnish	Vegetable	Salad
Turkey	Giblet	Oyster	Pineapple	Msh'd potato	Celery
	Cranberry	Raisin	Holly	Squash	Fruit
	Cran. Ice	Giblet	Celery leaves	Corn pudding	Apple/nut
		Sage	Cranberries	String beans	Apple/celery
		Chestnut	Parsley	Tomatoes	
		Sweet potato		Lettuce	
Chicken	Apricot	Celery	Celery leaves	Msh'd potato	Celery
	Giblet	Sage	Holly	Cream onions	Fruit
	Quince jelly	Sausage	Bacon	Corn fritters	Pear/cheese
	Mint jelly	Giblet		Peas	Pimiento
	Cran. Jelly			Hominy	
				Okra	
Duck/Goose	Apple	Raisin	Orange	Msh'd potato	Cabbage/nut
	Cranberry	Turnip	Prunes	Rutabaga	Waldorf
	Currant		Pickled beets	Turnips	Pineapple
			Apple	Parsnips	Orange
				Carrots	Pimiento
					Spinach
					Wild rice
Guinea hen	Butter	Celery/onion	Watercress	Msh'd potato	Tom. gelatin
	Currant jelly		Celery leaves	Cream onions	Apricot
			Olives	Corn fritters	Prunes
				Celery	Fruit
				String beans	Vegetable
					Wild rice
Squab/Pigeon	Butter	Potato	Toast triangles	Msh'd potato	Vegetable
	Vegetable	Bread	Olives	Carrots	Date
			Bacon	Turnips	Asparagus
				Spinach	Watercress
				Squash	Lettuce
				Sweet potato	Wild rice

❄ ROAST STUFFED TURKEY
November 1936

Even those who have roasted dozens of turkeys may have some surprises in store for them as to the best way of doing it. For the new theory is: roast uncovered in a moderate oven. That is, provided it's a young turkey.

1. To prepare fowl for roasting, wipe out the inside of the dressed bird with a cloth and sprinkle with salt. Pile stuffing in lightly and sew or skewer the opening. Fold back wings and tie legs and make a compact roast. Pat the skin with un-salted melted fat (turkey fat, lard, or vegetable shortening).

2. Roast it breast down without water and uncovered if the turkey is under a year old. The back fat of a fowl serves as a "baster." Baste occasionally as it roasts, using melted fat, or cover it before roasting with a cloth dipped in fat, or a piece of brown paper well greased. If you feel safer doing it the old way you may cover the roaster (omitting the cloth or paper, of course), but do not add water unless it is an older bird that needs steaming.

3. Roast at a moderate temperature (325 to 350°F) throughout. It is not necessary to sear it in a hot oven at the start, although you may start it out at 450°F and then reduce the heat quickly. Allow 25 minutes per pound for birds as small as 7 lbs. and reduce time per pound for larger birds down to 15 minutes per pound for a 20-lb. bird. This means that a small turkey will roast in 3 hours, a 10–12-lb. one in 3½ to 4 hours, and so on. To test for doneness, thrust a metal skewer in next to the thigh, and if there is no pinkish tinge to the juice, it is ready to serve.

❄ FOR THE HOLIDAY BIRD
By Lavilla Wright Macomber • November 1914

When making stuffing, only enough warm water should be added to the dry bread-crumbs to moisten, probably about 1 c. to 1 pt. of dry crumbs. Seasoning should be added to this water to blend well, a little butter should be mixed in with the crumbs and water, and 1 or more raw unbeaten eggs should be mixed in thoroughly. The fowl should never be filled more than ⅔ full.

ONION STUFFING:
Over 1½ c. white onion, chopped fine, pour 1 c. boiling water and ½ tsp. salt. Let stand till cold, drain, and mix with 1 pt. breadcrumbs soaked in 1 c. warm water to which has been added 1 tsp. salt, ½ tsp. paprika, and 2 or 3 sweet red peppers, chopped. Mix in thoroughly 1 tsp. butter and 2 unbeaten eggs. The best way to mix the eggs is with a slotted spoon, working slowly as for creaming sugar and butter. This makes enough stuffing for a large goose. Tart apple sauce should be served with it.

CELERY STUFFING:
With a vegetable brush, clean enough celery stalks and the best of the leaves to fill 1 pt. measure. Turn into mixing bowl and pour on boiling water not quite to cover. Cover and allow to stand till cold. Turn in 1 pt. breadcrumbs and a little more water if necessary to moisten, 2 tsp. salt, ½ tsp. white pepper, and a dash of celery seed. Add 1 tbsp. melted butter and 2 unbeaten eggs.

SAGE STUFFING:
Soak a little more than 1 pt. breadcrumbs in 1 c. well-seasoned beef or chicken stock. Add 1 tbsp. powdered sage, a little more salt and pepper if necessary, and 1 small onion finely chopped. Add enough melted butter or sweet cream to moisten and mix in 2 unbeaten eggs.

❆ WILD RICE DRESSING
November 1920

Wild rice is found in the sloughs of many of our northern states. It is even considered necessary to sow it after severe open winters in order that the wild ducks and geese may be lured by their love for this dainty into the lakes frequented by hunters. Because of the receptacle (a blanket) used by the Indians in gathering the rice, many women object to using it, and yet there are tales pursuing nearly every purchasable foodstuff which, were they known, would warn away the most fastidious. Wild rice is easily gathered and a little goes a long way. The sloughs on any farm where it will grow should yield some of this product, and use it during the winter as a breakfast cereal, as a vegetable with fat meats, and as a substitute for breadcrumbs in dressing for fowl of all kinds, stuffed roll of beef, and shoulder of veal.

Cook 1 c. wild rice in rapidly boiling salted water. When tender, drain, mix with an equal quantity of dry breadcrumbs. Handle lightly so as not to mash the rice too much. Season with salt, pepper, and sage, if liked. Add ½ c. melted butter and if necessary enough hot water to make just moist.

❄ SAVORY DRESSING
November 1938

8–10 c. stale bread cubes
broth to moisten
1 tsp. poultry seasoning
½ c. minced onion
1 c. celery, cut fine
turkey liver
2 eggs
½ c. melted butter

Add broth to bread to make slightly moist. Add seasonings, including turkey liver, cooked and rubbed to a paste. Add beaten eggs and butter last. Toss lightly.

Uses for Turkey Leftovers
December 1938

Stuffing Cylinders
Form turkey stuffing into cylinders, wrap in thin bacon slices. Broil or bake at 400°F till bacon is done. Serve with tomato sauce made by thickening a can of tomato soup. Or serve with hot, fluffy mashed potatoes and the rest of the turkey gravy.

Pancakes and Gravy
Pancakes or waffles with creamed turkey make a good supper dish. Add cut turkey to a well-seasoned cream sauce or turkey gravy, and serve hot over pancakes or waffles. Or mince cold turkey and moisten with gravy and heat. Spread over thin pancakes, roll them, and keep hot in oven till ready to serve.

❄ SWEET STUFFING
November 1924

2 c. stale breadcrumbs
½ c. chopped raisins
½ c. chopped walnuts
1 tsp. salt
⅛ tsp. pepper
½ tsp. dried sage
⅔ c. melted butter

Mix in order given.

❄ SALT PORK STUFFING
November 1924

1 lb. bread
½ c. fat salt pork
1 egg
salt, pepper, sage, and other seasonings to taste

Add enough hot water to crumbed bread to moisten well. Add the finely chopped salt pork and the well-beaten egg, along with seasonings.

❄ SAUSAGE STUFFING
November 1924

Use either white breadcrumbs or the crumbs from cornbread or Johnny cake. Moisten with hot water. Pour off the excess hot water. Add the sausage (about ½ lb. is sufficient for the average turkey). The amount and kind of seasoning depend upon the seasoning of the sausage. No butter is needed as there is enough fat in the sausage.

❄ POTATO STUFFING FOR ROAST TURKEY
Ladies' Home Journal, December 1917

Boil and mash 1 lb. white potatoes. Season with salt and pepper, then add 1 c. cornbread crumbs, 1 small chopped onion, 1 tbsp. butter, and 1 c. chopped celery.

❄ GIBLET GRAVY
November 1915

Sometimes the heart, liver, and gizzard are chopped after they are boiled until tender and added to the stuffing of the turkey. It is usually better to put them in a brown gravy. As the chopped particles tend to settle to the bottom of the bowl, persons who do not care for this addition can have the plain top and those who prefer the giblets may have a double portion. To make the gravy, melt and brown in a saucepan 2 oz. butter. Put in ¼ c. flour and stir till this is a rich dark brown, then gradually add 1 pt. stock from chicken, and the giblets. Stir until smooth and thick, season with salt and pepper.

❆ RABBIT CURRY
December 1914

Europeans frequently substitute rabbit curry or rabbit pie for the Christmas fowl.

Have a young rabbit cut in pieces as for frying by your butcher. Fry in 2 tbsp. bacon fat until a light brown. Remove from pan and drain on paper towels. In the same fat fry 3 sour apples and 2 onions, finely chopped, until tender and mash them to a pulp. Add 1 tsp. each curry powder and flour, 1 c. soup stock, and salt to taste. Return rabbit to broth in pan, simmer gently 2 hours—adding water if necessary. Serve with plain boiled rice.

❆ CROWN ROAST OF LAMB
December 1910

This method of serving a roast is not as well known as it deserves.

Have butcher tie together 2 racks of loin lamb chops in a circle. Strip down the meat part away from each rib, place on baking rack, and brush with olive oil. Cover bones with aluminum foil to prevent burning. Bake at 375°F for 15 to 20 minutes per pound of meat. Fill the center of the crown just before taking to the table with stewed peas well seasoned. Each rib should be decorated with a twist of white paper cut to represent a feathery plume.

❆ RAGOUT OF LAMB AND VEGETABLES
October 1929

Bring 3 pts. of lamb broth or chicken broth to a boil. Add 1 pt. peeled pearl onions, 1 pt. baby carrots, 1 c. small quartered and peeled turnips, 1 pt. small peeled potatoes, and simmer, covered, till vegetables are tender, about 45 minutes. Add any preferred amount of lean lamb in good-sized pieces, first sautéed in a pan in 1 tbsp. butter till butter and meat are brown. Season to taste—salt, pepper, celery salt, shaving of lemon peel and a few drops of the juice, tsp. Worcestershire sauce, tiny pinch of mace, six pimiento olives, quartered. Simmer all together for 15 minutes, then thicken slightly with a tbsp. each of butter and flour melted together and serve. The French use pieces of dry, crusty bread, added to excess broth at the last minute, in place of dumplings.

Variation: Add 4 cut-up tomatoes to the broth and vegetables, stirring occasionally, and 1 tbsp. sugar to the seasonings. Also add cauliflower sprigs and thin slices of zucchini, omitting the olives.

❄ BAKED SPICED HAM
February 1923

No other meat food lends itself to quite the variety of dishes as does the ham. There are many ways of using ham besides the usual boiled or fried ways.

1 medium-sized ham   Whole cloves
½ c. brown sugar

Plunge the ham into boiling water for 10 minutes. Reduce the temperature and cook below boiling for 2 hours. Remove ham from water and peel off the skin to near the shank end. Bake 1 hour at 350°F, basting frequently with equal parts vinegar and water. Take from the oven and rub the fat surface with brown sugar, insert whole cloves all over the fat part of the ham at intervals of 2 inches. Bake until tender without basting.

Another most satisfactory method for baking is to wash off the ham well, trim and slash in 1-inch squares, rub with brown sugar and ground cloves, add 1 c. boiling water and bake, basting frequently, at 350°F. This ham is flavory and tempting, with the squares of crisp skin separated showing well-browned fat.

Place the whole ham on a large platter, garnish with baked red apples, and serve from the platter at the table.

❄ BAKED HAM
December 1920

Select a 15-lb. ham. Parboil in water to cover 1½ hours. Remove the skin and dot the fat with whole cloves. Cover with a thick crust of 2 c. breadcrumbs and 1 c. brown sugar. In the baking pan with the ham, have equal parts of milk and water for basting. This gives an incomparable flavor. Bake at 350° for 4–5 hours (about 15 minutes/pound), to an internal temperature of 160°F.

❊ RELISH FOR HAM
May 1924

Here's an odd one: A dressing for ham. Add grated horseradish to whipped cream; add sugar and seasonings to taste. A little vinegar improves it if the horseradish does not have vinegar with it. Serve on either baked or boiled ham. I cannot tell you how it tastes, all I can say is, "try it some day."

❊ BAKED SLICE OF HAM WITH GRAPE JUICE SAUCE
December 1931

1 slice of ham ¾ inch thick
1 tsp. dry mustard

¼ c. brown sugar
milk to cover

Place ham in baking dish and rub with mustard and brown sugar. Pour milk over and bake at 350°F for 1 hour. Serve with Grape Juice Sauce:

1 tbsp. cornstarch
¼ c. cold water
¾ c. hot water

1 c. grape juice
juice of 1 lemon

Mix the cornstarch with the cold water; add hot water. Cook until mixture thickens, then add grape and lemon juices. Serve hot.

❊ JELLIED VEAL—KALVE DANS SMORGASBORD
December 1937

2 lbs. knuckle of veal
3 lbs. veal
4 slices onion
2 stalks celery

1 bay leaf
4 peppercorns
1½ tsp. salt

Saw knuckle of veal through in several pieces; cut meat in pieces. Barely cover with boiling water, add seasonings, and simmer until meat is very tender. Remove meat and cool, boil down stock, if necessary, to make 1 pt. and strain. Cut meat in small dice; add salt as needed. In the bottom of a mold arrange slices of stuffed olives and pour in a little stock. When this is set, add cooled meat and stock. Chill; turn out and garnish with parsley, hard-cooked eggs, and slices of pickled beets cut in fancy shapes.

Smorgasbord

by Miriam J. Williams

December 1937

"When our front door opens and company walks in, there may be five or there may be fifteen but around Christmas time it's likely to be nearer fifty," so Mrs. Adolph Abrahamson of Saginaw, Minnesota, *The Farmer's Wife* magazine's Scandinavian guest, was explaining as she busied herself in the Country Kitchen preparing good things for a "smorgasbord" meal.

Mrs. Abrahamson was one of our guest homemakers whom *The Farmer's Wife* magazine brings to its Country Kitchen from time to time to demonstrate some special type of cookery and pass on interesting recipes to our readers.

From a hospitable Norwegian family herself, and married into a Norwegian family where entertaining in the home is as much a part of living as baking rye bread and packing school lunches, Mrs. Abrahamson personifies friendly graciousness and charm. And, of course, she is a most capable manager and excellent cook. One has to be both to uphold the traditions of a Scandinavian community and prepare the good things.

"Smorgasbord" is literally translated as "bread-and-butter table," but in the old country it means a groaning board of cold appetizers served as the prelude to a meal. The Americanized version, Mrs. Abrahamson explains, is usually a hot and cold buffet supper. It is ideally suited to entertaining a crowd, for there is such a varied assortment that every taste is satisfied. Up in her Northern Minnesota community, less than a hundred miles from the Canadian border, smorgasbord is the traditional way to take care of large family-and-friend gatherings of the holiday season.

Several of the women get together two or three evenings before a big party or before Christmas to prepare cookies, cakes, and fancy breads. They make head cheese, sausage, pickled tongue, and meat rolls at butchering time, packing some in brine and storing an extra supply in a special cool place for just such occasions. They always have cheese of different kinds, always a fresh baking of rye bread and sweet rolls flavored with cardamom seed, always salads and relishes, potatoes and brown beans, spicy meatballs, and fragrant hot coffee.

Of course, there's pickled herring and anchovies and smoked salmon, and at holiday time there's lutefisk, a Scandinavian classic. Perhaps the crowning treat is a römme gröt, a delectable cream pudding.

❄ MEAT BALLS SMORGASBORD
December 1937

1 lb. ground beef	1 large onion, ground
1 lb. ground pork	2 tsp. salt
2 c. breadcrumbs	¼ tsp. allspice
2 eggs	½ tsp. cloves
1 pt. milk	

To make gravy (to be added to the skillet after the meatballs are cooked):

1 tbsp. flour	salt and pepper to taste
1 c. hot water	

The secret of these delicious meat balls is in using good meat, such as ground steak or shoulder, grinding the onion fine, and then working all ingredients together with the hand, big spoon, or electric mixer very thoroughly. The more milk worked in, the softer are the meat balls. Form into small balls—about 40 from this recipe. Brown in skillet in hot fat, part each of butter and bacon fat is good. Remove to casserole or kettle and pour over gravy made by adding flour, hot water, and seasonings to the pan fat. Cover and simmer or bake at 250°F about 1 hour.

Side Dishes

SALADS

Salads are one of the main ways and also the easiest by which to gain additional atmosphere for the holiday season. Among the many which can be used are cranberry, tomato jelly, green leafy, cinnamon apple salads, and others too numerous to mention. The many different shaped molds on the market, such as the star mold, ring, or wreath molds, help to add variety also.

When the table is crowded, we like to do away with the individual salad plate, in our family, and to have our guests help themselves to this course from one large plate. We call this "finger salad" or "finger relish" because we take it from the plate and eat it with our fingers. To prepare this salad we branch out into a whole group of vegetables, some of which are not commonly used raw, but all of which we find delicious without cooking. We follow just one rule in choosing the varieties: that we like to nibble them, raw.

Inspiration for this sort of salad came with appreciation of the real beauty of uncooked fresh vegetables. Do you know any flower more lovely than one of the tender inside leaves of red cabbage, broken to expose a bit of the white stem against the deep purple of the leaf itself? It seems a pity to mutilate such beauty with the chopping knife. We like better to break the leaves in two-inch or smaller lengths, and on each place a small dab of well-seasoned cottage cheese, or perhaps a bit of peanut butter made tart with boiled dressing.

❄ A FRENCH DRESSING FOR LETTUCE
October 1911

I think that word *salad* was born to do me good.

—Henry VI

For a palatable dish, the kind that "melts" in your mouth, good cooks recommend the following: first, freshen your lettuce in cold water. Then, while your lettuce is becoming crisp, take a small piece of garlic and rub your salad bowl with the same. In a separate dish mix 2 tbsp. oil (olive oil is preferred) with 4 tbsp. vinegar; add pepper and salt. Put your lettuce in the bowl and pour over your dressing and stir lettuce around. Then take a piece of bacon, cut in little squares, and fry out in a pan until crisp and all traces of grease are removed, then sprinkle over your lettuce. Dandelions may be treated the same way.

❄ SWEET CREAM DRESSING FOR SALAD
1934

1 c. heavy cream	½ tsp. salt
1 tsp. sugar	4 tbsp. lemon juice

Beat cream till stiff. Add seasonings, then lemon juice 1 drop at a time.

❄ RED DRESSING FOR HEAD LETTUCE
November 1924

1 tbsp. chili sauce	pepper to taste
5 tbsp. oil	paprika to taste
2 tbsp. vinegar	English mustard to taste
salt to taste	

Blend all thoroughly and add:

½ tbsp. chopped hard-cooked egg yolk	½ tbsp. chopped pimiento
	½ tbsp. chopped onion
½ tbsp. chopped hard-cooked egg white	½ tbsp. chopped chives, parsley, olives, or green peppers

❄ FRESH GARDEN SALAD
1934

1 qt. shredded lettuce	1 c. diced cucumber
2 c. diced tomatoes	1 tbsp. minced chives

Pour over the above ingredients a simple oil dressing of 2 parts oil, 1 part vinegar, pepper, salt, and a dash of cayenne which have been shaken together in a small jar till an emulsion forms. Toss lightly till salad is well coated. Radishes and other fresh crisp vegetables may be used.

❄ BELLE'S CABBAGE SALAD
November 1923

1 c. sugar	½ c. strong vinegar
2 tbsp. prepared mustard	½ c. butter
2 eggs	1 c. cream to whip
dash salt	about 1½ qt. finely chopped
dash cayenne	raw cabbage

Mix sugar and mustard; add beaten eggs, salt, cayenne, and vinegar. Cook over hot water, stirring until it thickens, adding butter as the mixture heats. Cool. This foundation will keep for months in a cool place. As desired, add ½ c. of the foundation to the whipped cream and mix with the cabbage.

❄ RAW CARROT SALAD
November 1924

2 c. raw carrots, grated	1 tbsp. chopped onion
½ c. chopped raw cabbage	Salad dressing (pages 37, 41)

This is even better than it looks! The salad dressing may be either mayonnaise, cooked, or French. ¾ c. grated cheese may be substituted for the cabbage.

❄ APPLE SALAD
December 1920

Select medium-size red apples. Cut off stem end straight across as if cutting off a cap. Scoop out the center of the apple and cut the shell in points all around. Mix the pulp with diced pineapple and celery and return it to the apple cups. Serve with any well-liked salad dressing. Or, substitute any salad better liked; chopped apple and celery with nuts is a favorite.

❄ CRANBERRY SALAD
December 1932

One of the most welcome arrivals on the market is the colorful cranberry which somehow seems to herald the holiday season. Cranberries have a tartness which makes them especially desirable to serve either in a cocktail or with the meat course. They are so versatile, however, that they are seen in many guises and in all courses ranging from cocktails, soups, salads to desserts, jams, jellies, and candies.

½ c. diced celery
2 diced apples
2 c. chopped cranberries

French dressing (page 37)
lettuce

Combine celery, apples, and cranberries; add dressing to taste and serve on lettuce leaves.

❄ CHRYSANTHEMUM SALAD
November 1931

8 medium oranges
1 c. diced apple
2 tbsp. lemon juice
2 tbsp. sugar
½ c. diced celery
½ c. broken walnut meats
lettuce
mayonnaise

Cut through skins of oranges ¾ of the way down and in very fine strips, being careful not to break strips apart [creating your chrysanthemum-shaped cups]. Remove orange pulp and cut in pieces, draining off juice to use in dressing. Marinate apple pieces in lemon juice to prevent discoloring and sprinkle with sugar. Combine orange, apple, celery, and nuts and fill orange chrysanthemum cups. Serve on beds of lettuce with dressing made by shaking or beating together equal parts of mayonnaise and orange juice.

❄ PEAR SALAD WITH HONEY DRESSING
November 1917

For each serving:
½ of a large peeled, cored pear, or 2 halves if the pears are small

For the dressing (for 6–8 servings):
3 egg yolks	pinch salt	whipped cream
½ c. honey	⅓ c. vinegar	

Beat the yolks slightly. Add the honey, salt, and vinegar. Cook in double boiler till thickened, beating all the while so it will be smooth. Set away to cool. Before serving, fold in a moderate amount of whipped cream just before adding to the salad, remembering that we are all now economizing with the use of cream. Garnish with canned red cherry or cranberry on top.

❄ ORANGE BASKETS
May 1922

12 oranges	2 c. strawberries
1 pineapple, peeled, cored, and chopped (juice reserved)	1 c. grape juice

Cut a triangular slice from each side of the oranges, leaving half the skin intact to form the bottom of the basket, and strip to form the handle. Scoop out the pulp with a sharp knife. Fill each basket with a mixture of orange, pineapple, and strawberries. To each basket add 2 tbsp. grape juice combined with pineapple juice left over from slicing. Serve cold. Garnish each plate with a sprig of something green.

❄ CHRISTMAS VEGETABLE SALAD
December 1932

1½ c. diced cooked beets
1½ c. steamed green beans, cut in 1-inch lengths
shredded lettuce leaves
French dressing (page 37)

Let beets and beans stand, separately, in dressing for at least 1 hour. Arrange in separate adjoining mounds on lettuce. Serve with dressing.

❄ LOBSTER SALAD
March 1911

The meat of one cooked lobster should be torn into shreds; scrape out the meat from the shell and set aside. Mix lobster meat with 3 tbsp. of mayonnaise dressing. Cover salad dish with crisp lettuce leaves, put a layer of lobster meat upon it, then a layer of celery cut into small pieces, alternately with a little dressing on top. Lay slices of hard-boiled egg around the salad.

❄ MAYONNAISE DRESSING
April 1917

1 tsp. salt
¼ tsp. white pepper
cayenne or paprika
2 egg yolks
2 c. olive oil
4 tbsp. vinegar or lemon juice
cayenne or paprika

Mix in a bowl which is ice-cold, using a silver fork or flexible knife. Have all the ingredients very cold. Mix the dry ingredients, add the slightly beaten yolks in the bowl, then add the oil, drop by drop, beating constantly as it is added. As the mixture thickens, add a few drops of the acid [vinegar or lemon juice]. When ¼ c. oil has been used, add the oil by spoonfuls. Beat hard. The beating makes the dressing stiff, and the oil makes it a permanent emulsion. If the mixture curdles, add it slowly to a fresh yolk.

FRUIT AND VEGETABLE DISHES

Trimmings for winter vegetables are quite the thing this season. They are quite simple and easily applied and bring out the real excellence of these modest but always-to-be-relied-upon standard goods. The trimmings must be applied discriminately and with a light hand to get the attractive and suitable result which will make an old standby seem like a new and interesting acquaintance. Before we apply the trimming we must be sure that the foundation is prepared by the best method. The right patterns for cutting your clothes and the right recipes for cooking the everyday foods, as well as for trimming them, are most important. The rules for cooking winter vegetables are few, but should be followed closely in the interests of flavor. Use boiling water to start the cooking. For strongly flavored vegetables such as onions, turnips, and cabbage, use a large amount of water to cook without a cover. In this way the strong odors and flavors will be carried away in the steam, we shall hardly notice the odor during cooking, and they will have a delicate flavor and color. Cabbage cooked 15 to 20 minutes in this way will be almost as white as when raw and will be digested easily by children as well as the adults.

❄ HARVARD BEETS
June 1922

½ c. sugar
½ tbsp. cornstarch
½ c. vinegar

2 c. beets roasted in the oven till nearly tender, then peeled and cooled
2 tbsp. butter

Mix sugar and cornstarch, add vinegar, and boil 5 minutes. Pour over beets which have been cut in thin slices, cubes, or fancy shapes. Cook on the back of the stove for ½ an hour. Add butter just before serving.

❄ SPICED CRANBERRIES
December 1931

2½ lbs. cranberries
2 c. brown sugar
1 c. mild vinegar
1 tsp. paprika

1½ tsp. cinnamon
½ tsp. ground cloves
½ tsp. salt

Wash cranberries and drain well, then add vinegar and cook till cranberries burst. Press through a coarse sieve, add remaining ingredients, and cook very slowly till thick.

❄ VEGETABLE PLATTER ROYAL
November 1936

Vegetables, of two or three different colors, arranged on one platter or tray make a handsome sight. An attractive combination is steamed spinach or pea timbales, diced buttered Hubbard squash, and glazed onions. Another combination is cauliflower (head cooked whole and melted butter poured over just before serving), glazed shredded carrots, and savory seasoned green beans. To prepare glazed onions, cook peeled pearl onions in boiling salted water till tender, drain thoroughly, sprinkle lightly with sugar, and dot with butter. Bake or broil till brown. If just two vegetables are used, choose a green one and a bright-colored one.

❄ ASPARAGUS TIPS WITH CARROTS
October 1929

Cook tender asparagus cut in pieces in a very little water. Drain, salt, add to sauce same amount of diced carrot. Season all with salt and pepper (sparse), a bit of sugar, and liberal butter. Let stand covered for 10 minutes, toss lightly with fork, and serve very hot.

❄ BRUSSELS SPROUTS
December 1920

Wash the sprouts carefully and remove the outer wilted leaves. Cover the sprouts with cold salt water, along with 1 tbsp. salt to each qt. water. Let stand for 2 hours or overnight. Cook in boiling water till tender and serve with melted butter.

❄ CABBAGE AND CHESTNUTS
January 1929

The French use chestnuts with cabbage to make a very appetizing dish. The chestnut, which is high in starch content, is more widely used as a vegetable in Europe than it is in this country, but American housewives are becoming more familiar with this article of food.

Shred ½ head of red cabbage and cook for 10 minutes in boiling salted water. Shell and blanch 1 lb. large chestnuts, keeping them whole if possible. Cook them in boiling water till tender. [*Editor's note*: Or use pre-cooked shelled chestnuts, available at specialty shops and many grocery stores during the holiday season.] Lay chestnuts in the bottom of a greased baking dish. Put in the partially cooked cabbage and 1 pt. milk. Cover and cook at 325°F till cabbage is tender, about 30 minutes. Drain, and if there is 1 c. liquor, thicken it to make a cream sauce, using 1 tbsp. flour and butter. Add more milk if necessary. Serve the cabbage in a deep dish with the hot sauce poured over it. If the chestnuts are whole, arrange them in a border around the cabbage.

❄ CABBAGE WITH BACON SAUCE
January 1929

1 medium head of cabbage	3 tbsp. bacon fat
2 tsp. salt	2 tbsp. flour
6 strips bacon	pepper
1 c. milk	paprika

Trim and cut cabbage in eighths. Plunge into boiling salted water and cook rapidly till tender without covering. Drain and pour bacon sauce over the cabbage. Fry the bacon till browned and put aside to keep warm. Make a white sauce from the bacon fat, flour, milk, and seasonings (see page 53). Garnish cabbage, over which sauce has been turned, with the slices of fried bacon.

❄ CARROT CUTLETS
January 1931

1 c. carrots, boiled and mashed	1 tbsp. onion juice
2 c. cold boiled rice	1 tbsp. celery salt
1 egg, beaten	breadcrumbs
salt and paprika	egg

Mix ingredients well. Form into balls and flatten them in shape of cutlets. Roll in breadcrumbs, egg, and again in crumbs. Sauté. Place a cube of jelly [any kind] on each cutlet and garnish the dish with parsley.

❄ CARROT SOUFFLÉ
January 1931

2 tbsp. butter	¼ tsp. salt
4 tbsp. flour	few grains paprika
1 c. milk	1 tbsp. minced onion
1 c. carrots, boiled and mashed	2 eggs, separated

Make a white sauce of the butter, flour, and milk by mixing flour into butter as it melts, then whisking in milk till thickened. Add carrots and seasoning, then the beaten egg yolks. Beat egg whites till stiff and then turn them into the first mixture. Turn into buttered baking dish. Set the dish in a pan of hot water and bake at 350°F for 30 minutes. Serve at once from the dish in which it was baked.

❄ GLAZED CARROTS
January 1931

Boil the carrots and cut lengthwise in halves, or quarters if large. Place in a single layer in baking dish. Over them pour a syrup of boiled cider, or maple sugar, or brown sugar. Bake at 350°F till brown, basting occasionally with the liquid. Serve with the syrup.

❄ CREAMED SPINACH
May 1911

Cook, drain, and chop fine 8 qt. spinach. Cook together 2 rounded tbsp. butter and 2 level tbsp. flour, put in the spinach, and stir and cook for 3 minutes. Add 1 c. cream in which baking soda the size of a pea has been dissolved and cook for 3 minutes longer. Season with salt and pepper, stirring all thoroughly, and serve immediately.

❄ SPINACH LOAF
November 1926

3 c. cooked spinach	½ c. grated Parmesan cheese
2 c. breadcrumbs	1 tbsp. lemon juice
2 eggs	salt and pepper to taste

Mix all ingredients well together and pour into buttered baking dish. Bake at 350°F for about 25 minutes. Serve hot.

❄ PARSNIPS WITH CHEESE
February 1926

3 c. parsnips, boiled till tender, peeled, and cubed
2 c. white sauce (page 53)
½ c. grated cheese
½ c. buttered breadcrumbs (page 53)

Arrange parsnips in a buttered baking dish in layers with white sauce and cheese. Cover with breadcrumbs, bake at 450°F for 15 to 20 minutes.

❄ PEAS IN TURNIP CUPS
November 1937
Contributed by Mrs. C. B.

Pare turnips of uniform size and cook in boiling salted water, uncovered, 25 minutes or till tender. Drain and cool. Remove center with vegetable or melon ball cutter or with a sharp-edged teaspoon. To serve, brush turnip cups with butter and heat in oven at 350°F. Cook 2 c. peas in water with the addition of a grating of onion, a sprinkle of salt, and ½ tsp. sugar. Drain; add 2 c. rich cream. Fill cups, place around the edge of serving plate or platter, and fill center with rest of peas and diced turnip, if desired, which has been seasoned and heated.

❄ MACEDOINE OF PEAS
October 1929

Combine 1 c. fresh peas, ½ c. of diced carrot, and ½ c. midget onions, peeled. Cook carrots and onions, tightly covered, ½ an hour; add peas, a pinch of sugar, salt to taste, liberal butter, and ½ tsp. lemon juice. Serve all very hot. Canned peas or frozen may be substituted for fresh ones.

❄ CORN CUSTARD PUDDING
Ladies' Home Journal, December 1917

To 1 c. corn kernels add salt and pepper to taste, 1 tbsp. butter, 3 well-beaten eggs, 1½ c. milk, and 3 tbsp. flour mixed till smooth in a little of the milk. Pour into a buttered dish and bake at 375°F for 20 to 30 minutes.

❄ TURNIPS WITH SOUR SAUCE
February 1926

1 qt. diced turnips	½ c. vinegar
3 tbsp. butter	½ tsp. salt
3 tbsp. flour	pepper
1½ c. water	

Cook turnips in boiling salted water, drain, and serve with a sauce made from the other ingredients: melt butter, stir in flour, slowly add water and vinegar and bring to a boil, stirring constantly. Season with salt and pepper and pour over cooked turnips.

❄ DUTCH STRING BEANS
1934

3 slices bacon	4 c. green beans
½ c. onion, sliced	salt and pepper

Cut bacon in small pieces and cook till crisp. Remove from fat and drain. Cook onion in bacon fat till slightly browned. Meanwhile, cook beans in a small amount of water for 10 to 15 minutes, till tender. Add to onions; season to taste with salt and pepper. Turn into a hot serving dish and garnish with bacon.

❄ SCALLOPED SWEET POTATO AND APPLE
November 1923

Sweet potatoes may be served plain, glazed, or scalloped with apple for a special treat.

Into a buttered baking dish put a ½-inch layer of pared, sliced sour apples. Sprinkle with sugar. Cover with a layer of sweet potatoes, season with salt and pepper, dot with butter, sprinkle generously with sugar. Repeat, having not more than three layers. Bake at 375°F; cover for the first 15 minutes of baking, then cook uncovered until the apples are soft—45 to 60 minutes.

❄ CANDIED SWEET POTATOES
January 1911

Boil medium-sized potatoes until nearly done, peel and cut lengthwise in slices ½ inch thick. Fill a baking dish with these slices, each thickly covered with brown sugar and dotted with butter. Add a little boiling water and bake 20 minutes at 400°F.

❄ SWEET POTATO CROQUETTES
January 1911

Take 2 c. boiled sweet potatoes and put them through a colander or ricer; add salt and pepper to season, a well-beaten egg, and a generous piece of butter. Shape into croquettes and fry in oil till browned on both sides.

❄ SWEET POTATO PUFF
November 1924

6 sweet potatoes
2 tbsp. butter

½ tsp. salt
whites of 2 eggs

Boil and mash the potatoes. Add butter, salt, and stiffly beaten egg whites. Fill buttered custard cups. Set in a pan of hot water and bake 20 minutes at 400°F. Serve in the cups.

❄ GOLDEN YAM CASSEROLE
November 1937

Pare yams, cook till tender in boiling water. Run through ricer. To each 4 c. add ⅓ c. cream, ¼ c. honey, salt to season, and ¼ tsp. mace or nutmeg. Pile in a buttered baking-serving dish, making depressions on top. When ready to serve, put marshmallows in depressions around the side, and heat at 350°F till lightly browned. Put lump of butter in center. Sprinkle with cinnamon or mace.

❄ BAKED SQUASH
December 1920

This will be improved if it can be reheated in the oven. Packing causes it to steam and renders the flavor less delicate. Split the squash; bake at 400°F without removing seeds and stringy portions, until tender. Scoop out, season with cream or milk and butter, pepper and salt, and a little sugar. Beat like mashed potatoes.

❄ SQUASH CHEESE SOUFFLÉ
October 1935

2 c. cooked, mashed winter squash
¾ c. milk and 2 tbsp. melted butter
salt and pepper
½ c. grated Parmesan cheese
2 eggs, separated

Squash may be first baked by cutting in pieces to remove the seeds, putting in baking pan cut-side down, and roasting at 400°F for about 40 minutes to 1 hour. Scoop out squash and mix with milk, seasonings and cheese, and yolks. Fold in whites beaten stiff. Bake at 375°F for 40 minutes or till firm in a pan set in hot water.

Pineapple Puddings

WORTHY OF A SECOND LOOK — A SECOND HELPING !

BY ANN CARROLL

Right out of our own kitchen comes this Christmas Pudding! It is your favorite pudding given a new dress, and new *zest*, with Hawaiian Canned Pineapple!

Puddings Hot. With a steamed Carrot Pudding (such as illustrated), our little trick is to line the well-greased mold with Pineapple slices before turning in the pudding mixture. Another idea is to include Crushed Pineapple in the pudding itself— or as a delicious sauce, just as it is.

Puddings Cold. Try adding Pineapple Tidbits to tapioca, bread or rice puddings. Turn out cup custards on chilled slices of Pineapple, or put a spoonful of Crushed Pineapple and currant jelly into the mold before turning in the custard. Add some Crushed or Tidbits to fruit gelatins and frozen desserts, or fold drained Crushed Pineapple into the whipped cream you use as topping. Alternate Pineapple slices with ladyfingers for the sides of icebox cake.

Yes, Hawaiian Canned Pineapple *does* have a way of adding flavor—to puddings as well as to fruit cocktails and salads, as a garnish for holiday meats. And best of all, it's such a *wholesome* fruit: vitamins A, B and C, many important minerals, plus natural sugars for quick energy. It's good, good *for* you—and convenient no end!

PINEAPPLE CARROT PUDDING

Mix together 1 cup each currants, raisins, grated potatoes, grated raw carrots, ground suet, sugar, sifted flour, 1 teaspoon each soda, nutmeg, and allspice, 2 teaspoons cinnamon, ½ teaspoon each ground cloves and salt. Turn mixture into a greased mold lined with slices of Pineapple, filling ¾ full. Cover, steam 2 hours. Serves 6 to 8. Once and a half the recipe was used in the pudding pictured above. Serve hot with a sauce made by boiling together ½ cup of sugar, 1 tablespoon flour, ⅛ teaspoon salt, 1 cup of the Pineapple syrup. When slightly thickened, add 1 tablespoon each butter and brandy or grated lemon rind. Serve it hot.

❄ MASHED WINTER SQUASH WITH PINEAPPLE
February 1926

Boil and mash a 2-lb. squash; add butter, salt and pepper to taste, and pineapple juice enough to soften. Add 1 c. shredded pineapple per qt. of mashed squash, beat well, reheat and serve.

❄ ZUCCHINI CUSTARD
October 1935

Cut cooked squash in dice; combine with custard in the proportions of 1 c. diced squash, 1½ c. milk, 2 eggs beaten slightly, ½ tsp. salt. Pour in custard cups, sprinkle tops with chopped parsley, and add a small lump of butter. Bake with cups surrounded by hot water at 375°F for 30 to 40 minutes.

❄ ST. NICHOLAS POTATOES
December 1920

Parboil 5 lbs. potatoes for 10 minutes; drain, peel, and slice. Place in a buttered baking dish in alternate layers with 2 c. peas, dotted liberally with pieces of chopped pimiento. When the dish is filled, pour over the whole a thin white sauce. Cover the whole with 1½ c. buttered breadcrumbs and bake at 350°F to a good warm brown.

❄ POTATO CROQUETTES
November 1919

Thoroughly mix 4 c. hot mashed potatoes, the well-beaten yolks of 2 eggs, 2 tsp. finely chopped parsley or celery leaves, 1 tsp. salt, ½ tsp. pepper, and ½ tsp. onion juice. Scrape an onion to get the juice. When well mixed, set aside to cool, then shape into croquettes, roll in breadcrumbs, and fry in sizzling butter till light brown.

❄ SCALLOPED POTATOES
November 1922

8 qts. potatoes
salt and pepper
1 c. flour
1 lb. butter
milk

Wash, pare, soak, and cut potatoes in ¼-inch slices. Put a layer in buttered baking dishes or shallow pans. Sprinkle with salt and pepper, dredge with flour, and dot with butter. Repeat until pans are filled; add hot milk to reach up to the top layer of potatoes. Bake gently until potatoes are soft.

❄ STUFFED BAKED POTATOES
May 1917

6 medium potatoes
¼ c. cream
2 tbsp. butter
½ tsp. salt
paprika
2 egg whites

Scrub potatoes thoroly and bake at 350°F till done—45 minutes to an hour. Remove from oven and with a very sharp knife cut each potato lengthwise, being careful not to break the skin. With a spoon scoop out the pulp of each potato, put in a bowl, and mash thoroly. Add the cream, butter, and seasoning and the beaten egg whites, saving a little of the egg to brush over the tops. Refill potato skins with mixture, brush over tops with egg white, return to oven to brown.

❄ FRENCH LYONNAISE POTATOES
October 1929

Dice 2 c. cold, boiled potatoes, add 1 c. diced cooked carrots, dredge with salt, pepper, and a dusting of flour. Sauté richly in butter or any nice fat in which minced onion has been simmering for 5 minutes. Serve very hot, sprinkled with minced parsley.

❄ WHITE SAUCE
1934

1 tbsp. butter	1 c. milk
1 tbsp. flour	½ tsp. salt

Melt butter in a skillet; add flour and salt, and stir to blend. Add milk and stir until thickened. This makes a thin white sauce, useful for cream soups and as a sauce for vegetables.

❄ BUTTERED BREADCRUMBS
February 1932

Allow ⅛ as much butter as crumbs. To prepare crumbs, use 1½ c. dry bread. Dry thoroughly in oven, then roll to crush (or pulverize in blender or food processor). Melt butter, add crumbs, stir until every crumb is coated.

BREADS

As I write I am wondering if any of you were, like myself, brought up in New England? If so you cannot help but remember how, for days, the preparations for the feast were going on. What a scene of enchantment seemed the great pantry with its rows of pies ... Its loaves of bread, both white and brown ...

—Maude K. Goodwill, December 1913

❄ HOT CROSS BUNS
March 1910

Take a bowl of bread dough after the first kneading. Set it aside to rise like the other bread dough; when light knead into it ½ c. currants that have been washed and dried, ½ c. sugar, and nutmeg to flavor. Knead no more than is necessary to mix the ingredients. Form into round biscuits, and place in a baking pan about ½ inch apart. Cut two deep gashes on top of each, crossing each other, and set to rise in a warm place. Just before putting into the moderately hot oven (400°F), brush the tops with melted butter or white of egg. Bake 10 minutes then reduce heat to 350°F and bake about 15 minutes more, until golden.

❄ ROLLS AND FANCY BREADS
1934

1 cake compressed yeast (substitute 1 package active dry yeast)
½ c. lukewarm water
1 pt. milk, scalded
6 tbsp. shortening
4 tbsp. sugar
2 tsp. salt
7 to 8 c. flour

Dissolve yeast in water. Scald milk with shortening and sugar. Cool to lukewarm; add yeast; add about 3 c. flour and salt to make a batter. Beat until smooth. Cover and let rise about 50 minutes in a warm place, until light. Add rest of flour or enough to handle. Knead thoroughly, place in a well-greased bowl; cover and let rise until double. Make into rolls or loaf. Let rise until double in bulk and bake. Small rolls bake in 30 minutes in a fairly hot oven (400° to 425°F); a loaf 45 minutes in a more moderate oven (375° to 400°F).

❄ DELICATE ROLLS
March 1938

1 pckt. quick yeast
1 tbsp. sugar
1 c. lukewarm water
1 c. milk, scalded and cooled, or
  lukewarm water
6 c. sifted flour
1 egg, beaten
4–6 tbsp. fat
3 tbsp. sugar
2 tsp. salt

Add yeast and sugar to lukewarm water, stir, and let stand 10 minutes. Add cup of milk or water and half the flour. Beat until smooth. Add egg, softened or melted fat, sugar, salt, and rest of flour. Knead into a medium-firm dough, adding more flour if necessary, until smooth and elastic. Let dough rise until doubled in a cozy place, fold or knead down, and let rise ¾ as much as the first time. Fold down and divide into rolls, shaping as desired. Let rise in greased pans until double in bulk. Bake about 20 minutes at 400°F.

❄ FANCY NORWEGIAN BREADS SMORGASBORD
December 1937

Make a good sweet roll dough (Rolls/Fancy Breads, 1934, page 54) flavor with 2 tsp. pounded cardamom; let rise and divide as follows:

Smolands kake (a cake)—Roll dough out thin as for roll. Put in a round pan and prick with a fork. Glaze with egg yolk, sugar, and milk mixture.

Jule kake (Christmas cake)—Add ¾ c. chopped candied peel, using red and green to give Christmas colors. Work in well, add raisins if desired, shape in round loaf.

Kaffe kake (Coffee cake)—Roll dough, cut in strips, and braid. Fit into a greased ring mold. After baking, frost with boiled or powdered sugar and butter icing and sprinkle with candied fruits.

Bake all the above at 350°F, till nicely browned.

Desserts

Spicy cakes, steaming puddings, savory odors of all kinds coming from the kitchen! Foremost among the associations which have grown up around the Christmas season is that of homecoming and its attendant feasting.

But the farm mother of today breathes a sigh of relief as she plans the menus she is to serve. No longer need she prepare a dozen kinds of pie or a half dozen kinds of cake. No longer need she fear the ills which follow Christmas time gorging. These meals can be just as healthful and well balanced, just as delicious as those of any other month.

In our own family we have established somewhat of a tradition of having roast pigeon as meat for our Christmas dinner. A couple of nights before the men climb into the haymow and take the birds from their roosts; then we all pitch in and help pick and dress them. We stuff them with our favorite dressing and put them in the oven 3 or 4 hours before serving time. They're delicious—if you have the pigeons to catch.

—Gertrude Brown, December 1928

❄ CHOCOLATE MOUSSE
September 1926

2 oz. bittersweet chocolate
1 c. sugar
½ c. milk
2 c. heavy cream

¾ tbsp. gelatin
3 tbsp. cold water
2 tsp. vanilla

Melt chocolate over hot water in a double boiler, add ¼ c. sugar, the milk, and ½ c. cream. Leave over hot water till cream is scalded. Add gelatin previously soaked in cold water, remaining sugar, and vanilla. Strain mixture into a bowl, set in pan of ice water. Stir constantly till mixture thickens. Fold in remaining cream beaten stiff. Pour into ice cream maker and freeze according to manufacturer's directions.

For coffee mousse, use ½ c. strong coffee, ½ c. sugar, and 1 pt. heavy cream with the same amount of gelatin in cold water as above. Dissolve the soaked gelatin in the hot coffee, adding the sugar and finishing as for chocolate mousse.

❄ CHOCOLATE BLANC MANGE I
November 1926

8 tbsp. cornstarch
6 tbsp. sugar
4 tsp. cocoa
¼ tsp. salt
4 c. milk
1 tsp. vanilla

Mix dry ingredients and moisten with 1 c. of the milk and the vanilla. Heat the rest of the milk and add to the first mixture. Cook in double boiler about 30 minutes. Pour into slightly damp single-serving ramekins or blanc mange molds and chill. Turn out to serve.

❄ CHOCOLATE BLANC MANGE II
1934

3 c. milk
½ c. sugar
6 tbsp. cornstarch

¼ tsp. salt
3 tbsp. cocoa powder
½ tsp. vanilla

Heat milk. Combine all dry ingredients, moisten with a little cold milk, and stir into hot milk. Stir till thick, cooking 30 minutes in a double boiler. Chill in individual molds and serve with whipped cream.

❄ LEMON FLOATING ISLAND
January 1910

Soak one ounce of gelatin and the thin, yellow rind of two lemons in one pint of cold water for one hour. Take out the rind; add one breakfast cup of white sugar and the juice of two lemons. Put the whole into a graniteware saucepan over a moderate fire, and stir until the sugar and gelatin are thoroughly dissolved, then pour the mixture into a bowl and let it stand until it begins to get firm. Beat the whites of two large fresh eggs to a stiff snow, then add them to the gelatin, beating the whole with a steady motion until it is firm and "rocky" in appearance. Pile it unevenly in the center of a glass dish, put cocoanut macaroons or lady fingers around the base, and pour around it a cold, boiled custard made as follows: to one pint of hot, sweet milk add three whole, well-beaten eggs and a cup of white sugar, with a pinch of salt. You can use the yolks of two eggs and one whole egg with the same result. Put the custard in a double boiler and stir it well until it is thick and smooth; then take from the fire and add a few drops of extract of lemon. This makes an attractive and delicious dessert.

❄ PRUNE SOUFFLÉ
October 1921

3 tsp. butter
3 tsp. flour
1 c. scalded milk
¼ c. sugar
4 eggs
2 c. Stewed Prunes

Melt the butter, add flour, and gradually the hot milk. Cook till thick. Add sugar and well-beaten egg yolks; cool and fold in stiffly beaten whites. Pack drained prunes into buttered baking dish and pour over custard mixture. Bake at 350°F for 35 to 40 minutes. Serve with cream.

To make the Stewed Prunes:

1 lb. prunes
1 qt. water
⅓ c. sugar
2 tsp. lemon juice

Wash the prunes thoroughly. Put in clean water and let soak several hours. Leave fruit in soaking water, cover, and cook slowly till skins are tender. Add sugar and lemon juice when almost done.

❄ PRUNE AND RAISIN PUDDING
November 1926

3½ c. milk
3½ tbsp. cornstarch
salt
½ c. raisins
¾ c. brown sugar
½ c. Stewed Prunes (see recipe above)

Scale 3 c. of the milk. Mix cornstarch and salt with remaining milk and add with sugar to hot milk. Stir till thick and smooth, add fruit, and cook over hot water in a double boiler for 30 minutes. Pour into large or single molds and chill. Serve plain or with whipped cream.

❄ NORWEGIAN PRUNE PUDDING
May 1929

½ lb. pitted prunes
2 c. cold water
1 c. sugar
1-inch cinnamon stick

⅓ c. cornstarch
1½ c. boiling water
⅛ tsp salt
1 tbsp. lemon juice

Wash and soak prunes in 2 c. water for several hours. Stew till soft in same water. Drain. Add sugar, cinnamon, and cornstarch well mixed. Slowly add boiling water and salt and boil 20 minutes, stirring constantly till spoon leaves streak in mixture. Remove cinnamon and add lemon juice. Serve hot.

❄ BAKED INDIAN PUDDING
November 1937

A famous New England recipe from Boston's Hotel Statler.

5 c. milk
⅔ c. molasses
4 tbsp. butter
⅓ c. sugar

½ c. cornmeal
1 tsp. cinnamon
¼ tsp. nutmeg
1 tsp. salt

Scald all but 1 c. milk; add molasses, butter, and rest of mixed dry ingredients. Stir and cook slowly till slightly thickened, about 20 minutes. Pour into buttered baking dish; add last cup of milk. Do not stir. Bake at 300°F, uncovered, for 3 hours without stirring. Serve warm with cream or vanilla ice cream.

❄ RÖMME GRÖT SMORGASBORD
December 1937

1 pt. very thick sour cream
½ c. water
½ tsp. salt

½ c. flour
1 pt. hot milk
sugar and cinnamon

Cook cream and water together very gently for 45 minutes to 1 hour, stirring occasionally. Add paste of salt and flour, with a little cold water, stirring thoroughly. Cook till thick and butter fat comes out of pudding on top. Remove fat and save. Stir in hot milk and whisk briskly with flat wire beater. Pudding should be very smooth and creamy. Pour into a bowl and make depressions on top for butter fat. Serve hot in dessert dishes and pass sugar and cinnamon to sprinkle on top. The pudding is not a success unless the butter fat comes out on top after flour is added.

❄ CRÈME DE MENTHE PEARS
November 1931

Pare, cut in half, and core 12 firm pears. Make a syrup of 3 c. sugar and 3 c. water. Add ½ tsp. mint oil. Drop the pears into the hot syrup and cook till clear. Serve with whipped cream or ice cream.

❄ APRICOT WHIP
February 1919

1 c. dried apricots, cooked in water till soft
3 egg whites
½ c. corn syrup
1 tsp. lemon juice

Rub apricots through sieve, add corn syrup, and cook slowly till mixture is consistency of marmalade. Cool. Whip egg whites till stiff, add lemon juice to apricots, and gradually fold them into whites. Pile lightly in buttered baking dish and bake in a pan of hot water at 300°F about 20 minutes. Some of the juice of the apricots is nice to serve with this. Prunes may be used in place of apricots.

❄ CRANBERRY WATER ICE
November 1912

Boil 1 qt. cranberries in 1 pt. water till skins are soft and strain through a cheesecloth. When cool, add the juice of 2 lemons. Make a syrup with 1 pt. sugar and ½ pt. water; when cool add to the cranberry juice and freeze.

❄ CRANBERRY PUDDING

January 1911
Contributed by E. I. Locke

Cream ½ c. butter; add gradually 1 c. sugar, 3 well-beaten eggs, ½ c. milk, 3½ c. flour, 2 tsp. baking powder, and 1½ c. washed and drained cranberries. Turn into a buttered mold, cover, and steam for 3 hours over a low flame. Serve with cream, sweetened and flavored with nutmeg.

❄ MAPLE NUT LOAF

1934

1½ c. brown sugar	2 c. boiling water	½ tsp. maple extract
7 tbsp. cornstarch	¼ tsp. salt	½ c. chopped walnuts
¼ c. water	3 egg whites	Custard Sauce

Mix sugar and cornstarch together and stir into a smooth paste with ¼ c. water. Stir in boiling water and cook in a double boiler for 15–20 minutes, till thick. Add salt to egg whites and beat till stiff. Stir into cornstarch mixture and add extract and nuts. Pour into a buttered mold and chill. Un-mold when ready to serve and serve with custard sauce.

To make the Custard Sauce:

1 c. milk	2 tbsp. sugar
2 egg yolks	¼ tsp. vanilla

Scald milk in double boiler. Beat yolks and sugar and gradually stir in hot milk. Return to double boiler and cook, stirring constantly, for 20 minutes, or until mixture coats spoon. Remove from heat, add extract, and cool.

❆ DATE TORT

December 1926

12 eggs, yolks and whites
  beaten separately
2 c. sugar
2 tbsp. flour
¾ c. water

2 c. English walnuts, chopped
3½ c. dates, chopped
1 tbsp. baking powder
Juice of 1 lemon

Mix all together. Bake 30 or 40 minutes in a buttered shallow pan set in water at 325°F. Serve with whipped cream.

❆ CHEESE TORTE

1934

1½ lbs. cottage cheese
8 egg yolks, beaten
1½ c. sugar
3 tbsp. flour
1½ tbsp. butter

1½ c. cream
⅛ tsp. salt
grated rind and juice of 1 lemon
8 egg whites, beaten stiff

Press cottage cheese through sieve. Beat yolks with sugar and mix with flour and butter till smooth. Add cottage cheese and remaining ingredients, folding in egg whites last. Pour into greased baking dish and bake at 350°F for 45 minutes.

❄ FIG PUDDING
December 1913

1 c. molasses
1 c. chopped suet
1 tsp. cinnamon
½ tsp. nutmeg
1 pt. chopped figs
1 tsp. baking soda
1 c. milk
2 eggs
3¾ c. flour

Mix together the molasses, suet, spice, and figs. Dissolve the soda with 1 tbsp. hot water and mix with the milk. Add to the other ingredients. Beat the eggs light and stir into the mixture. Add the flour and beat thoroughly. Butter one large bread mold; turn the mixture into the mold and steam 5 hours. Serve with your favorite sauce.

❄ BLACK PUDDING
December 1911

Cook 3 c. plump prunes till thoroughly done and press through a colander. To 2 c. of the pulp add 2 c. breadcrumbs previously soaked in milk and beaten smooth, 1 c. brown sugar, 2 tbsp. molasses, 1 tsp. ground cinnamon, and 1 pt. boiling milk. Heat all to boiling point, place in the oven at 350°F, and bake for an hour or more. Serve with a sprinkling of shredded cocoanut and bits of currant jelly.

❄ CRANBERRY STEAMED PUDDING
November 1929

½ c. butter
1 c. sugar
3 eggs
3½ c. flour
4 tsp. baking powder
½ c. milk
1½ c. cranberries

Cream butter and sugar and add eggs, well beaten. Sift dry ingredients and add alternately with milk to above mixture. Add berries and pour into buttered mold. Cover and steam 3 hours. Serve with whipped cream or thin sweetened cream.

She Sells Fruitcake

December 1937

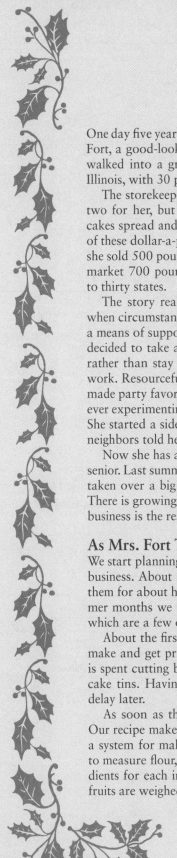

One day five years ago, Mrs. Theresa Walther Fort, a good-looking, happy young woman, walked into a grocery store in Cambridge, Illinois, with 30 pounds of fruitcake.

PHOTO BY SALTO

Mrs. Fort and one of her cakes

The storekeeper disposed of only twenty-two for her, but word of Mrs. Fort's fruitcakes spread and kept spreading. Popularity of these dollar-a-pound cakes increased until she sold 500 pounds last year and expects to market 700 pounds this year. Her cakes go to thirty states.

The story really starts fifteen years ago, when circumstances forced Mrs. Fort to find a means of support for herself and baby. She decided to take a position as a housekeeper rather than stay in the city in stenographer work. Resourceful and a good manager, she made party favors in spare time and was forever experimenting with some special dish for community suppers and socials. She started a sideline of fruitcakes for sale because she liked to cook and her neighbors told her she did it exceptionally well.

Now she has as a right-hand assistant a strapping son who is a high-school senior. Last summer Mrs. Fort and Richard moved to Geneseo where they have taken over a big old-fashioned house to start them in the tearoom business. There is growing demand for her Sunday dinner and parties, but the fruitcake business is the real story and here it is.

As Mrs. Fort Tells It

We start planning in the spring for our Thanksgiving and Christmas fruitcake business. About May 1 we pack 36 dozen fresh eggs in water glass, buying them for about half what they would cost us in the fall. Then during the summer months we make strawberry jams, jellies, apple butter, and grape juice, which are a few of the "additions" we put into the foundation recipe.

About the first of October we estimate how many pounds of cake we will make and get prices on ingredients in quantity. One evening in the early fall is spent cutting brown paper and heavy waxed paper to fit our various-sized cake tins. Having these papers ready for lining the tins saves considerable delay later.

As soon as the fresh crop of fruits and nuts arrive we start our baking. Our recipe makes 25 pounds of cake in one mixing, and we have worked out a system for making a hundred or more pounds each week. The first step is to measure flour, spices, sugar, etc. for four or five batches of cake. Dry ingredients for each individual batch are sifted into a heavy paper sack. Then the fruits are weighed and piled on separate trays. During leisure hours we cut the fruits. When we are ready to mix a batch of cake, it is a simple matter to assemble the butter, eggs, and liquids and combine them with the other ingredients which are measured and ready.

When the cakes are [done] we turn them out and remove the papers. After they have cooled thoroughly they are wrapped separately in waxed paper and packed in covered containers to ripen for at least a month. Several days before deliveries start we remove our cakes from their containers and decorate them. Each cake is brushed with molasses, diluted with water or egg white. Pieces of candied pineapple in natural or Christmas colors, cherries, and whole nut meats are generously placed over the top, then the cake is slipped into the oven for a few minutes.

It is fun, after the cakes of various shapes and sizes are gaily decorated, to put on their pretty wrapping before they go to market. On each cake is placed a tiny lace paper doily bearing instructions for storing the cake. Then the cake is placed on a lacy doily and carefully wrapped in clear, moisture-proof cellophane ribbon with a gay bow on top. Then off they go to sell at $1.00 a pound.

Dark Christmas Fruit Cake

2 lbs. butter
2½ lbs. brown sugar
1 c. molasses
1 c. milk
½ c. dark jam or jelly
½ c. fruit juice
13 eggs, separated
3 lbs. flour
1 tsp. each salt and cloves

1 heaping tsp. baking powder
½ tsp. baking soda
2 tsp. each cinnamon
  and nutmeg
2 lbs. raisins
2 lbs. currants
1 lb. dried figs, chopped
1 lb. citron, sliced
2 lbs. pecans, chopped

Figs, candied cherries, pineapple, orange, or lemon peel may be added. Browning the flour slightly gives a richer flavor. Cream butter and sugar. Add molasses and milk as well as jelly and fruit juice. Beat egg yolks and add. Sift flour, salt, baking powder and soda, and spices. Dredge the fruits with half the flour and nuts with other half. Fold in fruits and nuts and lastly the stiffly beaten egg whites. Bake at 275°F for 3 hours in paper-lined buttered pans.

White Christmas Fruit Cake
For 6 small or 3 large cakes

4 c. cake flour
1 tsp. baking powder
½ tsp. baking soda
½ tsp. salt
1 c. butter
1½ c. sugar
1 tbsp. lemon juice
1 lb. white raisins

½ lb. candied cherries, chopped
½ lb. candied pineapple, sliced
½ lb. citron, sliced
¼ lb. lemon peel, chopped
¼ lb. orange peel, chopped
1 lb. almonds, chopped
10 egg whites, stiffly beaten

Sift flour with baking powder, soda, and salt. Cream butter and sugar. Add lemon juice, fruits which have been dredged in flour, and almonds. Then fold in stiffly beaten egg whites. Bake at 250°F for about 3 hours in paper-lined buttered pans.

❄ PLAIN PLUM PUDDING
December 1911

1 c. sugar
1 c. suet chopped fine
1 c. raisins
1 c. currants
2 c. breadcrumbs

1 tsp. each salt, cinnamon, ground
  ginger, allspice
1 tsp. baking soda dissolved in 1 pt.
  buttermilk
1 qt. flour

Mix all together, adding flour last. Tie in a floured cheesecloth, allowing a little room for swelling. Drop in a large kettle of boiling water. Must be kept boiling steadily for 4 hours, and English custom is to pour a little alcohol on the pudding and set fire to it when taking it to the table. Serve with one of the sauces below.

HARD SAUCE:
Cream ⅓ c. butter with 1 c. sugar until very white and curdled looking; add the stiffly beaten white of 1 egg and 1 tbsp. lemon juice.

LIQUID LEMON SAUCE:
2 tbsp. butter
½ c. sugar
1 tbsp. cornstarch
juice of ½ lemon
½ tsp. lemon extract
1 c. boiling water

Beat thoroughly the butter, sugar, cornstarch and lemon juice, and extract. Pour water over, and cook in a double boiler till thick.

❄ STEAMED GINGER PUDDING
December 1932

1 egg	2½ c. flour
1 c. molasses	1 tbsp. ground ginger
½ c. butter, melted	1 tsp. baking soda
1 c. chopped figs	1 c. hot water

Beat egg; add molasses, melted butter, and figs and beat thoroughly. Add flour sifted with ginger and soda and when well mixed, add hot water. Put in two shallow greased pans and steam 1 hour. Serve with lemon sauce (page 68).

❄ SOUR CREAM GINGERBREAD
October 1924

1 egg	scant tsp. baking soda
¾ c. sour cream	3 tsp. ground ginger
½ c. molasses	2 tsp. cinnamon
½ c. sugar	½ tsp. salt

Beat egg, cream, and molasses; mix and sift dry ingredients; mix all together and beat well; bake at 350°F for 20–30 minutes in a shallow buttered pan.

❄ EGGLESS FRUIT CAKE
January 1913

1 c. sour cream
1 c. brown sugar
1 c. molasses
2 tsp. ground cinnamon
1 tsp. ground ginger
½ tsp. ground cloves
½ tsp. nutmeg
2 c. chopped raisins
½ c. shredded unsweetened cocoanut
pinch salt
1 tsp, baking soda dissolved in 1 c. hot water
3–5 c. flour, enough to make a very stiff dough

The dough must cleave from the sides of the mixing bowl and retain its shape when rolled in the hand. Press the dough into a buttered sheet pan, allowing it to double in bulk, cover it with two layers of waxed paper, and bake at 350°F until a toothpick thrust into the middle comes out clean. Place while hot in a covered tin cake box to keep moist. This is served without frosting in small, rather thick squares.

❄ ENGLISH FRUIT CAKE
December 1924

This recipe came down to me from English ancestors. The family custom has been to make the cake a little while before Thanksgiving. Some of it is used for this holiday feast but it is not in the very best condition until Christmas time. It will keep perfectly until spring, if allowed to and properly cared for, and so insures to the housekeeper a rich dessert ready for unexpected company or any other special occasion. As given, the recipe makes several loaves. If so much is not desired, it can be divided easily by measuring out only half the quantity of each ingredient mentioned.

¾ lb. butter	2 lbs. raisins
1 lb. sugar	½ lb. citron, cut into bits
12 eggs, beaten	¼ oz. powdered cinnamon
1 lb. flour	⅛ oz. powdered cloves
1 tsp. baking soda	1 lg. nutmeg, grated
1 c. clear, strong coffee	

Cream the butter and sugar together, then add the beaten eggs. Stir in a little flour [sifted together with the soda] and then a part of the prepared coffee, alternating them until both are used. Dredge the fruit well with a little extra flour and add this last. Stir all together. The mixture will be too stiff with the fruit for much beating. Divide into buttered loaf pans of any preferred shape and size. Bake slowly at 325°F for at least 1 hour.

The mixture calls for no leaven except the soda. However, 1 tsp. baking powder in addition, also sifted with the flour, produces a lighter and possibly more digestible cake. Some housewives might prefer it in this form.

This mixture makes a fine plum pudding if steamed instead of baked. Put it into buttered molds, cover closely, and steam or boil from 3 to 4 hours. Serve hot with any flavored sauce. Vanilla sauce follows.

Any leftover pudding can be reheated successfully by steaming it for about 20 minutes. With freshly made sauce it will be as good as when first cooked.

VANILLA SAUCE:

Cream ¾ c. sugar and 1 tbsp. butter. Put 1 pt. hot water into a saucepan over the fire [on a medium flame]. To this add 1 tbsp. flour first rubbed smooth in a little cold water. Cook, stirring constantly to prevent lumps or scorching, until it is just like a thin, smooth starch. Add this slowly to the butter and sugar, beating briskly all the time. The sauce should rise with the final beating and be light and foamy. Just before serving add 1 tsp. of best vanilla extract.

The same foundation sauce may be flavored with lemon, almond, pineapple, strawberry, cherry, or rose, to suit differing tastes. All are good with this pudding. If a sour sauce is preferred, omit other flavorings and add the juice of ½ a large lemon, with a little of the grated rind, or 1 tsp. lemon extract. If lemon is lacking, 2 or 3 tbsp. good fruit vinegar may be used in its place.

❄ NEW MINCEMEAT FILLINGS
January 1935

SIMPLE MINCEMEAT:

2 lbs. lean beef
½ lb. suet
4 lbs. tart quartered apples
1 tsp. ground cloves
2 tsp. cinnamon
2 tbsp. allspice

1 tbsp. salt
2 tbsp. brown sugar
1 c. corn syrup
1 qt. apple cider
juice and grated rind of 1 lemon

Boil beef in a very little water until tender. Chop fine. Chop suet and apples. Add all other ingredients except lemon and boil in a large kettle till apples are cooked, about 1 hour. Add lemon and mix.

SPICY MINCEMEAT:

8 lbs. lean beef and bone
10 lbs. tart apples
3 lbs. suet
1 lb. citron
3 lbs. raisins
3 lbs. currants
5 lbs. sugar
2 tbsp. salt

1 tbsp. mace
1 tbsp. nutmeg
1 tbsp. ground cloves
4 tbsp. cinnamon
4 tbsp. allspice
1 pt. grape juice
3 qts. beef stock

Boil beef till tender; cool and remove bones and gristle. Chop with apples, suet, and citron. Add other ingredients. Cook slowly for 1 to 1½ hours in a large kettle, stirring frequently. Make a lot of pies!

FAVORITE MINCEMEAT:

5 lbs. neck beef
2 gallons apples, quartered
1 lb. suet
5 lbs. raisins
3 lbs. brown sugar
3 tbsp. cinnamon
2 tbsp. cloves
1 tbsp. nutmeg
1 tbsp. salt
1 tsp. ground ginger
1 tsp. pepper
2 qts. apple cider

Boil then simmer beef till very tender, cool, remove from bone. Chop with apples and suet. Add other ingredients; cook slowly about 1 hour, stirring frequently. This makes about 10 qts.

❄ MY USES FOR HOLIDAY MINCEMEAT
December 1916
Contributed by Aldis Dunbar

One can bring back a sudden sense of Christmas by biting into a sprig of pine or hemlock or by encountering the savor of good homemade mincemeat. I first realized the possibilities of mincemeat, outside of "pie lines" one day when I was making an old-fashioned creamy rice pudding. When I came to put together my ingredients, I found to my dismay that the boys had eaten up all my raisins. But I had an inspiration! I used instead a cupful of mincemeat and baked the pudding as usual, allowing the little fawn-colored crust to form during the last half hour. My family hailed it with joy and since then, I have made desserts of many kinds, using mincemeat where raisins or other fruits were called for in the original receipts. They were called successful—and held the Christmas savor.

❄ CRANBERRY MOLASSES PIE
November 1929

1 qt. ripe cranberries
1 c. brown sugar
1 tbsp. butter

1 c. white sugar
1 c. molasses

Cook ingredients over a slow fire for 10 minutes. Line a buttered deep 9-inch pie dish with pie crust (page 73). Fill with cranberry mixture. Cover with strips of crust in a lattice pattern. Bake at 325°F for 45 minutes to 1 hour, or until berries are thoroughly cooked.

❋ PLAIN PIE PASTRY—2 CRUSTS
1934

Double this recipe to make two pies.

½ tsp. salt
1½ c. sifted flour

½ c. lard
3 or 4 tbsp. ice cold water

Add salt to flour and cut in shortening with a dough blender, sharp-tined fork, or finger tips, until pieces are size of small peas. Add a little water at a time, mixing with a fork lightly until it can be shaped into a ball. Divide dough and roll out one crust at a time. Avoid overhandling the dough either in mixing it or in rolling out the crust. Work quickly, especially in warm weather so that fat doesn't melt. To bake single crusts, lay in pie tin quite loosely and prick well over bottom or fit over the bottom of an inverted tin. Bake in a hot oven (450°F).

Tough crust may be due to too much water and too little fat, overhandling, or too slow an oven. Soggy undercrust may be due to not having the oven hot enough to bake the under crust before the filling soaks in, or to having the crust so rich or rolled so thin that the filling breaks through.

❋ FROSTING AND FILLING FOR CHRISTMAS LAYER CAKES
December 1911
Contributed by Lulu G. Parker

For decorating fancy cakes there are tiny frosting funnels in the market, but these are so seldom used in the average household that it does not pay to buy them. For making a fancy scrollwork or initials on top of a cake try using a funnel made of glazed writing paper held in shape with a pin. Squeeze the frosting through this. With a little practice one can work out any design. Chocolate creams may be split or any sugary candy, or cream candy, may be arranged on top of a cake when the frosting is soft. Nuts, raisins, citron, or candied fruits or orange peel may be used as well. [Following] are several good fillings and frostings for Christmas layer cake.

❄ SPONGE CAKE
June 1928

2 eggs, well-beaten until light-colored   1 c. white sugar
Add 1 tsp. vanilla and

Beat well again. Add 1 c. pastry flour into which 1 heaping tsp. of baking powder that has been thoroughly sifted. Sift into batter and cut it in, as you would pastry. Then add ½ c. boiling water and beat well again. Bake in two large layers.

Frost and fill with:

SOFT WHITE FROSTING
1 c. sugar   ⅓ c. water

Boil slowly together till the mixture hairs when dropped from a spoon. While this is boiling beat the whites of 2 eggs to a stiff froth. Add a pinch of cream of tartar and beat in the boiling syrup. Keep beating till it becomes thick and creamy, then flavor with 1 tsp. lemon or vanilla extract and spread between layers and on top of cake.

CARAMEL FILLING

1 c. brown sugar	½ c. hot milk	½ oz. bittersweet
1 c. molasses	1 tbsp. flour wet with	chocolate, grated
1 tbsp. melted butter	a little water	1 tsp. vanilla

Stir brown sugar, molasses, butter, milk, and flour together and boil, stirring for 5 minutes, then add ½ oz. grated bittersweet chocolate and 1 tsp. vanilla and boil 5 minutes longer. Stir in a bit of baking soda the size of a pea, cook until it forms into a creamy mass when dropped into cold water. Then remove from the fire, beat until creamy, and spread.

LEMON FILLING
Cream together 2 tbsp. butter and 1 c. sugar; add 2 beaten eggs and the juice and grated rind of 1 lemon. Mix well together and cook in a double boiler, stirring constantly until the consistency of jelly. When cold spread between layers of sponge cake.

MARSHMALLOW FILLING
Gum arabic (also known as acacia powder) is derived from the bark of the acacia tree and is a natural, tasteless emulsifier used in baking and candy making. It's available at specialty and baking shops, as well as from a number of online purveyors.

Dissolve 5 tbsp. gum arabic in ½ c. cold water, add ½ c. powdered sugar, and boil until thick enough to form a soft ball between the fingers when dropped into cold water. Beat the white of 1 egg stiff, flavor with 1 tsp. lemon or vanilla extract, and pour the hot syrup over the egg. Beat and spread on cake with a knife dipped in hot water.

UNCOOKED ICING

¾ c. confectioner's sugar: put it into a bowl and wet it with hot milk. Add the milk 1 tbsp. at a time; it will not take more than 3. Beat it until smooth and spread.

CHOCOLATE FROSTING

Make as above, but melt 2 oz. bittersweet baker's chocolate and thoroughly mix it with the sugar before milk is added.

❄ SPICE CAKE
October 1928

1 c. butter
2 c. sugar (cream these)
3 eggs (break one at a time in
  batter and beat)
4 c. flour
2 tsp. baking powder, heaping
vanilla

1 or 2 c. raisins
1 tsp. cloves, ground
1 tsp. cinnamon
1 tsp. nutmeg
1 c. sweet milk

Beat well and bake in an oiled cast-iron skillet at 350°F.
Ice with the following: 1 c. sugar and ¼ c. water boiled together until the mixture threads. Cool a little and pour over stiffly beaten white of 1 egg, beating hard all the time.

❄ VERY BEST FRUITCAKE
1934

¼ lb. citron, shredded
¼ lb. lemon
  peel, shredded
¼ lb. orange
  peel, shredded
½ lb. candied
  cherries, halved
½ lb. nuts, chopped
½ lb. dates, chopped

½ lb. candied pineapple,
  chopped
¼ lb. shredded
  unsweetened cocoanut
½ lb. raisins
2 c. flour
1 tsp. allspice
½ tsp. nutmeg
½ tsp. ground cloves

1 tsp. salt
1 tsp. baking powder
½ lb. butter
½ c. sugar
⅓ c. honey
3 eggs
6 tbsp. orange juice

Dredge fruit in ¼ c. of the flour. Sift remaining flour with dry ingredients. Cream butter with sugar, add honey, then stir in eggs. Add dry ingredients alternately with orange juice. Pour batter over fruit and mix till all is thoroughly blended. Line two buttered baking tins with three layers of waxed paper, allowing ½ inch of paper to extend over sides of tins. Pour batter into pans and bake at 275°F for 2–3 hours, with a flat pan containing 2 c. water at bottom of oven, till cakes are done.

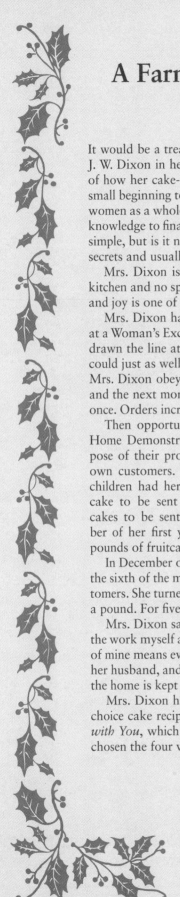

A Farm Woman's Christmas Cakes

December 1925

It would be a treat, indeed, if the readers of *The Farmer's Wife* could visit Mrs. J. W. Dixon in her North Carolina home and hear from her own lips the story of how her cake-making business has grown, like Jack's beanstalk, from a very small beginning to something beyond even her dreams. One topic in which farm-women as a whole are mightily interested in is how to turn some of their practical knowledge to financial account. The story of how Mrs. Dixon did this seems very simple, but is it not true that the secrets behind all legitimate success are "open" secrets and usually very easy of application?

Mrs. Dixon is the mother of a family of seven. She had only a small farm kitchen and no special conveniences "But," she says, "my work was a real joy"— and joy is one of the vital ingredients of success.

Mrs. Dixon had been selling Boston brown bread, cheese straws, and salads at a Woman's Exchange. Unexpectedly, someone ordered a cake. Mrs. Dixon had drawn the line at cakes but the manager of the Exchange said that a good cake could just as well be turned out of that little farm kitchen as good brown bread. Mrs. Dixon obeyed the hint Opportunity had given her, went to work at once, and the next morning carried a basket of cakes into the Exchange. They sold at once. Orders increased steadily until the Exchange closed for the summer.

Then opportunity spoke again: the farmwomen of the county organized a Home Demonstration Booth at the city market where farmwomen could dispose of their products. Mrs. Dixon turned in cakes and the cakes made their own customers. Then two grocers asked for them and the mother of seven children had her hands full. She tells us that someone ordered a large fruit-cake to be sent to Paris, France, for Christmas, and there were orders for cakes to be sent as gifts to other cities outside her own state. That December of her first year of making cakes for sale; she turned out, on order, 200 pounds of fruitcake and more than 200 other cakes.

In December of 1924, Mrs. Dixon closed her books to all new customers—on the sixth of the month for fruitcakes and on eleventh of the month to all old customers. She turned away orders for at least 200 pounds of fruit cake at one dollar a pound. For five days before Christmas she filled orders for layer cakes.

Mrs. Dixon says: "As these cakes are my own hand embroidery, I do most of the work myself and cannot take care of all the business offered me. This business of mine means everything to a woman who positively would not leave her home, her husband, and children and go into the city for a position. The atmosphere of the home is kept sweet and clean and our children are taught a lesson in thrift."

Mrs. Dixon has given *The Farmer's Wife* permission to publish some of her choice cake recipes which are included in her copyrighted book, *Making Cakes with You*, which she published in answer to demands for her recipes. We have chosen the four which she considers her top-notch Christmas cakes.

The Four Top-Notchers

December 1925

Dark Fruit Cake
The quantities listed for this cake will make 8 lbs. of Christmas cake.

Prepare following fruits:

Cut 5 lbs. raisins

Measure 1 lb. currants

Cut 1 lb. citron and 1 lb. figs

Cut ½ lb. crystallized pineapple and
  cherries

Chop ½ lb. pecans and walnuts

Chop 1 lb. blanched almonds

Peel and chop 4 mellow apples

Measure 2 tsp. each of ground cinnamon, mace, cloves, nutmeg, and allspice.

Have ready the pans you wish to use, greased thoroughly and lined with greased paper.

Then prepare batter:

1 lb. butter

1½ lbs. soft brown sugar

12 eggs, separated

1 lb. flour

1 c. molasses

1 tsp. baking soda

Cream butter, add half the sugar gradually, and cream till fluffy. Beat egg yolks till creamy and add other half of sugar. Combine these mixtures and add flour, beat till smooth. Beat whites till stiff and fold in. add 1 c. molasses with 1 tsp. baking soda stirred in, add spices, mix well.

Dredge all the nuts and fruit with extra flour—takes about 4 c., sometimes more. Put them in a large bowl or tray and dredge slowly—this is important. Add these to batter and mix thoroughly. It will be very, very stiff.

Fill pans ¾ full—batter does not rise much—but you will wish to decorate top and in steaming, the cake should not touch cover. Now the stiff batter is in the pans we are ready to put the decorations on top. Have ready extra slices of citron figs, crystallized pineapple and cherries, whole almonds, and half walnuts. Arrange these in a very artistic way on top of cake, cover each cake pan with a cover that fits well over the top (unless you have a regular steamer), place in steamer, and cover well. If you have no cake steamer, any vessel with cover may be used. Let water come up about ⅓ of height of tin containing cake. Have water boiling when cakes are put into steamer, keep it boiling, and replenish it when necessary. In a deep vessel, the lower half can be filled with water and the tins elevated above water. This is better and easier as water does not have to be replenished. Never let steamer go dry.

Steam 1 and 2 lb. cakes for 3 hours

Steam 3 and 4 lb. cakes for 4 hours

Steam 5 and 7 lb. cakes for 4½ to 5 hours

Steam 8 and 10 lb. cakes for 8 hours

If the cake is beginning to leave the sides of tin when taken from steamer, it is not necessary to put it in the oven. If you feel it is not quite ready, you may return it to the steamer for a while longer or place it in oven—leave oven door open and watch it carefully to prevent discoloring decorations. These cakes should cool a little so that they may be handled very carefully in being removed from the tins.

Sallie White Cake

Prepare the same as the Dark Fruit Cake and use the same decorations. These tops resemble beautiful rosettes. Our little daughter says they look like real Christmas trees!

12 eggs
1 lb. butter
1 lb. flour
2 lb. sugar
2 lbs. citron
2 lbs. shredded
  unsweetened coconut

1 lb. blanched and
  chopped almonds
¼ lb. crystallized pineapple
¼ lb. crystallized cherries
½ lb. English walnuts,
  black walnuts, and
  pecans mixed

Steam this cake for 4½ or 5 hours. I consider it the best cake in the world!

Raleigh Special Layer Cake

Assemble following ingredients:

1 c. butter
2 c. sugar
4 eggs, separated

1 c. water
3 c. sifted flour
2 rounded tsp. baking powder

Prepare four layer-cake pans, grease well, and dredge with flour. Cream butter thoroughly; gradually add 1 c. sugar and beat until fluffy. Beat egg yolks until very creamy then add second c. sugar gradually and beat well. Add this to first mixture and beat thoroughly. Begin adding water, just a little at a time—if possible add all the water before beginning to add the flour but if creamy mass begins to separate, then add a little flour and then remaining water. Fold in flour, a cupful at a time, and continue in this folding until this is a smooth batter. Beat egg whites until stiff but not dry. Fold these into batter. Sift into this batter baking powder and beat this just a few minutes—to be sure baking powder is evenly distributed. Pour batter into pans. Bake in a quick oven (400°F) for 15 or 20 minutes.

Make Boiled Icing and add to Ambrosia Filling:

1 c. grated coconut
1 peeled orange, cut into pieces

½ c. crushed, drained pineapple

Add to the boiled, cooled icing first the pineapple. Spread this on layers, add bits of orange and sprinkle coconut over this, add another layer, spread icing, dot with orange bits, and sprinkle coconut on top. Build up your cake and cover top just as you did the layers.

"Lady Webb" Cake

1 c. butter
2 c. sugar
4 c. flour

6 egg whites
1 c. water
2 heaping tsp. baking powder

Mix and bake in three layers at 350°F. For the filling use double the amount of Boiled Icing and add to this:

1 c. grated coconut
1 c nut meats

1 c. chopped raisins
juice of 1 orange and 1 lemon

Spread between layers and on top. Add coconut sprinkled on top. An additional ¼ c. chopped raisins may be dredged in flour and added to batter for middle layer of three-layer cake.

To Make Boiled Icing:

1¾ c. sugar
¾ c. boiling water
3 egg whites

1 tsp. any desired extract
1 level tsp. baking powder

Reserve 1½ tbsp. sugar. Dissolve remaining sugar in boiling water—if cover is placed over saucepan for a few minutes it will prevent sugar from adhering to the sides of pan. Let this boil very rapidly. When heavy drops fall from a spoon when spoon is held high above saucepan, then it is time to beat egg whites—a tiny pinch of salt may be added to whites before beginning to beat. We wait until syrup begins to thicken before beating egg whites because if beaten egg whites stand, they will liquefy. When eggs are well beaten, add the reserved sugar and beat well into eggs until stiff but not dry.

Test boiling syrup again. If it silks to a long thread which flies out, it is ready to be poured very slowly over beaten egg whites mixed with extract—beating vigorously. After beating about 5 minutes, add baking powder. Continue beating until it is cool and you have a smooth, creamy filling which should stand up well.

NATIONAL
The Farm Journal
December, 1928
1928 SCHEDULE
LETTER FILE CHILDREN

MAKING FESTIVE GIFTS AND DECORATIONS

The quintessential do-it-yourselfer, the farmer's wife was nothing if not adamant that the best gifts, for friends and family alike, were those made by hand. She paid the same delightfully lavish attention to the decorations that festooned her home and dinner table.

TABLE TALK

Homemade Holiday Sweets Are Gifts That Always Please
By Anna Barrows • December 1916

There are many charming receptacles for holiday gifts and especially for candy gifts. If both the container and the candy are homemade, the gift will be all the more individual. Besides decorated boxes there are cornucopias that can be made of colored and fancy paper. Pretty baskets can be fashioned. The candy stocking always pleases children: make a stocking, any size desired, out of lace or net or mosquito netting, fill with pretty candies, and finish off with bright ribbon and a sprig of holly.

The gift of sweets need not necessarily be of candy. A mince pie, a plum pudding, a loaf or fruit cake, or rich spicy cookies also are attractive Christmas gifts and in many cases would be more acceptable than candy; these may be wrapped in specially decorated holiday paper, held in place by Christmas seals or by ribbon with a bunch of holly slipped under to look gay.

Also under the head of sweets come dates, figs, plums, prunes, and raisins. The Farmer's Wife reaches some persons who raise their own supply of these delicacies. What better gifts to distant friends than packages of the choicest offerings from the home trees and vines, daintily wrapped and mailed with the season's greetings? With the aid of nuts, candied cherries, and marshmallows [crystallized orange or grapefruit peel, cranberries, or even some firm home-canned peaches or apricots], delicious combinations can be affected.

Candy, Cookies, and Cakes

CANDY

❄ PINOCHI
November 1910

1 c. white sugar
3 c. brown sugar
1 c. milk

1 lump of butter half the size of an
  egg (approx. 2 tbsp.)
1 c. walnuts, broken

Boil all except nuts until mixture hardens when dropped in a cup of cold water. Add 1 c. broken walnuts and stir fast until hard enough to pour. Turn onto a flat, greased tin and cut in squares.

❄ COCOANUT DROPS
December 1912

Beat the white of an egg to a froth, adding nearly as much shredded unsweetened cocoanut as it will take up. Add enough confectioner's sugar to make the mixture thick enough so that it will just drop from a spoon. Drop teaspoonfuls on oiled paper or a greased tin, putting the drops far enough apart so that they will not run together; put them into a moderately hot oven (375°F) and bake 15 minutes, or until puffed up and delicately brown.

❄ CHOCOLATE CARAMELS
November 1910

2 c. molasses
1 c. brown sugar
1 c. milk
½ lb. bittersweet chocolate
1 lump of butter the size of an egg (approx. 4 tbsp.)

Beat all together then boil in a double boiler until mixture thickens in cold water. Turn into flat tins well buttered. When partly cool cut into squares.

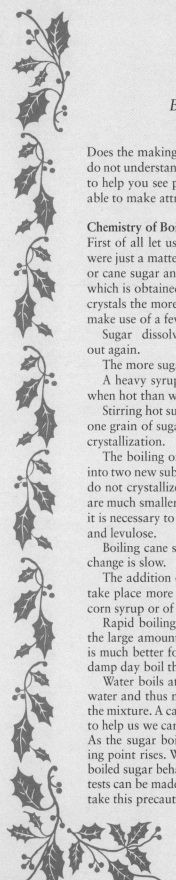

Domestic Science
How to Make Candy
By Mrs. A.R. Kohler • December 1911

Does the making of candy seem a difficult and rather uncertain task, which you do not understand because of frequent failures? If so this paper has been prepared to help you see plainly the "Reasons Why" in candymaking so that you may be able to make attractive and delicious candies with unfailing good results.

Chemistry of Boiling Sugar

First of all let us consider what we are trying to do when we make candy. If it were just a matter of sweetness and flavor we could add our flavor to lump sugar or cane sugar and our candy would be done. But we want a certain consistency which is obtained by controlling the size of the crystals of sugar. The smaller the crystals the more creamy the candy. To be able to control these crystals we must make use of a few simple facts in the physics and the chemistry of sugar.

Sugar dissolves readily in water but if allowed to stand crystallizes out again.

The more sugar in the solution the more quickly it will crystallize.

A heavy syrup of sugar crystallizes much more readily and in larger crystals when hot than when cold.

Stirring hot sugar causes the sugar to crystallize in large coarse crystals. If only one grain of sugar be left undissolved in the boiling solution it will tend to start crystallization.

The boiling of sugar brings about a chemical change. Cane sugar is changed into two new substances which are called dextrose and levulose. These substances do not crystallize so readily as cane sugar does, and when they do, the crystals are much smaller, therefore to make creamy fudge or fondant or any other candy it is necessary to change a considerable proportion of the cane sugar to dextrose and levulose.

Boiling cane sugar in water changes it to dextrose and levulose, although the change is slow.

The addition of some acid as cream of tartar or vinegar causes the change to take place more rapidly. The addition of some dextrose in the form of table or corn syrup or of molasses causes the change to take place more rapidly.

Rapid boiling tends to cause the formation of large crystals. On a rainy day the large amount of moisture in the air affects the candy by making it sticky. It is much better for a beginner to choose a dry, clear day. If it must be done on a damp day boil the candy a little stiffer than would be necessary on a dry day.

Water boils at the sea level at a temperature of 212°F. If we add anything to water and thus make it heavier, we raise the temperature of the boiling point of the mixture. A candy thermometer can be bought for seventy-five cents. With this to help us we can test our candy accurately and be absolutely sure of our results. As the sugar boils, water evaporates, the mixture grows heavier, and the boiling point rises. Without a thermometer certain tests are made from the way the boiled sugar behaves. When one has had some experience in making candy these tests can be made almost as accurately as with a thermometer. However, we must take this precaution: pull the candy off the fire while making the test. Otherwise it will go on boiling and our test will not be accurate. If the test shows the candy has not reached the proper stage put it on the fire again and continue boiling.

Here are eleven tests for boiled sugar together with the temperature tests:

Small thread, 215°F. When dropped from a spoon a small thread is formed.

Large thread, 217°F. A stronger, stiffer thread appears at this test.

Pearl, 220°F. A little bead of sugar collects on the end of the spoons.

Large pearl, 222°F. A larger bead collects.

The blow, 230°F. Take a clean broom splint and twist it to form a loop about half as big as a cent. Dip this into the syrup. If the syrup holds inside this loop, similar to a soap bubble, and spreads open in ragged edges when blown, this stage is reached.

The feather, 232°F. If the syrup when blown spreads out into feathery strings, this stage is reached.

Soft ball, 238°F. Forms a soft ball when dropped into ice water.

Hard ball, 248°F. A hard ball if dropped into ice water.

Small crack, 290°F. If allowed to thread in ice water it is brittle.

Crack, 310°F. Cracks if poured on the bottom of the vessel containing ice water.

Caramel, 350°F. When sugar has boiled until it is a light yellow color, it has reached the caramel stage.

Various Kinds of Candy

With these things in mind let us consider the making of two or three types of candy. If we understand the reasons why in these it will be a comparatively easy matter to take any recipe that you may find anywhere and make it into just the kind of candy that it should be.

Fondant is perhaps the most satisfactory kind to make for Christmas candies. With it as a basis all kinds of cream candies and bonbons may be made. Any flavor desired may be added to it, it can be colored most attractively by vegetable colors, it can be combined with fruit, nuts, or small cakes, and can be dipped in chocolate to form chocolate bonbons. To have a variety of bonbons, make a considerable amount of fondant. Divide it into smaller portions; flavor each portion differently, color them if so desired and shape into bonbons. The fondant is made of granulated sugar. To five cups of sugar add a cup and a half of water and one-fourth teaspoon of cream of tartar. Put these into a smooth granite or aluminum pan, which is rather deep. Stir so as to dissolve sugar. Be careful that no crystals of sugar adhere to the side of the pan. Heat slowly and boil without stirring until the soft-ball stage is reached. If any sugar gathers on the side of the kettle while boiling wash it off with the hand. First dip the hand in a pan of cold water, quickly wash off a small part of the sugar with the tips of the fingers, and repeat until all the sugar adhering to the side of the pan is removed. If this is done quickly there will be no danger of burning the fingers. When the fondant is done boiling, it may be set aside to cool in the pan in which it was cooked, unless a cold marble slab is available. If cooled in the pan be careful to have it cool evenly and not get hard around the edge as it would if set in cold water. If the slab is to be used oil it slightly. Let the fondant cool just a little and then turn it carefully on the slab. Working it or pouring quickly while it is still hot will cause it to "sugar." The cold slab, however, will cool it off so that is can be worked at once. This should be done with a wooden spatula. Stir until it is white and creamy. When too hard to stir, knead with the hands until it is perfectly smooth. If the slab is not used, let the fondant cool in the saucepan until the hand can be easily be borne on it. Then stir with a wooden spoon in the same way. Knead it on a large plate. When perfectly smooth, put it into a bowl, cover with oiled paper so as to exclude all air so that a crust may not be formed, and let stand for at least twenty-four hours. Standing makes it creamy.

Apply these same methods in the making of any candy that has to be stirred, like fudge. Do not stir it while it is cooling unless it is necessary to stir just a little occasionally to prevent burning. When hard enough, set aside to cool before stirring. By following this method, remembering always the reasons why for each step, creamy fudge will be assured.

A variety of candy is made by beating the syrup into the beaten whites of eggs. This is done in making Sea Foam. To two cups of brown sugar add one-half cup of water. The brown sugar has not been refined like the cane sugar. It has some molasses and other substances left in it and so we do not need to add the cream of tartar. Boil as for fondant until the large-thread stage is reached. Set aside to cool. Beat up the whites of two eggs until stiff and dry, then beat into them the syrup, a little at a time. Add nut meats, one-half to one cupful as desired, and one-half teaspoon of vanilla. Continue beating until the candy is stiff enough to drop from the spoon. Drop on oiled paper.

Sometimes corn syrup is added as in the making of Russian Cream. To two cups of granulated sugar take one-fourth cup of water. Boil until it reaches the hard-boil stage and set aside to cool. Beat the whites of two eggs until stiff and dry, then add the syrup gradually, beating all the time. When the syrup has all been added and the mixture is beginning to thicken add one cup of nut meats and pour into a buttered pan. This is delicious as it is, or it can be further varied by cutting into suitable shapes and dipping them into melted chocolate.

Another delicious candy is made from the carameled sugar. To two cups of sugar add one cup of boiling water and one-eighth teaspoon of cream of tartar. Boil until it reaches the caramel stage. Remove the pan from the fire and set in a pan of cold water for an instant in order to stop boiling at once. Then set the pan into another pan of boiling water. Take nut meats separately on a long pin, dip in syrup to cover, remove, and place on oiled paper. Fruits can also be glacéd. Such fruits as grapes, strawberries, sections of oranges, and candied cherries are most commonly used. Whatever the fruit be careful the skin is not broken, otherwise the juice of the fruit would dissolve the candy. In the case of grapes leave a small bit of the stem. With the oranges be careful not to break the skin of the sections when separating them. A pin cannot be used in dipping but a loop made of wire stiff enough to hold the candy should be used instead. Glacéd fruits keep only a day and should be made only in cool, clear weather.

Whenever corn syrup is used in making candy no precautions need be taken to prevent the mixture from sugaring. This is true in such candies as caramels, and a much longer time is required to cook this candy than the other varieties.

❊ BUTTER SCOTCH
November 1910

2 c. sugar
2 tbsp. water
1 lump of butter the size of an egg (approx.
  4 tbsp.)

Boil without stirring until mixture hardens on a spoon. Pour on buttered plate and mark in squares. When cool break off as marked.

❊ CANDIED CITRUS PEEL
May 1937

An especially attractive gift I once saw was a shallow, round tin box full of candied orange and grapefruit peel. The grapefruit peel had been colored green in the process and the orange peel colored red. The box was divided by pasteboard partitions into quarters and the red and green placed alternately. The natural orange color of the candied orange peel harmonizes well with the green. Making candied peel is not expensive, either, for the peel can be removed from the oranges or grapefruit served for breakfast or in salads.

Strips of orange, lemon, or grapefruit are cut . . . and these are boiled until tender. Then the juice is drained, and, to 4 orange peels, a syrup made of 2 c. sugar and 1 of water are added. The mixture is boiled until the strips appear transparent. Then they are lifted from the syrup, and, when slightly cooled, rolled in sugar. They should be dried on a flat dish or paper slightly, then stored in a covered container to keep fresh and tasty.

❊ CANDIED APPLE SLICES
1934

2 c. sugar   few grains salt
½ c. water   5 tart apples
½ c. corn syrup   red cinnamon candies

Heat sugar, water, corn syrup, and salt. Boil till syrup threads. Peel and slice 1 apple at a time and drop slices in hot syrup. Cook slowly till transparent. Add cinnamon candies during cooking to color syrup. Remove apple slices and drain. Roll in sugar and dry on waxed paper. Prepare another apple, thinning syrup with 4 tbsp. water each time. Let apples stand 24 hours then roll in sugar again. Let stand another day, and roll in sugar a third time.

Holiday Candies
Let the Children Know the Joy of Making
the Christmas Goodies
By Bertha Bellows Streeter • *December 1914*

Decide a week or two before Christmas just what kinds of candy would be most enjoyed by all the family; a list of all the requisites for making it, added to the shopping list, will insure having all the materials at hand when they are needed. Another thing to be planned is share that the children may take in the delightful task. If there are nuts to be cracked, meats to be picked out, flavors to be chosen, or corn to be popped, do not think of doing those things yourself if you have children capable of doing them. Helping Mother make the Christmas candies is a memory every mother should give the children. When everything is at hand and all the little tasks of preparation have been done by the children, the real work is only play to even a busy mother.

The night before Christmas Eve is always looked forward to in the home of one of my friends, as the family devoted the evening to making Christmas candies, and it often happens that the friends of the boys and girls come in to help. Even Father helps pull the old-fashioned molasses taffy that everybody likes. This is made by boiling together, without stirring, four cupfuls of brown sugar, four tablespoons of molasses, the same amount of vinegar, eight tablespoons of water, and four of butter. At the last the taffy is pulled into a long, thin strip and cut with the scissors into pieces about an inch long.

These are generous recipes, as this family is a large one and fond of candy. In many homes half the quantities specified will be sufficient.

They always have a Christmas tree at this house of many children. The little folk delight in making popcorn balls for its decoration; sometimes these balls are not so true as they might be if shaped by more skillful hands, but they are far more beautiful in the sight of the children because they make them themselves. It is great fun to get together small articles, like rings from prize packages, tiny dolls and candies with mottoes on them, and tie each in a small piece of oiled paper with a long string. In the afternoon the children pop the corn and pick out all the little burned pieces. Then Big Sister makes the syrup, then pours the syrup over the popcorn, and the children make up the balls quickly, inclosing a favor in the center of each and leaving the string free for fastening the ball to the tree.

❄ SEA FOAM
January 1911

2 c. light brown sugar	1 egg white
1 c. boiling water	

Boil until a little stirred upon a cold plate will form a firm, creamy ball. Pour boiling hot over the stiffly beaten white of 1 egg; add any desired extract for flavoring, and turn out onto a buttered jelly roll pan to a thickness of ½ inch. ½ c. of any nuts, finely chopped, added to the whole before turning into the pan, makes a still more delicious confection.

❅ AMERICAN TOFFEE
January 1911

Melt gradually 1 lb. light brown sugar, 4 tbsp. maple syrup, 4 tbsp. butter, 1 tbsp. water, and a little lemon juice. Let it boil until a little dropped into cold water will be crisp. Pour onto buttered jelly roll pans, having the toffee ¼ inch thick. When nearly cold mark into squares. These squares are delicious if dipped into melted chocolate.

❅ SOFT NUT CANDY
April 1911

Boil together 2 c. powdered sugar, 1 c. maple syrup, and ½ c. cream until a firm ball is formed when a little is dropped from a spoon into cold water. Remove from the fire, add 2 c. hickory nut meats chopped fine, and beat as it cools. When nearly cool drop in small quantities on buttered wax paper.

❅ CREAMED WALNUTS
April 1911

Beat the white of an egg very light and add sufficient confectioner's sugar to make a very stiff dough. Moisten this with a little cream added drop by drop until of the consistency of soft putty. Flavor with a squeeze of lemon juice and form into small balls, pressing a walnut half into each.

❅ CREAM CANDY
February 1912

To 2 c. sugar add ½ c. water and boil without stirring till it forms a soft ball when dropped in water. Remove and let stand until it begins to cool. Then beat thoroughly with a silver fork. This candy may be colored with fruit juice or seasoned any way preferred and makes an excellent cocoanut candy by adding ½ c. grated unsweetened cocoanut to ½ c. of the candy.

Making the Christmas Candies at Home

By Lulu G. Parker • December 1912

If there are young people in the home a few afternoons or evenings ought to be spent by them in making the Christmas candy. For homemade candy is not only more pure and more wholesome than most inexpensive candy that is found in the shops, but it may easily be quite as good as the most costly which is sold there. When one remembers that cheap candy is often a combination of saccharine, which tastes like sugar but is a dangerous drug, cornstarch, coal tar dyes, glue, and tallow, they hesitate to give it to the children.

On the other hand a few pounds of sugar, a little flavoring, milk, and butter, with such raisins, shredded cocoanut, and shelled nuts as the pantry affords, may be turned by the exercise of a little heat and patience into delicious sweets which will harm no one.

If the children or young folks do their own candymaking, the house-mother should have it agreed that they wash their sticky cooking utensils and leave the kitchen in order when they have finished.

❄ PEPPERMINT CANDY
February 1912

To 2 c. sugar add ½ c. milk and 1 tsp. peppermint extract. Cook for about 10 minutes and remove to a buttered plate, beating it thoroughly as it cools.

❄ BUTTER TAFFY
November 1910
Contributed by R. Raymond

---

3 c. brown sugar
½ c. molasses

¼ c. vinegar
¼ c. water

Boil together until mixture hardens in cold water. Add 2 tbsp. butter and 1 tbsp. vanilla extract. Cook 3 minutes then cool on buttered pans before cutting.

❄ TAFFY CANDY
March 1912
Contributed by Blue-Eyed Bess

2 c. sugar
½ c. water
¼ c. vinegar

Boil briskly; do not stir while boiling. Cook to the soft-crack stage, then add 1 tbsp. any flavor extract and turn out onto a pastry marble. Pull taffy [you may want to wear cotton gloves for this] by stretching and twisting into a thick rope, folding into a horseshoe, and working again into a longer rope that is quartered and stretched again. When creamy white, cut into pieces with scissors.

❄ TAFFY APPLES
December 1923

1 dozen apples
2 c. sugar
½ c. corn syrup
1 c. water
1 dozen skewers
few drops cinnamon flavoring

Select bright red apples in uniform size, wash, and dry. Insert the skewer in the blossom end. Put the sugar, corn syrup and water in saucepan and cook at a slow bubble, stirring till sugar is dissolved. Continue cooking without stirring until a temperature of 300°F is reached.

Sugar crystals that form on the side of the pan may be washed off with a small piece of cloth tied to the tines of a fork and dipped in water. Remove from the fire and place in a pan of hot water to prevent cooling while dipping the apples. Add flavoring. Stand the apples in a rack or some device in order that they may cool with an even covering of candy.

❄ PEANUT BRITTLE
December 1913

Shell and chop roasted peanuts till there is 1 pt. Place in frying pan 2 c. sugar. Stir sugar over low flame until it first lumps, then gradually melts. When it is a pale coffee color and clear, add nuts and quickly pour into buttered tin pan. Pour as thin as possible and when cold, break up.

❄ PEANUT BUTTER CREAMS
December 1930

2 c. brown sugar
½ c. milk
2 tbsp. peanut butter
1 egg white
½ tsp. vanilla
peanuts

Boil sugar and milk till it threads. Add peanut butter. Beat egg white and vanilla till stiff and add boiling syrup, a little at a time, continuing to beat till thick and stiff, then drop by teaspoonfuls on waxed paper. Press half a peanut on each cream.

❄ FOR THE CHRISTMAS CANDY BOX
December 1916
Contributed by Pearl S. Lyons

Fondant can be made by either one of two methods. It is not at all difficult if the directions are carefully followed.

To make cooked fondant:

6 c. sugar
2½ c. water
¼ tsp. cream of tartar

Utensils: Large porcelain kettle, marble slab or table top with iron rods to fit around edge or a large platter; also a wooden paddle.

Put the ingredients into the kettle and stir over a low fire until all the sugar is dissolved, then boil rapidly without stirring until a soft ball forms when tested in cold water. Wipe the sides of the kettle frequently during boiling to prevent crystals from forming around the edge. This may be done with the hand dipped quickly in cold water, or with a little wet cloth or fork. When the soft-ball stage is reached pour the mixture on the well-greased slab or platter and let stand until it is nearly cold and the touch of a finger leaves a dent. Move the fondant back and forth with the wooden paddle, working around each side then thru the center and keep the mixture well together so it will all be of the same consistency. When firm enough, knead with the hands like dough until smooth throughout. Put into an earthen bowl, cover with a wet cloth of several thicknesses and let stand 24 hours before working into various shapes.

❄ FUDGE
December 1913

Boil together slowly, till it reaches the soft-ball stage, 2 c. sugar, 1 c. milk, ½ oz. bittersweet chocolate. Remove from the fire and add 2 tbsp. butter and 1 tbsp. vanilla. Beat until creamy and just as it starts to thicken, pour quickly on buttered pan. Cut into squares when firm.

❄ FUDGE CHOCOLATES
December 1916

2 c. milk
4 c. sugar
4 oz. bittersweet chocolate
2 tbsp. butter
1 tsp. vanilla

Cook the milk, sugar, and chocolate together. Stir constantly until a soft ball is formed when tested in cold water. Add the butter at once and remove from the fire. Allow to get cold, then add the vanilla and beat hard until the mass holds its shape. Turn out on marble slab or earthenware platter. Mold and knead with the hands until perfectly smooth. Break off uniformly sized pieces and roll into balls 1½ inches in diameter. Let stand on waxed paper for 24 hours, then dip each in the melted chocolate prepared by this method: melt ½ oz. semi-sweet chocolate in a double boiler. Dip each ball separately, using form or the hand. Place on waxed paper to set.

❄ FUDGE VARIATIONS
December 1912

2 c. sugar
½ c. milk or cream
butter the size of a walnut (1 tbsp.)

Put these on the fire in a heavy saucepan and boil, stirring all the while, until a little dropped into cold water will form a waxy lump if worked with the fingers. Before starting the cooking, prepare three or four buttered pie tins, having melted 2 oz. of chocolate and a drop of vanilla in one; peanuts, raisins, or broken-up walnut pieces in another; and cut-up marshmallows in a third. Combinations of seeded dates, candied fruit, cocoanut, etc. will occur to the candy cook. When the sugar and milk are through cooking, pour some of it into each of the pans and beat until smooth and creamy. Mark off into small squares before it becomes quite cold. If one person must work alone she would better make only two pans at a time, and beat the one containing chocolate first. Any flavoring may be used.

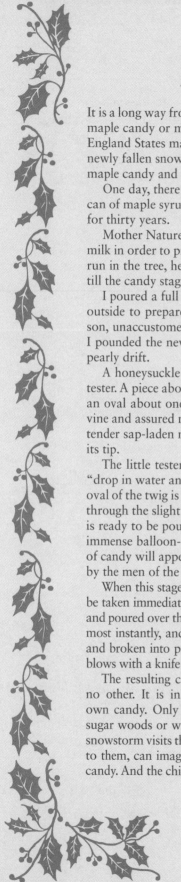

Maple Sugar Candy

By Richard S. Bond • January 1923

It is a long way from a Vermont sugar woods to Philadelphia and yet the delicious maple candy or maple wax that is made in such quantities in the northern New England States may be made any place where there is a cold snap with plenty of newly fallen snow, a can of pure maple syrup, and knowledge of how they make maple candy and "sugar off" in the woods.

One day, there were fully three feet of snow banked against our back door. A can of maple syrup was in the cellar. The know-how had been stored in my head for thirty years.

Mother Nature, as expressed in the sugar maple, needs no vanilla, or butter, or milk in order to produce candy. She needs nothing but heat; heat to make the sap run in the tree, heat to boil it into a syrup, and heat to boil the syrup still more till the candy stage has been reached.

I poured a full quart of maple syrup into a pan and while it heated, I stepped outside to prepare my snow bed and get my candy tester. My thirteen-year-old son, unaccustomed to sugar camps or maple candymaking, watched eagerly as I pounded the newly fallen snow into a compact mass for a full square yard of pearly drift.

A honeysuckle vine that had trailed up the porch furnished the "blower" or tester. A piece about 18 inches long was clipped and the tip curled until it formed an oval about one inch long and half an inch across. A piece of thread tied the vine and assured me of an oval hole that would stay put. In the sugar woods, the tender sap-laden maple or birch or beech twig would permit a knot to be tied in its tip.

The little tester takes the place of that portion of a candy recipe which says "drop in water and when it forms a hard ball." As the boiling syrup thickens, the oval of the twig is inserted for an instant, raised to the lips and a gust of air blown through the slight film stretching across the opening of the twig. When the candy is ready to be poured on the snow, a slight blow through the hole will throw an immense balloon-shaped bubble from the stick. Sometimes half a dozen bubbles of candy will appear before the film has been exhausted. This is the method used by the men of the northern sugar camps.

When this stage is reached, the candy should be taken immediately to the prepared snow bed and poured over the surface thinly. It hardens almost instantly, and in a moment may be lifted and broken into pieces of desired size by sharp blows with a knife or small hammer.

The resulting candy can be compared with no other. It is in a class by itself—Nature's own candy. Only those who have visited the sugar woods or who are willing when the first snowstorm visits them to bring the sugar woods to them, can imagine the flavor of pure maple candy. And the children can eat it freely.

❄ PRALINES
December 1916

2 c. confectioner's sugar
1 c. maple syrup

½ c. heavy cream
2 c. pecan meats

Boil the sugar, syrup, and cream till the soft-ball stage is formed when tested in cold water. Remove at once from the fire and beat hard till creamy. Add the nut meats quickly and drop by spoonfuls on oiled paper.

❄ MAPLE FONDANT
December 1916

1 c. maple syrup
1 c. sugar
1 c. water

⅛ tsp. cream of tartar
walnuts

Combine the ingredients, stir until the sugar is dissolved, and boil without stirring until the soft-ball stage is formed. Keep the crystals from forming on the sides of the kettle by wiping the inside quickly and gently with the hand, a cloth, or a brush dipped in cold water. Put out on a buttered marble slab, table top, or large platter. When the mixture is cool and may be dented with the finger, work hard and thoroly with a wooden paddle 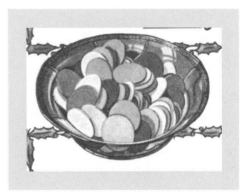 or spoon till it holds its shape. Then knead with the hands till smooth and creamy. Put in a large earthen bowl, cover with a damp cloth, and let stand 24 hours. Roll into small balls 1¼ inches in diameter and put a walnut meat on each side, flattening the ball.

❄ COCOANUT BALLS
December 1918

1 c. shredded unsweetened cocoanut
2 tsp. vanilla
4 tsp. peanut butter

Mix in a bowl, shape into 1-inch balls with the hands, put on wax paper, and set in the icebox or a cold place to harden.

❄ PARISIAN SWEETS
December 1918

1 lb. dates
1 lbs. dried figs
1 c. raisins
1 c. walnuts
¼ tsp. salt

Clean the fruit well and put through a food chopper. Cut the nuts up quite fine and mix through the fruit mixture. Sift a *very little* cornstarch on the board to keep from sticking and roll the mixture into a long roll 1½ inches in diameter. Slice into slices ¼ inch thick. The roll may be rolled in grated cocoanut before slicing.

❄ BURNT SUGAR CANDY
December 1927

3 c. sugar
1½ c. cream
1 c. black walnut meats
a little salt

Place 2 c. sugar on a medium fire with the cream. At the same time, put the other 1 c. sugar in an iron skillet with no water or wetting and melt over hot fire, stirring constantly. When melted, and when the sugar and cream are boiling hard, combine the two mixtures. Cook, stirring constantly, till it forms a soft ball in water. Add nuts and salt and beat till cold, turn out on a greased board, and cut in squares.

(Note: when the two mixtures are first poured together the melted sugar forms hard lumps but they soon melt down.)

❄ RAISIN CLUSTERS
December 1931

½ lb. sweet chocolate
1 c. roasted peanuts
¼ tsp. salt
2½ c. raisins

Break the chocolate in pieces and place in the top of a double boiler. Allow water in lower part to steam but do not boil. Remove from fire and let stand 5 to 10 minutes, stirring occasionally to aid in melting. Remove from fire and add to chocolate the remaining ingredients. Mix thoroughly and drop by teaspoonfuls on waxed paper to harden.

At Christmas Make Good Cheer!
Each and Every One May Lay a Fagot on the Yuletide Fire
December 1916

Dear Martha:

I have your letter asking me to do some Christmas shopping for you and I write to say that I decline your commission! You give me a list of friends and relatives here in town and the sums you can spend on each, and you breathe a sigh that the University for the children and the cost of the new silo have made the sum so small and then you ask me to get the best things I can find for the money. My gift, you are making.

My dear, you made my gift last summer, you and your intimate friend Nature, and I am returning your check, for you made most of these other gifts at the same time . . . My dear, don't you see how you could so easily send yourself and your life and your own surroundings to each of us who are city-bound here? . . . It will cost you no more worry than a morning's selection and an afternoon's packing and no more money than parcel-post charges.

Alice has had a pretty hard time this year; that long illness has not left much surplus for Christmas dainties. So tuck a little butter or some eggs into a dressed fowl; or a wee young pig would not be a bit too much holiday jollity for her. Or, send doughnuts, filled cookies, or gingerbread—you make them so well and they are so good . . .

I've finished my lecture and I'm hoping that you will find it as palatable as I shall your goodies. I shall send you the most citified gift I can find because that

is I and I am anticipating that mine from you will be redolent with the sunshine and pure air and peace that are you!

Your very best friend,
—Mary

❄ FRENCH LOAF (IN THREE LAYERS)

December 1927

I. WHITE LAYER

3 c. light brown sugar
1 c. cream
few drops vanilla

½ c. blanched, chopped almonds
1 tbsp. butter

Boil sugar, cream, and vanilla till soft-ball stage. Remove from fire and stir till cold. Add nuts. Put in bottom of buttered loaf pan.

II. PINK LAYER

3. c. light brown sugar
1 c. cream
½ c. Brazil nuts, skinned and sliced thin
1 tbsp. butter

Cook as above. When done, color with red fruit coloring, flavor with strawberry, wintergreen, or cinnamon (wintergreen is best). Stir until cold and place over white layer.

III. BROWN LAYER

3 c. light brown sugar
1 c. cream
2 oz. unsweetened chocolate

1 tbsp. butter
½ c. walnut meats, chopped

Make as above and place on top of pink layer. This makes a large loaf of candy that keeps indefinitely and may be sliced as needed.

❄ BOYS LIKE THESE

By Miriam J. Williams
December 1938

Your box of goodies, for the boy friend who is to be remembered on some special occasion, need not be elaborate but the contents must be really good. Try to arrange each good thing in a separate section or row, using cardboard partitions or trays, if necessary, so that a variety is offered yet each is by itself. Use plenty of fresh waxed paper to pack things nicely. Cover the box to give it a handsome tailored look, decorate with his initials cut out of contrasting paper, and then tuck in a snapshot of yourself which smiles "A Merry Christmas."

❄ AMY'S CARAMELS

1 c. white sugar
1 c. white corn syrup
pinch salt
2 tbsp. butter

2 c. cream
1 tsp. vanilla
1 c. chopped walnuts

Combine first 4 ingredients and 1 c. cream. Boil to soft-ball stage, stirring constantly. Then add second cup of cream slowly, while it is still cooking. Cook until it makes a firm, pliable ball when it is dropped in cold water (entire cooking takes about 45 minutes). Then add vanilla and nuts and pour into 8-inch or 9-inch square pan. Let stand 12 hours before cutting. Wrap each cube in waxed paper.

❄ CHOCOLATE FLAKES

½ lb. semi-sweet dipping chocolate
½ tsp. vanilla

½ c. chopped nuts
2 c. cornflakes

Melt chocolate in a double boiler. Remove from heat, stir till smooth and partially cool, add other ingredients. Drop in clusters on waxed paper. Put in cool place till set. Crispy and good but must be kept cool.

❄ SPICED NUT MEATS

1 c. sugar
5 tbsp. water
1 tbsp. cinnamon
1 tsp. vanilla

2 c. large nut meats,
such as walnut
halves

Combine sugar and water, cinnamon, and vanilla and bring to a boil. Boil 2 minutes. Remove from fire, add nut meats, stir till syrup looks cloudy. Turn on waxed paper or greased surface, breaking apart into clusters.

❄ GLACÉD FRUIT AND NUT BALLS
December 1920

1 c. dates
1 c. dried figs
1 c. raisins
2 c. nut meats

Wash and dry fruit and nuts. Chop fine, mix well, and roll into shape. If desired, glaze with the following glacé mixture:

2 c. corn syrup
¼ c. water
1 tbsp. vinegar

Boil together till brittle when tested in cold water. Place pan in pan of hot water and begin to dip the balls at once. Put balls on waxed paper to cool.

❄ FRUIT SWEETS
December 1920

1 c. dates
1 c. dried figs
1 c. raisins
1 c. nut meats
1½ tsp. orange juice
grated orange peel
⅛ c. honey

Chop fruit and nuts fine. Add orange juice, rind, and honey. Mold into balls and dip in cocoanut or chopped nuts.

Popcorn Jamboree

By Ruby Price Weeks • December 1938

Making popcorn is fun. Making popcorn balls is *more* fun. But the *most* fun of all is to have the whole gang in the kitchen doing all at once!

Why not have a party some night and make popcorn balls for children at the church or community Christmas tree, for a children's home or some group of children who don't have many treats?

You will find there will be much less confusion if each person has a definite task. Have some of the group pop, while others shell more corn. Let someone else make the sirup.

If you invite a number of people, plan to have some decorate baskets in which the popcorn balls will later be arranged and delivered. For this use splint or heavy paper baskets such as those in which vegetables or fruits are packed. Let two persons work together, furnishing them with attractive paper, string in the colors which you are using for the popcorn balls, paste, and a pair of shears. A simple prize might be offered to the couple making the most attractive container.

While the balls are cooling and getting firm enough to wrap is an excellent time for *all* to wash up the dishes and put the kitchen in order.

If you wish, you may provide each person with paper and pencil for writing two-line verses to be enclosed with each popcorn ball—between the paraffin and cellophane wrappings. The message should supposedly be from Santa Claus. (Can't you see the youngsters reading and comparing their verses?) Prizes are in order here, also.

Cut cellophane squares to form the outer wrapper, large enough so that when wrapped around the corn ball and held in place with string or ribbon, the four corners will form points at the top and make a most attractive package.

Popcorn may be made in anything from an iron kettle to the most modern electric popper. Nothing is better than the good old-fashioned method: allow one tablespoon of fat (lard, vegetable cooking fat, or oil) to five tablespoons of popcorn. Put in hot skillet; add 1 tsp. salt. Shake slowly until it starts popping, then faster. When finished, removed unpopped kernels.

If corn is dry, sprinkle with water before popping, or let it stand outside in a shady place to absorb moisture.

To Make Popcorn Ball Sirup:

1 c. sugar	½ c. unsalted butter
¼ c. molasses	2 tbsp. hot water
1 tbsp. vinegar	¼ tsp. salt

Heat sugar in a smooth, heavy skillet, stirring constantly until melted. Pour quickly into a saucepan in which other ingredients have been heated slowly together. Boil until brittle when tested in cold water. Pour over corn. Add chopped nuts or dates, if desired. Shape with buttered hands while warm.

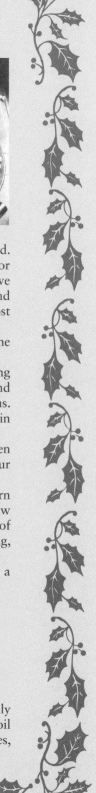

❄ CREAMED DIPPED ORANGE SLICES
February 1928

Separate 3 seedless oranges into slices without breaking inner partitions. Make the following cream: 2 c. sugar, 1 c. water. Put on to boil. After it boils do not stir but drop in cream of tartar the size of a pea. When a little dropped in cold water forms a soft ball, remove from stove and pour on marble slab or on a large china platter. Turn with wooden paddle until it creams, then put in top of double boiler placed over hot water. When melted dip in slices of orange with a wire fork, without pricking the skins.

❄ CANDIED POPCORN
December 1913

Boil 1 c. sugar, 3 tbsp. water, and 1 tbsp. butter till it is almost at the soft-ball stage. Then throw in 2 qts. nicely popped corn. Stir quickly till the corn is all coated. Take the kettle from the fire and stir constantly till cool, when every grain will be separate and crystallized with sugar. Care should be taken lest the corn should burn. Nuts of any kind may be added with the corn if desired.

COOKIES

❄ THE CHRISTMAS SWEET TOOTH
December 1924

Our preparations for Christmas have never seemed complete without "all kinds" of cookies for the children. The prime favorites are a rather rich confection, slightly troublesome to make; but they are worth the painstaking that a perfect result demands. Grown people, as well as children, approve them.

The mixture calls for:

1 c. sugar
1 c. butter
2 whole eggs
4 egg yolks
1 tsp. vanilla
1 lg. tbsp. vinegar
1 tsp. baking soda
flour—3 to 4½ c.

No liquid is used except the vinegar. If milk or water is added, the dough will be easier to work but the cookies will lose their characteristic quality and become ordinary. If the vinegar is extremely sour, it may be weakened slightly with water.

Cream the sugar and butter. Add the eggs and yolks well beaten and vanilla. Put the vinegar into a cup; stir in the baking soda and as it foams, add it quickly to the mixture and beat all together thoroughly. Work in sifted flour little by little to make a soft, smooth dough. As the dough is very sticky and crumbly, it can be more easily managed if only a part of it is rolled out thin at one time. Cut into shapes. Fill one set of buttered baking pans then take a fresh piece of dough and roll again, always keeping the board well floured. Cut out and place the rounds in more pans so the edges do not touch. They should be about ½ inch apart to allow for rising and spreading. Sift a little powdered sugar over the cookies and bake them quickly at 400°F, with care to prevent scorching. The work is easier if two can attend to it, one to roll and cut out the cookies, the other to watch the baking. When taken from the oven, they should be spread on a table covered with a clean, dry cloth and left until they are cool and crisp. Then they may be packed away until needed.

These cookies may be cut into any fanciful design as they are not crumbly after baking and they will hold their shape well. For a special children's party this may be desirable. The plain rounds taste just as well, however, and if they are topped with a stiff jelly or thick jam, just before serving, they appear sufficiently festive for any occasion.

If stored in a cool, dry place the cookies will keep almost indefinitely, if allowed to. As time passes, they may seem to become very dry, but they soften at once in the mouth. Their greatest enemy is moisture.

❆ SAND TARTS
October 1928

1 c. unsalted butter, softened
1½ c. sugar
2 eggs, beaten
3½ c. flour

½ tsp. cinnamon
¼ c. granulated sugar mixed with
   1 tsp. cinnamon

Cream butter and sugar, add the beaten eggs, and sift in flour and sugar. Roll very thin, brush with egg white, and sprinkle with cinnamon sugar. Place on buttered baking sheets and bake quickly at 400°F. Citron, raisins, orange peel, blanched almond slivers, pecan halves, or maraschino cherries make good decorations for these if wished.

Variation: Substitute brown sugar for white and add ¼ tsp. salt.

❆ CHRISTMAS BROWNIES
December 1930

½ c. butter
1 c. brown sugar
1 c. chopped dates or nuts
¼ c. rolled oats
1 tsp. salt

2 tsp. baking powder
1 tsp. cinnamon
½ tsp. nutmeg
2 c. flour
½ c. milk

Cream butter and sugar together. Add dates or nuts and oats. Sift salt, baking powder, spices, and flour together. Add alternately with milk to the first mixture. Drop from spoon on a tin and bake about 10 minutes at 350°F.

❆ CHOCOLATE COOKIES
December 1930

½ c. butter
1 c. sugar
1 egg, well-beaten
2 oz. melted bittersweet chocolate

2 c. flour
¼ tsp. salt
2 tsp. baking powder
¼ c. milk

Cream the butter, add the sugar, and blend well. Add the well-beaten egg and chocolate and beat. Add remaining dry ingredients and milk alternately. Chill dough and when firm, roll out and form in rolls the size of a tumbler. Chill again till firm, then cut into thin slices. Bake on greased pan or cookie sheet at 350°F about 10 minutes. If dough is put in refrigerator it may be kept several days if wrapped in wax paper.

Christmas Cakes and Candies

By Mabel K. Ray

What can I give cousin Laura for Christmas? For the woman who makes lovely cakes and candies the question is easily answered, as no more acceptable gifts could be given to friends or relatives. In fact such gifts carry with them truly individual thoughts from the giver.

Boxes of assorted cookies, candy, and cake, either fruit cake or other kinds, are all suitable presents. Possibly you have pounds of fruit cake or plum pudding in store now—ready to give as presents.

Packing the Gift

Packing the candy, cookies, or cake in the box in a pleasing arrangement may seem very difficult at first. However, with a little practice and forethought as to color variations and shapes, the trick will soon be learned. No matter how one packs the gift box or with what, a good rule to remember is to pack it so that the articles hold their positions and are not jumbled together upon arrival at their destination. What could be more disappointing than to have one's interest aroused by the outside of the package then inside find—just hash. After all that work and a good product to begin with, too!

After packing the container, wrap with Christmas tissue, and tie with cord or ribbon in harmony as to color with the gift box. If the box is to be given to a friend present in the home at Christmas or nearby, a sprig of holly, mistletoe, evergreen, or bittersweet may be tucked on top where the package is tied and lend much cheer.

❄ HONEY CAKES
December 1928

1 lb. sugar	1 tsp. cinnamon
1 lb. honey	ground cardamom seed from 3 pods
1 tsp. baking soda dissolved in 2 tbsp. water	¼ c. water
	juice and grated rind of 1 lemon
1 lb. flour	4 c. pecan meats, chopped fine
¼ tsp. cloves	¾ c. ground lemon peel, chopped fine

Put the sugar and honey in a saucepan; heat until the sugar is dissolved and the boiling point is reached. Remove from the fire and pour the mixture into a large bowl. Add the baking soda, dissolved in the water, immediately. Then stir in the flour and spices which have been sifted together, and ¼ c. water with the lemon juice and rind. Add the nuts and citron (all chopped fine), mix well, roll very thin, and cut. If dough is allowed to cool before rolling, the process will be very difficult. Allow cakes to stand overnight before baking. Bake at 350°F.

❄ GERMAN SPRINGERLE

February 1928
Contributed by Mrs. A. W., Illinois

7 eggs, separated
3 c. powdered sugar
1 tsp. grated nutmeg
1 tsp. cinnamon
1 tsp. vanilla
1 square chocolate, grated
2 tbsp. butter
1 tsp. baking powder
1 c. flour

Beat yolks and sugar, spices, vanilla, chocolate, and butter which has been slightly softened to facilitate mixing. Fold in beaten egg whites. Mix baking powder with ½ the flour and stir or knead into mixture. Turn onto well-floured board and knead in as much flour as dough will hold. Roll very thin and mold over single springerle mold or mold of any kind. Press dough on mold to make design distinct. Cut cakes out, lay on the table. Cover with clean cloth and let dry until morning. Bake at 350°F for about 20 minutes.

❄ DUTCH CHRISTMAS CAKES

December 1928

1 c. unsalted butter, softened
1 c. sugar
1 tsp. grated orange rind
6 tbsp. orange juice
4 to 5 c. flour
2 tbsp. sugar sifted with 1 tsp. cinnamon, for sprinkling
2 tbsp. sugar mixed with ½ tsp. grated orange rind, for sprinkling

Cream the butter and sugar, stir in the orange rind and juice, then work in the flour. The dough should be very stiff, so it is necessary to work in the last flour with the fingers. Chill then roll very thin; cut and sprinkle half of the cookies with cinnamon sugar. Sprinkle the tops of other cookies with grated, dried orange rind and granulated sugar. Place on buttered baking sheets and bake at 350°F till done.

❄ MOLASSES COOKIES
December 1928

½ c. lard
2¾ c. sugar
1 c. molasses
4 eggs, slightly beaten
2½ to 5 c. flour
¾ of a whole nutmeg, grated
1 tsp. cinnamon
1 tsp. ground cloves
1 tsp. mace
1 tsp. baking powder
¼ tsp. baking soda
1 qt. pecan meats

Cream the lard and sugar; add molasses and eggs. Then sift in 2 c. of flour with the spices, baking powder, and soda. Stir in the chopped pecans and enough additional flour to roll easily. Cut, place on buttered baking sheets, and bake at 350°F, watching closely, for these cakes burn easily.

❄ OLD ENGLISH GINGERNUTS
December 1928

½ c. unsalted butter, softened
2 c. sugar
2 eggs
4 c. flour
2 tsp. ground ginger
1 tsp. each of cinnamon and ground cloves
½ c. walnuts, chopped
sugar for rolling
citron pieces or walnut halves for garnish

Cream butter and sugar, beat in eggs, then the flour sifted with the spices. Add ½ c. chopped walnuts. The dough will seem quite stiff. Shape into little balls with the fingers, roll them in granulated sugar, and press a piece of citron or half an English walnut into each. Place on buttered baking sheets and bake at 350°F, till golden.

❄ NORWEGIAN KRUMKAKE

December 1928

Contributed by Mrs. W. J., Minnesota

Editor's Note: This recipe requires a krumkake iron, a contraption resembling a waffle iron that sits atop a stove burner and embosses a slight design on the cookie as it "bakes." The cookie is then rolled into a cone shape while warm.

1 c. unsalted butter, melted
1 ¾ c. sugar
2 c. flour
6 eggs
1 tsp. vanilla
1 c. cold water

Mix ingredients to remove lumps and bake on krumkake iron until golden. Remove and roll right away.

❄ SWEDISH SPRITZ COOKIES I

December 1924

Contributed by Mrs. A. J., Iowa

1 c. unsalted butter, softened
1 c. sugar
1 egg
2 tsp. almond extract
2½ to 3 c. flour to make a stiff dough

Cream butter and sugar; add egg, extract, and flour. Force through a cookie press to form into rings or fancy shapes. Place on unbuttered baking sheets. Bake in a hot oven (400°F), taking care not to burn.

❄ SWEDISH SPRITZ COOKIES II

December 1924

2 sticks unsalted butter, softened
⅔ c. sugar
3 egg yolks
1 tbsp. almond flour
2½ c. flour

Cream butter and sugar, add egg yolks, then almond flour and flour. Mix well. Force through cookie press into desired shapes and place on unbuttered baking sheets. Bake at 400°F for 6–10 minutes.

❄ SANDBAKELS
December 1924

1 lb. unsalted butter, softened
1⅛ c. sugar
1 egg
4 c. flour
½ tsp. salt
1 c. almond flour

Cream butter and sugar then add egg. Add remaining ingredients. Press small bits into cookie forms [*Editor's note: traditionally, small fluted tart-like tins*] and place on baking sheets. Bake at 350°F until delicately browned.

❄ SWEDISH SPRITSBAKELSER
December 1924

1 c. unsalted butter
1 c. sugar
1 egg
1 tsp. almond extract
2½ to 3 c. flour

Cream butter and sugar; add egg, extract, and flour. Dough must be forced through a cookie press and formed in rings or fancy shapes. Place on buttered baking sheets and bake at 400°F, taking care not to burn.

❄ SWEDISH ALLSPICE COOKIES
December 1937

¾ lb. unsalted butter, softened
2½ c. sugar
1 c. dark corn syrup
1 c. heavy cream
1 tbsp. cinnamon
1 tbsp. ground cloves
2 tsp. allspice
1 tbsp. baking soda
12 c. flour, approximately

Cream butter and sugar. Add corn syrup and heavy cream, and mix alternately with dry ingredients sifted together. Chill in refrigerator then roll out very thin. Cut in Christmas trees, diamonds, rounds, and place on buttered baking sheets. Bake at 375°F for about 10 minutes.

❄ LOVE KRANDSE

December 1924
Contributed by Miss S. R., Nebraska

1 c. unsalted butter, softened
½ c. sugar, plus extra for dipping
3 c. flour
4 egg yolks, hard cooked and pressed through a sieve
1 tsp. vanilla
1 egg, lightly beaten
granulated sugar

Cream butter and sugar and mix with flour. Add the egg yolks and vanilla. Roll the dough thin and form in small wreaths. Dip in beaten egg and sugar. Place on buttered cookie sheets and bake at 350°F till just done.

Gifts From Your Cook Stove

Better Than Trinkets Bought in the Shops
By Annette C. Dimock • December 1923

The older I get the surer I am that people have a hankering for home-cooked Christmas gifts. This rule for ginger snaps makes half a bushel! So we call them:

Half-Bushel Snaps

5 c. molasses
1 c. boiling water
4 c. sugar
1 lb. butter
2 tbsp. cinnamon
2 tbsp. ground ginger
2 tbsp. baking soda
flour

Put all ingredients except baking soda and flour into a saucepan and heat until the butter melts. Remove from fire and add 2 tbsp. soda. Cool. Add flour to make a dough which can be rolled very thin and finish like any cookies.

It matters less what we give as a Christmas greeting than the spirit in which we make our gifts. I once buried a hatchet by sending a birthday cake to a mere acquaintance who "had a mad" on. And we are now as good friends as at first. Let's scrap our hatchets and bake them into good things for our friends.

❊ DROP CAKES FOR HOLIDAY BASKETS
December 1923

1 c. sugar (brown or white)
½ c. unsalted butter, softened
2 eggs
½ c. light sour cream
½ c. corn syrup
1 tsp. each cinnamon and ground cloves
1 tsp. baking soda
1 c. each raisins and figs or dates, chopped
2½ c. flour
½ tsp. baking powder
½ c. black walnuts

Cream the sugar and butter; add eggs, then sour cream and syrup. Next add the spices and soda dissolved in 2 tbsp. hot water. Mix fruit with ¼ c. flour to keep from settling. Add remaining flour and baking powder to the batter until stiff enough to drop, then stir in fruit and nuts and drop on buttered baking sheets. Bake at 350°F until golden brown.

❊ CHOCOLATE HONEY ROUNDS
December 1923

½ c. unsalted butter, softened
⅓ c. sugar
⅔ c. honey
2 eggs
2 squares bittersweet Baker's chocolate, melted and left to cool slightly
3 c. flour
½ to 1 tsp. ground anise
½ tsp. baking soda
1½ tsp baking powder
½ tsp. salt
2 or 3 tbsp. cream

Cream butter; add sugar and honey, then eggs and cooled melted chocolate. Mix until very creamy. Sift in dry ingredients and add a little cream to blend. Shape into balls, place on buttered baking sheets, and stamp into rounds by flattening with a glass covered with a damp cloth. Bake at 350°F for about 10 minutes. These are better after storing a few days in a covered tin.

❊ HOLIDAY CRULLERS
Ladies' Home Journal, December 1917

1 c. sugar
½ c. butter
2 eggs, well beaten
½ c. milk
½ tsp. mace or nutmeg

½ tsp. salt
4 c. flour
4 tsp. baking powder
lard or oil for frying

Cream sugar and butter together, then add eggs; mix till smooth. Add milk, spices, and flour to make a stiff dough. Roll to ¼-inch thickness; cut with a cruller cutter (or cut into 4-inch lengths, make a slit down the middle, and pull one end through to make a knot). Fry in deep, hot fat and drain on paper towels or brown paper, then sprinkle with powdered sugar and cinnamon.

❊ ROLLED HONEY WAFERS
Ladies' Home Journal, December 1917

¼ tsp. ground cardamom
¼ c. butter
¾ c. honey
⅞ c. flour

Sift flour and spice into butter and honey. Mix well and spread thin over buttered cookie sheet. Mark off 3-inch squares and bake at 300°F till lightly browned. Cut into squares while warm and roll into tubes. Cool.

CAKES

❄ PLAIN FOUNDATION CAKE
December 1917

¼ c. butter or shortening
½ c. sugar
1 egg, well beaten
1½ c. flour
¼ tsp. salt
½ c. milk or water
3 tsp. baking powder
1 tsp. vanilla

Cream the butter and sugar thoroly then add the well-beaten egg. Sift the flour and salt and add alternately with the liquid, keeping the mixture of an even consistency. Mix quickly, beat hard, and fold in lightly the baking powder, sifted over the top, and the vanilla. Turn into a greased 8-inch pan and bake at 350°F for 30–40 minutes. Makes one layer.

Variations of Plain Foundation Cake:
White Cake: Use 3 egg whites in place of whole egg.
Gold Cake: Use 4 egg yolks in place of whole egg.
Mocha Cake: Use cold coffee in place of the liquid called for.
Chocolate Cake: Add 2 oz. melted bittersweet chocolate and a little less flour.
Nut Cake: Add ½ c. chopped walnuts, slightly floured.
Spice Cake: Add ½ tsp. cinnamon, ½ tsp. mixed allspice, nutmeg, and cloves.

Variations in Tins and Shapes:
Loaf Cake: Bake in a small loaf pan or double the ingredients and bake in large loaf pan.
Layer Cake: For a small cake cut the one layer in two and frost, making a two-layer cake half-size, or double size the amount and bake in two layer pans.
Cupcakes: Drop the mixture into well-greased muffin pans, filling the pans ⅔ full and baking about 25 minutes. These make dainty little cakes for all purposes.
Fancy Cakes: Heat tiny fancy-shaped pans, then brush with a good brush dipped in melted butter. Drop 1 tsp. cake mixture into each pan and bake 10–15 minutes. Or a one-layer cake may be cut into fancy shapes with a cutter but there is a waste unless great care is taken to plan the pieces.

❆ KRINGLER
May 1928
Contributed by Mrs. J. W. E., North Dakota

1 pt. milk
1 yeast cake
flour to make thick batter—3 to 5 c.
½ c. butter
1 c. raisins
1 c. sugar
citron
grated lemon rind
3 eggs

Scald the milk; when lukewarm dissolve a yeast cake in some of the milk. To this add enough flour to make a smooth thick batter. Set to rise in a warm place for 2 or 3 hours till doubled in bulk. Then add butter, raisins, citron, lemon rind, sugar, and eggs. Add enough flour to knead. When the dough does not stick to the board it is divided into three portions. Each portion is rolled out in a long, narrow strip and the three strips are braided together. Place braided dough in circular shape, cover with a towel, and put in a warm place to rise. Then moisten top with milk and stick in pieces of blanched slivered almonds. Sprinkle with sugar. Bake at 350°F for about ½ an hour.

Cakes and Puddings

By Mabel K. Ray • December 1932

With the holiday season comes the special time for making fruitcakes. Every family likes them and they make fine gifts. Some homemakers will follow favorite recipes handed down in the family for generations; others will wish for new recipes. So we are offering some fruitcake recipes which you will agree are good if you try them. Several are from "Our Readers." We are including also some new pudding recipes.

In baking fruit cakes it is well to line the pans with waxed paper since this will not only keep the cake from burning but will help keep the moisture in the cake during storage or the ripening period, which should be several weeks. Fruitcakes should be cooled, wrapped loosely in waxed paper, and then stored in a tightly closed container.

If you wish to decorate the top of fruit cakes with almonds, candied cherries, and fruit peel, do it after removing the cake from the oven by brushing the top with molasses diluted twice, arranging a design with the peel and nuts, then drying in the oven for a few minutes.

Fruit Cake

1 c. unsalted butter
1 c. granulated sugar
1 c. brown sugar
4 eggs, beaten
1 lb. raisins
1 lb. currants
1 lb. citron
1 tbsp. cinnamon

1 tsp. ginger
1 tsp. nutmeg
1 tsp. cloves
4½ c. flour
1½ c. sour milk
1 tbsp. baking soda dissolved in 3 tbsp.
    hot coffee

Cream butter, add sugars, and cream well together. Add beaten eggs. Dredge fruit in part of flour. Sift flour and seasoning together. Add fruit and flour alternately with sour milk. add soda in coffee; mix. Bake in two loaf tins in 300°F oven for 1½ to 2 hours.

Coffee Fruit Cake

½ c. shortening
1 c. light brown sugar
2 eggs, separated
¼ c. strong coffee
½ c. half-and-half

1¾ c. flour
3 tsp. baking powder
½ lb. raisins
⅛ lb. sliced citron
¼ lb. figs cut in strips

Cream shortening; add sugar then yolks and coffee and half-and-half. Sift flour and baking powder and add slowly. Add fruit, slightly floured, and fold in beaten egg whites. Bake in greased loaf pan at 300°F for 90 minutes.

Old Fashioned Plum Pudding

½ lb. raisins
½ lb. currants
2 oz. chopped citron
2 tsp. nutmeg
½ tsp. cinnamon
½ lb. sugar
½ lb. suet, chopped fine
4 c. flour
3 eggs, separated
milk enough to make a stiff batter

Dredge fruit and citron with flour. Combine dry ingredients. Add yolks and mix thoroughly, then add enough milk to make stiff batter. Fold in beaten egg whites last. Turn into thickly floured square of unbleached cotton cloth, tie securely, leaving some space for pudding to swell, and plunge into boiling water. Boil gently five hours.

Steamed Ginger Pudding

1 egg
1 c. molasses
½ c. unsalted butter, melted
1 c. chopped figs
1 c. hot water
2½ c. flour
1 tbsp. ground ginger
1 tsp. baking soda

Beat egg; add molasses, butter, figs and beat thoroughly. Add flour sifted with ginger and soda and when well mixed, add hot water. Put in greased shallow pans and steam 1 hour. Serve with lemon sauce.

To Make the Lemon Sauce:

1 c. sugar
2 tbsp. cornstarch
juice and grated rind of ½ lemon
1 egg
2 tbsp. unsalted butter
2 c. boiling water

Mix sugar and cornstarch; add lemon juice and rind and slightly beat egg. Add butter and boiling water and cook over low flame till clear. Serve hot or cold.

Other Gifts

What do we need to make a Merry Christmas? Is it money to spend, or can we make of it something else that all of us can more easily spare?

In years gone by we knew a certain John and Mary who got to thinking that money means everything—even to the making of a Merry Christmas. So when there came a December when money was scarce with them, they agreed one night, after the children had been put to bed, that there should be no Merry Christmas for their family that year.

Bravely they set out to fulfill their agreement, but when they came to the very day before Christmas, the eager hopes of the children haunted them and gave them no rest. Coming suddenly face to face, John and Mary said almost together, "We cannot, we dare not, let this Christmas go by without making it as merry as we can—for the children, for ourselves!"

But how? They found a way, because love always does find a way!

It was strange how their will to be of good cheer led them to the discovery of so many simple things, without price, that were good material for making Christmas merry—their home, of course, and the love that dwelt in it; also understanding of the drama of sacrifice and real heroism that had been played in that home through the months. But more—the will to be of good cheer quickened their ingenuity! How they flew about the tasks of fashioning this and that out of little or nothing!

Christmas came, Christmas went, and between the coming and going there was joy in that home—simple joy, it's true, but joy.

The first Christmas was a sign of what Christmas should be—made mostly of love and will to find good cheer. We dare not neglect to let any Christmas go by without making it as merry as we can—for the children, for ourselves.

—December 1931

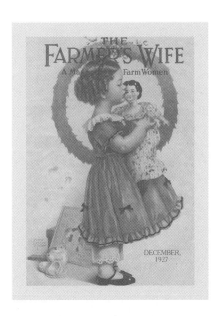

Christmas Gifts from the Farm

Where Else on Earth Are There So Many
Good and Beautiful Things?

By Marion Aldrich • December 1919

Last Christmas I spent with a schoolmate who lives in the country. I had gone to her home in the early Autumn to board because I had much writing to do and needed quiet. At the same time I needed the sweet, pure country air. When we first began talking of Christmas, fully six or eight weeks before that date, Ruth, my friend, began the old-time plaint: "I know I shall get a lot of pretty things from my city friends and relatives, and what on earth can I get in this old ark that is fit to send them?"

"This old ark" was the village general store, where we were when we brought up the subject of Christmas giving. "Ruth Preston," I answered her, "with all the opportunities you have for making the most delightful, unusual, and really worthwhile gifts, you should worry about Storekeeper Wiggin's limited stock of cheese and chewing tobacco."

"What do you mean?" gasped Ruth.

"Well, you never lived in the city, cooped up in an apartment, or in a house in a big town where the nearest woods and nearest garden were miles and miles away? Did you now?" She admitted that she never had.

"Imagine that you did live in such a place. What would you say if you were to receive a beautiful little baby fir tree eighteen inches high, a luscious deep green, growing in a pretty little wooden tub painted deep red? Suppose it came to you carefully wrapped in wet burlap so that the express people could see what it was and keep it right side up?"

"It would be pretty," admitted Ruth.

"And suppose you lived in a big elevator apartment with a tiny kitchenette and a new maid every week or so and all the goodies you had you made yourself or got at a café or dug out of cans with a can opener. How would you like to get a great fat mince pie, packed in a box so carefully that it couldn't crush or break?"

I had set her to thinking. Soon after that we brought up the subject once more. I sent back to the city for two dollars' worth of narrow, red ribbon, holly ribbon, Christmas labels, tags, and stickers.

"What are you going to send him?" I asked Ruth one day as she mentioned her very wealthy brother who had lived in a distant city for twenty years.

"Oh dear, Tom has so much money that anything I could afford would look cheap!" she complained. "Neckties are silly and I don't know the latest styles. I'd like to surprise him once—"

"Make fifty of those old-fashioned big sugar cookies, such as your mother used to make for you and Tom when you were youngsters. I know how they taste—I want one right now! Wrap each one in white tissue, stick a tiny fancy label on, to fasten the tissue together, pack them firmly in a box, and send them along to him." Watch his mouth water!

Ruth did it and the letter she got from her brother brought the quick tears to her eyes.

To my brother's wife I sent a small crate of mixed vegetables. She was delighted. I sent them early enough for her to use them for the Christmas dinner. There was a small Hubbard squash, some choice potatoes, onions, beets, carrots, turnips, a cabbage, some apples, a dozen hard winter pears, and a little jar of delicious crabapple jelly I tucked in.

To our old school teacher, still striving to teach the young idea how to shoot, Ruth and I joined in making a big, rich fruit cake.

To a friend who had a number of small children, Ruth sent half a dozen jars of pure honey.

I don't know how many little jars of jellies and chili sauce and baby pickles and jams and other preserves and condiments we sent along for presents.

To a doctor friend—the one who sent me to inhale the country air for six months—I sent two dozen big, rich duck eggs, quite fresh. On each egg I pasted a tiny sticker, a little Santa or Christmas tree or stocking or something of that sort. I placed these in a wire case which holds each egg firmly, marked them plainly, and they reached the good doctor without a break or a crack.

Every year Ruth's great-aunt sends her something of value. This great-aunt owns a string of business blocks in a big city and keeps a lawyer busily attending solely to her estate. At my suggestion, Ruth prepared a goose for the oven, stuffed it, sewed it up in a white cloth, and packed it in a box, the corners of which she filled with apples and onions for roasting. This she sent to Great-Aunt, not without fear and trembling.

"The very idea of sending her something to eat," she gasped, "She'll think it an insult." She invited a select few in to dinner, she wrote, and boasted of the "home-grown goose straight from my dear niece who lives on a farm." And all her guests raved.

To friends who had children we sent baskets of native nuts: walnuts, butternuts, hickory nuts, chinquapins, and the like. We also made some delicious maple kisses, wrapped them in waxed paper, packed them with sprigs of evergreen, and sent them along.

If you have popcorn, tie up four bunches, six ears in a bunch, with red ribbon and send it as a present. Country popcorn "tastes different," you know. It does. I've tasted it.

For Your Christmas Giving

By Lenore Dunnigan • December 1927

A particularly useful gift to the schoolgirl who loves books is the good looking and inexpensive book cover made of black oilcloth. It is lined with black satin, bound on the edges with orange bias binding, and decorated on the front with a flower cutout of red and green felt.

Bookcover

The attractive notebook cover above can be used for a writing portfolio. It is cut from black oilcloth and lined with cherry-colored sateen. The front is effectively decorated with a stencil design in rose, blue, yellow, and green.

A thoughtful gift for the one who likes things for the house is the charming table runner and pillow to match, illustrated below. They are made from wool homespun in a lovely shade of blue, with bindings of bright orange felt. The interesting embroidery design is worked in soft shades of orange, yellow, tan, henna, brown, and green wools.

Table Runner

The runner measures 18 inches by 64 inches with ¾-inch bindings of felt. The bindings are cut 1¾ inches wide, folded through the center, the edges turned in, basted over the edges of the runner, and stitched. The conventional flower and acorn design forms an attractive border at each end. The single embroidery motifs are repeated along the sides of the runner. French knots, satin stitch, twisted running, and outline stitches are the stitches used. The beauty of the finished articles is in the blending of soft colored wools and the accuracy and fineness of the work.

The same design decorates the pillow, which is cut 16 inches by 16 inches with ¾-inch bindings of orange felt. The same colors used on the runner are repeated in the pillow. The back is of homespun.

Pillow

The shopping bag illustrated below is fashioned of blue homespun and a part of the embroidery design used on the pillow and runner adds color to the front.

The bag is cut 12 inches wide at top, 14½ inches at bottom, rounding off the corners. It measures 14½ inches deep. It is lined with unbleached muslin. Top is bound with orange felt. Handles are cut 2½ inches wide and 16 inches long. They are folded lengthwise through the center, edges turned in, and stitched and sewed to the bag 1¾ inches from each edge.

Any simple embroidery pattern can be used for decorating the articles of homespun. Coarse linen crash, monk's cloth, and loosely woven wool homespuns in tan, brown, green, wisteria, and blues, with contrasting binding of felt can be used. The design would be lovely in bright wools or draperies of crash, theatrical gauze, or homespun fabrics.

Shopping Bag

How to Build Dolly a House
A Real One That Will Cost Little Cash
and Will Give Great Joy
By Ellis Meredith • December 1921

Anybody who has the price can buy a doll's house but they are expensive. Anybody who has a little imagination and a few slender resources and fairly deft fingers can make a doll's house that will be a thing of beauty and a joy for a considerable time.

To make a doll's house, first catch—not the doll but the little girl AND the doll. The girl should not be less than six not more than ten years old, and the doll should be from four to seven inches tall and should be a "lady" doll. If she is a paper doll, that will do just as well. I notice of late that fashions in dolls run to hugeness, requiring as much material and care when it comes to clothes as the little mother herself, and nothing short of a whole room or an outdoors playhouse would be a proper accommodation. The doll's house I prefer is one that can be set away in the corner of the living room, or some other room, where it will not take up a lot of space and be a nuisance to the grownups, who have some rights, though not so many as they think!

The next thing to decide is how many rooms the house is to have. A living room and bedroom are the easiest to furnish but a kitchen is a great addition—even if it requires another small box nailed on. I allow about a foot breadth, by ten inches in depth and twelve to fifteen inches in height for each room. Then I go to the nearest grocer and tell him I want a box to make into a doll's house and he gets interested and lets me paw around until I find something that will do.

Having the box, the next step is to put in the partitions, if there are to be any, and even if the box is pasteboard, it is better to make the partitions out of thin, smooth board. The side of the box which is to be the floor should be scraped and sandpapered until quite smooth before the partitions are put in. If there happens to be a little shellac or paint or varnish, this gives an "air" to the floors. I don't hold with carpets, but a scrap of white oilcloth makes a lovely kitchen floor! In most homes there are to be found remnants of wallpaper but it must be small in pattern; the ceilings should be plain. If there is not any wallpaper, plain wrapping paper makes a good wall. The outside of the box can be papered with any dark or gay-colored scraps of paper one happens to have, with dark brown paper, or with calico, or cretonne. Two screw-eyes with a plait of heavy cord, knotted at the ends, makes a good handle for the house— a great convenience when moving time comes.

By the time the floors and walls are done, the house begins to have an expectant air, and should be provided with windows, which are the eyes of any house. If they are to look out as well as in, you must decide on the season, and not show a glimpse of trees and flowers through one and snow and ice through another!

Windows can be made in three ways. The very elaborate way is to get small transparent slates and make fine net curtains, and either glue or nail the slates in place. I prefer to economize, so sometimes I take scenic postcards and make a sash, with a dividing bar across the middle, paste the sash on the card and then glue the card in place. Then I put up my curtains—usually a bit of net, or "footing," though a fine barred muslin, or paper, makes a good curtain, and the effect is quite realistic. But the easiest windows, and really the best, are those you cut from an advertisement, and it was the four windows in a rug advertisement in *The Farmer's Wife* that made me think of the doll house. Well, you can take one of those lovely interiors found in advertisements and place it on a wall of your house, hang up portieres, and produce a vista of most inviting aspect. Even with the picture windows the curtains should always be real.

My last "vista" of this sort was a small blue room, so I made it an imaginary room for a little girl-doll, just off her mother's room. I made the portiere of blue voile, a frill across and side drapes, and put it on a long hairpin, straightened out and crooked at the ends, and put through tiny screw-eyes. It made a decided addition.

Of course the wise housebuilder will assemble her materials—brads, thumb tacks, scraps of ribbon and lace and velvet, or muslin, or plain flour sacking. If there is a boy in the house who uses tools, he can make furniture all right, but if there isn't, I gather up boxes and use them. A spool box makes a very good couch, with a little cotton fastened on with glue, and a fringed "robe." A box a trifle wider makes a good bed, treated the same way, with a roll made of pasteboard and neatly covered. Of course, Dresden ribbon upholsters a bedroom beautifully, but the unbleached domestic, made with a frill, cross stitched in blue or red, is just as effective for the bed covering, the dressing table, window seat and chairs, which are made of more boxes—round and square, or big spools, or typewriter ribbon cores, or the heavy pasteboard toilet paper cores. Once you start on this it is surprising how many things can be evolved from what we think of as mere rubbish.

This Christmas, if I succeed in finding the girl, I mean to make a Colonial kitchen, in which the big fireplace is the main thing. Now a fireplace is easy to make, and most satisfactory. If you have a handy boy, he makes a mantel, with side pieces. Lacking the boy, you find a pasteboard box, imitation wood, of a dark color preferred, and then dampen the pasteboard, so as to bend it back, giving say three-quarters of an inch in depth. A search through advertising pages will nearly always produce pictures of bricks that can be used before the fireplace and for the back of it but now and then a fire picture will give realistic flames; and then you gather twigs, pile them up, fasten them together with tiny wire, run a few ravelings of red and blue and yellow silk if you have it through and around the twigs, and then nail it in place, and you have a "really, truly" log fire.

This is my own invention, as are the bookcases which I always install, for what is a house without books? These books cannot be pulled out, but like Mrs. Cratchit's ribbons, they "make a jolly good show for a sixpence." Here again a box with partitions is necessary, and then—the fluted brown packing paper that can be had for the asking from any merchant if there is none about the house. Cut it the width for your shelves, say three-quarters of an inch, to an inch wide for the bottom shelf, leaving enough to tuck in and glue at the ends, and with colored crayons color as you please, or draw lines, top and bottom, and the "flutes" look like real book backs. Any doll will find them charming!

At the ten-cent store—blessed resort of the destitute—I buy the table and chairs sets; four chairs and a table for ten cents. If they are tin or dark wood, I let it go at that, but if they are plain white wood, I glue tiny squares of ribbons on the seats, or even give them a coat of gold paint if I desire a Louis Quinze effect! Kitchen sets can be bought for ten cents in tin or wood, and I allow myself the luxury of tiny candles, ten cents a dozen, with candlesticks at a cent apiece.

A house must have flowers, and while tiny flower pots can be bought they are expensive and usually too large. What to do? I looked over a box of discarded millinery and found some wisps of green and a few faded little flowers, which responded to the touch of the crayon wonderfully; then I assembled the family thimbles, varying in size from Friend Husband's down to a number six. I melted paraffin and filled them, and stuck in my flowers as the wax cooled, let them get hard, then dipped them in boiling water, and out they came, and while still warm I set them firmly on top of the mantel, the bookcase, and the table, where the warm wax sticks fast, and they look like glasses of water.

Framed pictures can be cut from advertisements and they add, but I felt that I should have a rug, in addition to the fringed piece of Canton flannel, before my fireplace. I longed for a polar bear skin so I rummaged around until I found a scrap of white eiderdown about four inches square. I cut out something the general shape of a mud turtle, with longer legs than usual, sewed a scrap of it so as to turn for a head, stuffed it out, sewed on blue bead eyes, tiny bits of the eiderdown for ears, and an infinitesimal scrap of red ribbon—flannel would have done—made the tongue. It was a love of a pelt! Grey would make good wolf skins.

The other advertisement that specially caught my attention was one of monogrammed china. I may never have a set of the china, but if I make that colonial doll kitchen, I shall certainly use that china as a background. It is arranged perfectly for the purpose and the doll doesn't live who wouldn't be delighted with the result.

There are a few items that I permit myself to buy because I can't make them; one year I found some delightful little brooms about four inches long so that year I bought brooms and also "little bitsie" bird cages. I always buy a wee cat when I can but I do not put it in the same room as the canary!

Perhaps I have not made this very plain. It is such easy work when one gets the knack of it but the main thing necessary is resourcefulness, because what I want to get over is that any woman of ordinary intelligence with the material to be found in any average house can make a lovely gift for from nothing up—even the most extravagant doll houses have never cost more than a dollar—that will mean long hours of pleasure to the little girl who gets it. I once made a boys' playhouse but that is another story. In these days when everything costs so much and children's toys are often prohibitive in price, I think there must be women and girls who would like to try my plan, for I have never known it to fail, and it is no end of fun for the maker. Be a house builder!

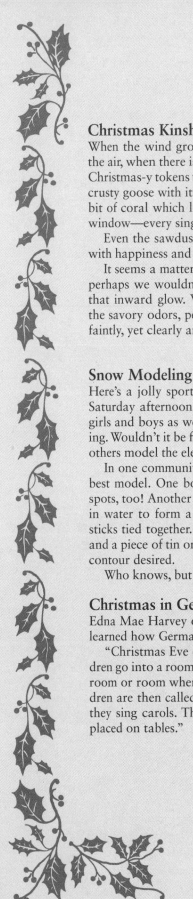

For Our Girls

December 1931

Christmas Kinship

When the wind grows colder and tiny white pellets shot from a leaden sky fill the air, when there isn't a single shop window in all the town that isn't filled with Christmas-y tokens that fairly tempt the imagination—from the fat, golden-brown crusty goose with its festoon of vegetables in the grocer's window to the delicate bit of coral which lies in its satin case beneath the holly wreath in the jeweler's window—every single thing seems to sense the spirit of kinship abroad.

Even the sawdust hearts of the painted dolls must feel it for they fairly glow with happiness and blush quite rosily.

It seems a matter of course to greet the passerby with a friendly smile though perhaps we wouldn't have thought of it at any other season. But then—there's that inward glow. We fairly had to smile. Perhaps it's just the holly, the pine, the savory odors, perhaps it's nonsense, or perhaps it's—as the bells say, ever so faintly, yet clearly and sweetly—"Peace on earth good will toward men."

—Elinor Haymond, West Virginia

Snow Modeling

Here's a jolly sport and a dandy way to spend the noon hour at school, or a Saturday afternoon. It's snow modeling, and it's becoming quite a fad with big girls and boys as well as the little ones. It's a great recreation for the club meeting. Wouldn't it be fun to have a snow circus? Let some one make the tents, while others model the elephants, monkeys and clowns.

In one community last winter a contest was held to see who could make the best model. One boy made almost an exact image of his dog Towser—brown spots, too! Another had two cats fighting. In making these things, snow is mixed in water to form a heavy slush. This may be packed around a frame made of sticks tied together. A wooden paddle is convenient to use in packing the snow, and a piece of tin or a knife is used to carve away excess and secure the lines and contour desired.

Who knows, but this might be a way of discovering talent in sculpturing?

Christmas in Germany

Edna Mae Harvey of Pennsylvania has a "pen pal" in Germany. From her Edna learned how Germans celebrate Christmas and is passing it on to the rest of us.

"Christmas Eve every person goes to church. On their arrival home the children go into a room. The parents at this time go into what is called the Christmas room or room where the tree is kept, to kindle the candles on the tree. The children are then called in to the room. Each one takes his place by the tree where they sing carols. Then they are allowed to look at their gifts which have been placed on tables."

Suggestions for the Coming Christmas

Christmas Presents from Strange Places

By Lulu G. Parker • *December 1911*

If your friends are plentiful and your purse is slim, perhaps these ideas will help you to fill some of the Christmas stockings:

Christmas out of the Scrap Book

Holders from bright flannel for use around the stove: roll of material for doll clothes for the child who likes to sew. This can be made more complete if you can add a few patterns for the dolls' clothes; jabots from scraps of lawn, lace, or embroidery; cutout blocks for a quilt top for some quilt maker. Crochet or woven rag rugs made from new pieces of cotton goods are now in good repute for chambers and bathroom floors.

Christmas out of the Old Magazines

Posters form the colored covers for the boys' and girls' rooms; scrapbook pictures and cutout picture puzzles for the children; booklets made from plain unruled paper in which are pasted bright, entertaining stories. These being so light are just the thing for an invalid.

Collect good plans for parties and suggestions for games to make a scrapbook for the woman who likes to entertain. Or a series of fancy-work ideas for the needleworker. From the pictures in the magazines there is no limit to the contest cards which can be made. A very little searching will discover pictures to illustrate titles of books, or names of flowers, famous men, or cities. These may be pasted on blank cards to be passed around for guessing at parties. About two dozen cards should make a set. These should be numbered and an extra card should give the answers for the use of the hostess. To illustrate—

Names of flowers: A picture of several young men and a button sewed on card represents Bachelor Button.

Picture of an automobile or locomotive and name or map of some country stands for carnation.

Picture of sheep represents Phlox.

Names of cities: Picture of a boy on a bicycle represents Wheeling, Va.; several lions, Lyons, France; advertisement for sausage, Bologna. By consulting an atlas one can find names of cities easily illustrated, and then find pictures without trouble.

And if a country woman has a city friend to whom she wishes to send a truly splendid gift, nothing can be better than a basket dinner. For this take a brand new splint basket and if you have time to paint it green, so much the better. Lay in it first a full double sheet of white tissue paper in such a way that after the basket is filled, the paper can be folded over all its contents. A dressed fowl, vegetables of two or three different kinds, all scrubbed to immaculateness, a glass of homemade jelly, and, for dessert, a can of fruit and a pint jar of real country cream will furnish a dinner that will make your city friend bless the day when she first made your acquaintance. Or, if you want to send a simpler gift, let it be a couple of dozen eggs, but do them up in some pretty and original way. A woman of my acquaintance received just such a gift last Christmas. The eggs were packed in white cornmeal, in a pretty box, and in such a way that just nine eggs were peeping from the surface of the snowy meal, and on these, in red watercolor paint, one letter on each egg was the message, MERRY XMAS. A red ribbon had been laid in the box first of all, then a sheet of white tissue paper, and after the eggs were packed, the paper was folded over, and the ribbon tied in a pretty bow to which was fastened the card with the donor's name.

Hints for Those with Empty Purses

As this has been a year of droughts and a shortage of crops in many sections of the country, to some Christmas giving is likely to be a perplexing question; to most of us, the holiday season would lose much of its charm if shorn of this pleasure of joyful preparation and the glad bestowals of love tokens.

Do not be disheartened at the slimness of your purse and Christmas prospects. You may not be able to give costly presents, indeed you may be obliged to forgo Christmas shopping altogether this year, yet that need not deter you from bestowing pretty and useful gifts on those whom you love best.

Bibs and caps for the babies can be fashioned from almost nothing. Bootees can be made from old kid gloves, scraps of flannel, or heavy outing. Small boxes may be transformed into beautiful receptacles for holding gloves, handkerchiefs, collars, neckties, veils, jewelry, and even silverware, by covering them prettily on the outside and putting in a dainty lining.

Do the work neatly, stitching in loving thoughts and tender memories, and your gifts will be received with gladness and carefully cherished.

Dos and Don'ts for Christmas

Do, if you can keep it, sign this pledge. It was circulated by some enthusiastic young reform-er and called "Yours for a courageous, sincere, and Christly Christmas"—

"I will give no gift which I cannot afford.

"I will give no gift which has not love behind it.

"I will give some gifts which shall not be exchange gifts at all but genuine generosity to someone to whom it will mean very much."

Don't do up a parcel in such poor wrapping paper or in such a flimsy manner that the wrapper may be easily torn and separated from the contents.

Don't fail to put your name and address, preceded by the word "from," on the upper left-hand corner of every piece of mail.

Don't forget to mail parcels early.

Don't say that you expect nothing. You know that would not be so.

Don't sigh for a baby grand piano if a barrel of flour would do you more good.

Don't forget, if you are going to play Santa Claus, that cotton is not as innocent as it looks.

Don't go around complaining that the true spirit of Christmas has departed. That is not the way to bring it back.

Don't forget you were a child once yourself.

Don't give simply for the purpose of showing that you can afford to do so.

Don't value the gift by the amount of its cost.

Don't put aside until tomorrow the good cheer you may spread today.

Christmas Potpourri

By Mary Octavia Davis • December 1937

A collection of odds and ends about Christmas, old and new, pagan and Christian, but worth remembering and fun to do.

Hang mistletoe and holly with evergreen about your house. Be sure you burn it, though, either on Candlemas Day, February 2, or Twelfth Night, January 6, or the "elves and goblins who live in the woods will be up to mischief in your house."

Trim your tree this year with something different. Hang gold and silver suns, moons, and stars, as the peasants did years ago.

Tie a sprig of mistletoe on your packages as a symbol of "Peace on earth, good will to men."

Hang an evergreen wreath outside your door, to shelter the homeless elves whose homes have been taken to make some child's Christmas tree.

Burn a candle in your window, a symbol of the light that has guided the world since the birth of the Babe of Bethlehem. (Be especially careful of fire.)

If you are a bride-to-be, make a big stocking and hang it outside your door as Spanish girls do. Santa may come by and put coins in it for your dowry money.

Leave hay and carrots in a convenient place for Santa's reindeer to eat while Santa comes down the chimney to fill the stockings. Holland children leave the hay in their wooden shoes outside the door. In the morning the hay is gone and the gifts are there.

When you tend your stock Christmas Eve, give them extra hay and oats; give kitty cream instead of milk and the dog a bigger bone; so that, according to old superstitions, when midnight comes and the animals speak to one another, they will have only good things to say of you.

Save eggshells as you do for Easter. Dye them or roll them in colored powders. Insert string tied to an inch-long matchstick. Trim your tree with these. An old Russian custom.

For an invalid who must spend Christmas in bed make a French Arbre de Nau. Take a hoop, not too big; wire evergreen sprays around it, making a green hoop.

Wrap nuts, sweets, glazed fruits, things that will keep, in colored cellophane and wire among the evergreens. Then for fun put on tiny toys such as puzzles, tricks, bubble pipe, and jack-in-the-box.

For table decorations try cellophane straws tipped with sealing wax and sewed into shapes as trees, pompons, candles; put candles in tins from the dime stores lacquered to match your color scheme; sprays of evergreen tied to small candle for place card or put on breakfast trays; gumdrop tree made from colored gumdrops and gilded thorny branch; use large tree for centerpiece and make small ones for place cards.

Christmas tree balls banked in evergreen for centerpiece and small ones tied to evergreen spray for plate favor. Clothespin dolls dressed as druids bringing in the Yule log through cotton snow as a centerpiece and small Yule log with spray of holly for place card.

If your family is scattered, and most of you will not get home to spend Christmas with Mother and Dad, then start a family chain letter, everyone sending a letter to one person to have them bound, or one member writes a letter to another member, this one in turn writes a letter sending the old letter and the new letter on to the next one. By Christmas the letter should be a sort of family album of the past year.

Dip oranges, lemons, limes, apples, and tangerines in clear thin shellac. Wire into wreaths and table pieces with evergreen, holly, and pine cones. This is known as a Della Robia wreath.

Wrap handkerchiefs, lingerie, hose, as candles in gold or silver paper or stuff in cornucopias of Christmas wrapping paper—wrap very small boxes in red- or green-checked gingham with spray of red berries—wrap jellies in round bottles in cellophane with squat red candle at the top—string small gifts along a gold or silver cord—cut out figures from old Christmas cards and paste on packages.

And above all save time to have a very Merry Christmas!

Give Her a Recipe File
December 1923

Every woman loves a good recipe and to have the favorite one at hand at the right moment is indeed an advantage. It is here that the card-file has found its way from the downtown business office to the efficient kitchen. When it reaches the kitchen it is a "recipe card-file."

Many homemakers are finding great help in a systematic arrangement of their best recipes. Instead of writing them in a book, as we used to do, they are written, printed, or pasted on small cards of uniform size and conveniently filed in a box especially designed for the purpose.

Directions for a light fluffy omelet may be turned to at a moment's notice. A recipe for company dessert is at the fingertips when company drives into the yard. Father's favorite fudge frosting and the fruit cake for Christmas are in the card-file ready for use when needed.

This recipe file is a small wooden box, only a little larger than the cards which stand upright in it. Because it is small and very good looking it may be placed conveniently on the kitchen shelf, cabinet, or table. Each box contains a set of cards on which to paste the recipes and also a set of index cards which separate the different classes of dishes—Soups, Desserts, Cake, Bread, and so forth.

Recipe cards are slipped into the space in front of the index card and there you are—the recipe is all ready for use. When in use the card is simply removed from the box and placed where it may be easily read. After use it is returned to the indexed file.

Filing recipes can become a real hobby and distinctly a source of pride when following a system like this. And, if you happen to be one of the very up-to-date housekeepers who budgets her time, the time saved from vain searching through scrapbooks and miscellaneous clippings will probably count high in minutes, perhaps hours.

Even with this new system we cannot entirely dispense with tried and true cook books and booklets. We all have at least one of them to which we are thoroughly devoted and without which we could not be the prize cook of the neighborhood. But we may if we choose copy some of the most frequently used recipes from these books on the handy file-cards. We also clip recipes from our favorite magazines and get them from our friends. And, of course, we are not limited to the handwritten cards as attractive, printed, and beautifully illustrated cards are now available.

As a Christmas remembrance, a recipe card-file should contain at least a dozen of your favorite recipes or it may be equipped with a set of the printed cards. An original Holiday wrapping completes this very personal and practical gift.

Christmas Comes in a Wooden Shoe
By Edna Bowling • December 1927

"Oh, let's have a Christmas tree," said Anne at an impromptu meeting of the Cloverleaf Club held in the hall of the high-school building. "There will be one at church, and then the community one, besides Christmas trees we all will have at home. I know! Let's put our gifts in wooden shoes, that's what they do in Holland."

"Wooden shoes? Where would we get them?" asked Marie and Lucy and Hilda all at once.

Ruth, who was president of the club, looked thoughtful. "I think Anne has a good idea," she said. "Won't you choose someone to work with you, Anne, and then plan the meeting?"

"I'd love to," said the bright-eyed Anne, "if Lucy will help. Will you, Lucy?"

Of course Lucy did, and right then the other girls started wondering what Anne and Lucy were planning. But not one inkling did they have until they arrived at their leader's home for the club meeting.

They found her house gay with evergreen over windows and doors, with Dutch children and Holland scenes, cut from crepe paper, tacked about the living room. At the door each girl was asked to put on a pair of "wooden shoes" made of heavy brown wrapping paper pasted over cardboard soles. Anne and Lucy decided they weren't going to have any too small, so they used as a pattern Anne's father's boots.

Business meeting and demonstrations were quickly finished in spite of the suppressed chuckles at the president and secretary trying to be dignified in their great shoes.

At game time Anne and Lucy were ready with gray paper and scissors which they gave to the girls, who raced to see which one could first cut out a pair of skates. A tiny Hans Brinker made of dates was presented to Hallie who had the best pair of silver skates.

After that there was a skating race across the room, placing the skates heel to toe across the floor. A snowball fight, using big balls of white crepe paper wound over cotton, thrown across "canals" of gray paper fastened to the backs of chairs, proved much fun. "Storks," the girls found, was a funny game in which their wooden shoes were no asset! The Dutch Maiden's Morning proved to be a relay race in and out of the many petticoated costume of Dutch girls.

Other games, too, and then on to the dining room where they found on the table a great "wooden shoe" made of brown wrapping paper, wire, and cardboard. A plump Kris Kringle, cut from crepe paper and stuffed with cotton, perched on the toe; and from the top of the shoe scarlet ribbons stretched to each place with tiny paper shoes filled with candy at their end.

Each girl followed her ribbon into her shoe to find her gift. Immediately afterward, Lucy and Anne served hot chocolate topped with marshmallows, and cookies cut in animal and bird shapes.

Some of the gifts the girls found are pictured here.

For Jenny there was a saucy clown doll with a costume of five attractive handkerchiefs. The doll was made of inexpensive cotton with features painted with fabric paints. Her hair was made of loose strands of golden wool.

Lucy displayed a darning bag which Marie had made for her of two 12-inch circles of green gingham bound with yellow bias tape. The strap, edged with tape, was fastened to the center of the upper circle, in which there was also a bound opening cut from the center to one edge. A friendly black kitten complacently unraveling a ball of yellow yarn was outlined on the bag.

Hilda and Katherine, bread club girls, both received holders—but such different ones! Hilda's holder was of yellow and white flannel braided in three strands, with the last row of braiding sewed on scallop fashion. Katherine's holder was a Little Red Hen with head outlined in black and a rocheted comb.

At the end of Anne's ribbon was a dainty Holland maid, whose serviceable tan dress, made to fit over a wooden clothes hanger, was roomy enough for all of Anne's laundry.

Handicraft Helps
Nouvart Tashjian • December 1920

Christmas gift-giving is still with us! It is a lovely custom, if observed with common sense and discretion. It is the purpose of the Handicraft Helps department of *The Farmer's Wife* to furnish from month to month seasonable suggestions for handwork which women and girls with a reasonable genius for using the needle can make at home . . .

Our great American poet and philosopher, Ralph Waldo Emerson, said of gifts what we all know to be aboundingly true: "It is a cold, lifeless business when you go to the shops to buy something which does not represent *your* life and talent but a goldsmith's."

Most of us have little money to spend at the "goldsmith's"—but all of us can give something, and when it is made by our own hands, it means a thoughtfulness and caring-ness beyond the mere spending of coin.

Baby's Knitted Sweater

Material: One skein of three-fold white saxony, and one skein of baby blue saxony.

Directions: With colored wool cast on 60 st.

Knit 3, purl 3, for 12 rows.
With white wool knit plain until you have 33 ridges.
At each end add 28 st for sleeve.
Knit plain 20 ridges.
Knit 48 st bind off 20 st for neck.
Knit 48 st.

Now work one shoulder at a time. Work 4 ridges. Add 1 st at each row for 12 rows. Make 20 ridges in all from shoulder, then bind off 28 st for sleeve. Work 5 more ridges.

Now work other shoulder same as this one, then have all st on one needle and knit 28 ridges.

With colored yarn make a rib of 12 rows, knit 3, purl 3 with colored yarn, pick the stitches at the neck (52 st) and knit plain 2 rows. At each end at shoulder add 1 st at every row. Work 8 ridges in all then bind off.

With colored yarn make a chain stitch, 5 inches long; make 3 small loops like clover leaf, and another larger leaf for buttonhole.

Crochet a small ball with the colored wool for button. Sew up the sides and sleeves. Always wash carefully so as not to shrink.

Sewing Book

A very practical gift for Mother, or Sister, who has just been married, is a sewing book. Cut two inches of heavy cardboard that are each seven inches wide and twelve inches long. You will need four pieces of cretonne seven and one-fourth inches long to cover the cardboard on both sides. Before putting the cretonne on the cardboard you can make the pockets and the tabs. Take a piece of cretonne seven and one-fourth inches wide and four and one-fourth inches long and sew it on the bottom of the cretonne that will cover the left side of the book, to make a pocket for holding odds and ends. On the same side [sew] a cross strip of cretonne seven and one-fourth inches wide and two and one-fourth inches long for holding spools of thread. Make about five pockets for the spools, sewing a seam about every one and one-half inches apart to hold different-sized spools nicely. Above this, a small strip to hold the thimble can be sewed. On the cretonne which will cover the right side of the book sew two narrow tabs for scissors, one about two inches from the top and one about two inches and one-half from the bottom, or measure to fit any special size of scissors. A piece of flannel two inches square will hold several sizes of needles. It takes only a minute or so to sew on tabs for pins, and other necessary articles which you may think of, and they add a great deal to the usefulness of the book.

After you have all the pockets and tabs which you think will be needed you can easily cover the cardboard. Join the two pieces of cardboard together with three strips of cretonne three inches long and one inch wide, one two inches from the top, one in the middle, and one two inches from the bottom. Basting thread in black and white and also spools of number 50 in black and white should be on hand, a tape measure and a small pencil can be put in the big pocket, and small crayons in white or yellow can always be used by the sewer for marking hems and so forth. A pocket put in for Mother's glasses would be very handy. The book can be folded and put away when not in use and the knowledge that all the sewing utensils are within easy reach is very comforting to a busy woman.

Chair Rest

Grandma's back gets tired when she sits for any length of time in a hard-back chair. A long, soft pillow with a cord fastened to it to hang over the back of any chair will be a welcome gift from a small member of the family.

Match Scratcher

Where gas or electricity has not yet made its appearance, lamps must still be used. In this case the youngsters can make useful and pretty match scratchers for presents to their elders or to one another. A ribbon bolt can be secured at any merchandise store. Use ribbon one inch wider than the bolt and shirr both edges of it. Slip ribbon over the bolt and tighten both sides. Cut out two pieces of sandpaper to fit the sides of the bolt. Stick them on with library paste. Sew baby ribbon on for hangers.

Hairpin Case

A hairpin case can be made very quickly and does not cost much. Use a strip of linen about eight inches long and three inches wide, in whatever color you wish, and piece of lace net the same length. Run a narrow hem on all sides of the linen and then carefully sew the net to the linen body. You can make a pocket for holding hair nets by lapping the case over about three inches at the end. Tack this pocket down on two sides. Two strips of narrow ribbon twelve inches long sewed on the opposite end from the pocket does nicely for a hanger. Tie ends of ribbon into a succession of little bows at top for a dainty finish.

Slipper Spool Case

Spools, emergency needles, and pins are all carried in the dainty little case shown in the photograph.

Sunbonnet Work Bag

This work bag will delight any dainty needleworker. It can hold pins, needles, embroidery, cotton or silk, tiny embroidery scissors, thimble.

Jolly Jenny

Jolly Jenny is a doll which all babies dearly love. She came to the editorial office of *The Farmer's Wife* straight from her farm home, leaving her little baby-mother long enough to have her picture taken and patterns made of her jolly self, so that every farm baby can have a Jolly Jenny, too.

Jolly Jenny can be made in about an hour and absolutely without cost. All that is needed to make her, complete from the top of her jolly cap to the tip of her saucy toe (including, of course, her adorable smile) is: two stockings, a bit of Turkey-red cotton, cotton for stuffing, and a corset stay.

Some Fancy Work for Christmas Gifts
Simple, Easily Made
December 1910

Embroidered Pincushion

Cut two round pieces of linen the same size and embroider the edges in scallops; work eyelets in both to correspond exactly and some simple design or initial on one piece. Make a small round cushion of pink or blue silk; stuff loosely with cotton, which may be sprinkled with sachet if desired. Insert cushion between the embroidered pieces and run baby ribbon of corresponding shade through the eyelets, finishing with bow.

PIN CUSHION

Gentlemen's Four-in-hand Tie

Make a chain of thirty stitches.

1st row—make 6 tr. In 3rd st form needle. 1 dbl. In 6th st. this makes a shell. Repeat 4 times making 5 shells in all and making the last double in the very end of chain.

2nd row—3 ch., 6 tr. In last double, a double in top of last shell, 6 tr. In next double, double in top of next shell, repeat to end of row.

Reduce to 3 shells and work 16 inches for band around neck.

Widen to 6 shells and work 14 inches and fasten off thread. This must be worked very tightly or it will soon become stringy and ill shaped. The same stitch may be used for a belt making more or less shells according to the width desired.

Ladies' Necktie

Showing two ways of finishing the ends.

Make a chain of 16 st.

1st row—A double in 2nd st from needle, dbl. In 6 following st., 1 ch. Dbl. In 7th again and in the 6 following st., 1 ch, turn so as to bring the thread on the inside between the work and the needle.

2nd row—Pass by 1 dbl. And work a dbl. In each of 6 dbls, 1 dbl. In chain st., 1 ch, another dbl. In ch., and a dbl in top of each dbl. To end of row. Repeat until desired length; fasten off and finish either with fringe made by double thread 4 times, draw loop through stitch, then draw ends of thread through loop. Fill the end of tie with these threads. Divide the threads evenly and knot across once by taking half of one bunch of threads and tying it around next bunch.

Take half of second bunch and tie around the third and so on to the end, then trim the ends evenly, or finish with small raised rose.

This may also be made wider for a belt if so desired.

Christmas Toys You Can Make

By Carroll P. Streeter • December 1936

Our own children have had so much fun with the following homemade Christmas presents—and I have had so much fun making these things—that I am pushing along the suggestions to anyone who may be interested.

1. From *The Farmer's Wife Magazine*'s booklet, *Homemade Toys and Play Equipment*, I took the idea of making a doll cradle out of a double-handled basket. Simply screw a piece of one-inch board to the bottom of the basket (so that some child won't step through it), and mount this board on a couple of coat hangers for rockers. Take off one of the basket handles and attach it where the other is fastened on. Put a canopy for the cradle over these handles, which become ribs to support it. Paint the basket, and that's all there is to it.

2. Perhaps the most used plaything in our house has been blocks. Blocks are expensive, but you can get a gunny sack full of them for a quarter by going to the lumber yard or carpenter shop and asking for odds and ends of 2x4, 2x2, and 2x6. Cut them into shorter lengths, varying in multiples of two inches—that is cut some four inches long, some six, some eight. Then the pieces can always be fitted together evenly, in an amazing number of combinations. Sandpaper the edges just enough to smooth them and paint. We used red, blue, green, and yellow.

3. From the booklet already mentioned I got the idea for a train. The base of the engine is a piece of 1x4 board, pointed at the front. On this board screw a tin can which has a couple of wooden discs fitted inside to give the screws something to hold to. A spool makes a smokestack and a half spool becomes a steam dome, bell, or whatever you want to call it. Build a little square cab behind the can, paint the engine red and blue, and you have a toy that will please any child.

   For cars use cigar boxes, with hooks on one end and screw eyes on the other. Leave the covers on the boxes, as it is more fun to haul a concealed load.

4. For days when children play in the house, something to draw pictures on is a lot of fun. Blackboards are dusty and chalk may be ground into the rug. At our house we like better a simple four-legged easel, made of 1x4s and hinged at the top. It holds big sheets of print paper which you can get, with holes punched, for a little money at any newspaper or job printing plant. Put a trough along the bottom for crayons, and have a small chain to keep the easel from spreading too much. The paper can be held by bolts (open end out). If you make both sides of the easel alike, two children can draw at once.

5. A "play house" or "store" which can be set up in the house is made of two pieces of plywood, each about 4 feet square, hinged together. In one cut windows, in the other a door. Set it up in a corner of the room and the walls of the room make the other two sides. When done with it, simply fold it up and put it away.

Ends of fruit crates make excellent "roofs" and "floors." By nailing two of these pieces together you can make a gable roof, and it is easy to notch a short piece of 2x2 to put on top as a chimney.

In Toyland

December 1930

Whoever heard of Christmas without a ball? Children will love this one crocheted of wrapping cord in blue, green, yellow, orange, red, and purple. If you do not have the colored twine, why not dip some white in the dye bath when other dyeing is being done?

The secret of this ball is the filling—beans! Won't it look gay hanging at the end of a Christmas tree branch or sticking out the top of the stocking?

A yarn doll is a delight to the toddling youngster. It is light in weight and is so easy to carry around by one of its conveniently long arms or legs.

The materials necessary are the cotton for the filling, and white, pink, and blue yarn, with a small amount of black.

First, wrap white yarn 65 times around an 18-inch cardboard. Slip a thread through all the loops at one end, tying them together. Cut the loops at the

other end. Next, shape a piece of cotton to form the head and body. Place the tied ends of the yarn over the head, making them lie straight and smooth. Tie a thread around the neck and bring the yarns down snugly over the body of cotton, dividing them to form the legs. Wrap the legs tightly with light blue yarn, finishing them with short, fluffy tassels.

For the arms, wrap a 12-inch cardboard 30 times with white yarn. Twist blue yarn around the whole group. Pull the arms through the body and make tassels for each hand.

The trunk is covered with a row of pink loops. Wrap the yarn around a pencil ten times. Slip a threaded darning needle under the loops and take a stitch in the doll, pulling the loops off the pencil. Continue until the body is covered. Pink and blue yarn make the cap, done in double crochet stitch.

The horse is easily made of unworn pieces of an old coat, while oilcloth, outing flannel, or gingham is used for the cat.

Presents to Make
December 1930

Letter File. With a coping saw cut from ¼-in. board the two sides of your letter file, using the frame around these directions for your pattern. Sandpaper until smooth. Paint one side and the edges of each black. When dry glue a flower or any other design from wallpaper or a magazine on each painted end. Put under a weight to dry. Cut another strip of board as wide as the bottom of the file and about 2½ inches long. Nail this to the ends and paint the inside black; when dry give all a coat of white shellac.

Book Ends. Enlarge pattern by adding an inch at top and bottom and ½ inch at sides. Cut patterns with a folded paper to make sure sides are alike. Saw two ends over pattern out of ½-inch boards and sandpaper them. Cut two pieces of galvanized sheet iron 4 inches square; punch mail holes in one edge. Nail these to bottom of book ends. Paint or enamel, decorate, and shellac as you did letter file. Paste a square of felt—pieces cut from an old felt hat will do—on the bottom of each piece of iron to keep it from scratching the table. (If letter file and book ends are made for Sister they may be painted and decorated to match the color scheme of her room.)

Your Own Christmas Card. Use the tree on this page for a pattern. Put it in the center of a tall correspondence card. It may be cut from green paper with a red paper base and a gummed gold star pasted on the tip, or it may be all of black paper. Or it may be painted in color or crayon or done in black ink. Under it write "Merry Christmas" and this poem (or make up a better one.)

> The wish beneath
> This Christmas tree
> Is all for you
> And comes from me.

Letter File   Your Christmas Card   Book Ends

A Christmas Suggestion
December 1910

A busy woman remarked last year that Christmas giving would be easy if it were not for the time spent in selecting some different gift for each one of her forty odd friends and relatives. For this year she determined to simplify the work by making three lists, one for gentlemen, one for young ladies and girls, and one for women. After counting the number in each she made enough pretty crochet ties of different shades for the first list, a dainty linen handkerchief trimmed with tatted made by her own deft fingers for each on the second, and a soft, bright pair of house slippers for each on the third. The last was the most difficult, but by making a part of smaller size than the rest she was able to check down the list when purchasing the soles and the result was quite as satisfactory as though the slippers had been knitted one pair at a time.

—*Laila Mitchell*

Little Gifts for the Flower Lover

The woman who delights in raising flowers will be glad to find in her Christmas stocking—a few of your choicest seeds in a dainty envelope, a slip of your favorite flower, a jardinière that is the right size to hold one of her plants, a roll of crepe paper to cover her flower pots of the right color to harmonize with her walls, a little powder bellows to shoot insect pests, a package of patent plant food or fertilizer, a bundle of neat wooden labels to mark her seed beds, or a book about plant culture.

—*Lulu G. Parker*

Handicraft Gift Ideas
December 1938

Every homemaker enjoys practical gifts that can be put to immediate everyday use; pictured here are three washcloths which are hand crocheted, making a smart set in white and a color to harmonize with bathroom accessories. For the set of three, choose two balls of white and two balls in color, using mercerized crochet cotton with a number 0 hook.

The first cloth is crocheted in a solid square, the second features alternate blocks of white and the matching color, and the third has three blocks of color running diagonally through the white center. All have contrasting overcast edges.

For attractive hot pan holders of the same design use carpet warp or crochet cotton, doubled. Reduce the number of stitches in each section to make the holder the desired size. Finish with a loop or ring in each corner.

In every baby's stocking there should be a soft, cuddly toy on Christmas morning. This one can be a bunny with cotton-tuft tale or a pussycat with long whiskers. The foundation of this one is a child's white half sock. Cut the toe to shape the ears and slash the top for legs. Add arms. Stitch, leaving an opening for stuffing. Stuff the heel so the animal sits comfortably. Printed cotton overalls complete this simple gift.

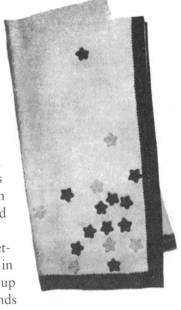

The square lunch cloth is a last-minute gift that can be made in no time. Round-thread cream color linen is cut in a 36-inch square. Band edges with deep maroon bias tape. Directly inside stitch maroon and gold rickrack band intertwined to make a single border.

Scattered over the cloth in each corner are five petalled flowers of maroon and gold rickrack, sewed in place with invisible stitches. To make flowerets draw up one edge of a five-point piece of rickrack and sew ends with invisible stitches.

Embroidered Accessories

Embroidery is a popular decoration this year. A belt might be done in pleasing colors of yarn on an otherwise simple wool dress, with a bag repeating the design and colors. Floral motifs shown at the lower right are beautiful in harmonious colors.

A bolero, belt, and matching bag are accessories to change the "key" dress which every smart woman owns. A scarf of bright wool, worked in white angora yarn, will also be a happy selection for the teenage girl.

Even conventionalized animal designs may be cleverly worked in embroidery floss, like the elephant shown here.

So little material is required for these items that the piece box will provide them. Flannel, velvet, broadcloth, and felt are only a few of the suitable fabrics.

Gifts for Her/for Him

December 1937

"What can I give him—or her"—as the case may be, is the theme song of letters reaching our office every day. You want to give a gift very much desired, yet not too personal; you want it to look like quality yet not be too expensive. There are really dozens of ideas; in fact, we were hard put to know which to leave out. Here are our recommendations:

A new glistening umbrella in a gay color will drive away the blues on a rainy day. This one has a removable handle.

The seed pearl bag with its gold mounting will shoot your rating sky high. The chiffon hankie is the perfect accompaniment or a very nice remembrance given alone. To the girl who is a good pal give a charm bracelet, then add other charms throughout the year.

Keeping a scrapbook for Kodak pictures, poems, or clippings is a favorite hobby with girls. This one has a fascinating reproduction of an old map and suggests a flattering interest in worldwide affairs.

The girl who loves gifts for her room will appreciate dresser lamps. This one is an approved height and what is more it has a lovely blue and silver plaid shade. Pairs are available.

Perfume for Cousin Beth

Fragrances are lovely this year, and bottles are the most attractive ever. In a white-and-copper package come a subtle flower combination called Sonata.

A Manicure Kit for Mother

The one shown holds cuticle scissors and pedicure shears that really cut, tweezers, nail file and other manicure essentials.

She'd like a good hand lotion, too, to use after her manicure, after dish washing, and before she goes outdoors. If she likes a thick, creamy lotion, there's one in a square-cut, gilt-capped bottle and another in a modernist red and white container. An amber-colored, quick-drying lotion comes in a Christmassy red package.

Give Sister a Beauty Box

One of these in dainty blue and pink holds a rose-scented powder and a popular cream. Another holds four purpose cream, lipstick in a rose and silver case, powder, and rouge. Perfume, lipstick that instantly matches its color to yours, powder and rouge make up the third, a gay little red and gold kit.

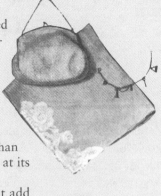

"Something Different" for Friend Joan

A little red, white, and blue gadget only a little bigger than her lipstick holds four cosmetics, and she'll be delighted at its cleverness.

So that she can replenish the cream supply you might add a jar of cleansing cream or one of powder base, or both. We show a moderately priced jar of cold cream that any girl would like.

For Him

Hair tonic, cologne and shaving lotion in a fascinating combination of bottles will please the boy friend who is always perfectly groomed.

If he travels he will appreciate an oiled silk lined case for comb, brush, shaving equipment, and such items. Cases come fitted or not as you please.

A desk pen which can be converted into a pen to carry in his pocket is a gift any man would enjoy.

A leather belt with an initialed buckle were oft-mentioned items when we asked boys what they liked for gifts. A sterling buckle with an engraved monogram is a lasting gift. Less expensive is a tie clip with a hobby charm.

"Give him a suede jacket" is the advice given by many men when questioned. Jackets come in a wide range of prices, qualities, and colors, so you surely will find the one you want.

A Shaving Set for Brother

The young man who's just started shaving will enjoy having his own shaving cream or soap, talcum, and after-shave lotion. One company features an inexpensive, red-and-green packaged Gift Box for Gentlemen.

The Joy of Christmas Giving and Receiving

Zara's Christmas Gifts

By Essie Bock • December 1913

"Zara! Zara!" I laughed this afternoon when I entered her mother's kitchen where Zara was sitting at the table, nothing but glue and scraps. Even a scrap of paper had stuck in her hair. "Zara," I said again, "What are you doing?" By then I had thrown my hat in a corner, pulled off my sweater, and I saw what she was doing. She was cutting the picture of a bedstead from a catalog. "Gone back to doll days?" I teased.

"Making Christmas gifts," she returned. "You must be rich, May, if you can afford to buy them for all the little folk you wish to remember."

"I should think not," I replied. "There are just a couple dozen little folk that I don't remember."

"Why not?" Her dark eyes turned my way for just a moment then went to the headboard of the bed which was difficult to cut. It was very fancy.

"I haven't the money, and you know it," I retorted.

"This bottle of glue cost ten cents and I am going to make seventeen Christmas presents without spending a cent more."

I was interested. "You are always doing something wonderful, Zara. I want to learn how, so you must tell me. I've got ten cents for glue."

"The next most difficult thing to get is the cardboard, but I have been saving it all the year. Every postal card, business, you know, and all the lightweight macaroni, mush, and cracker boxes, I save. Then—"

"What a cute little team," I interrupted. On the other end of the table, where I had not yet noticed it, was a paper wagon—the picture of one I should say standing, and in front, just as if hitched to it were six splendid horses. "How did you fix that?"

"Just cut out the horses and glued them on cardboard twice their size, cut the neck to the back and from the tail to the hips, doubled the top piece down and cut all around the animal and when finished he stood up. Some of the pictures have no feet so I have to draw some from another. I have a piece of old carbon for that."

"Where do you get them?"

"Out of mail-order catalogs. The big ones always have horses, even if some of them are small." And while she was telling me all about it she showed me a lot of little teams, some hitched to buggies, some to carriages, and two to wagons. And she always had the vehicles the right size for horses. "Papa gets two or three harness catalogs, too, and they have splendid pictures. I like this team best," she added, as she showed me six dapple greys, exactly alike, heads down and pulling, hitched to a big wagon. And up on the seat she had put a little man.

"And I suppose you will tell me it is just as easy to get pigs and cows and chickens?" I challenged.

"Easier," was the assured response. "Especially the chickens, think of the hundreds of poultry books. And Papa gets catalogs on cattle and sheep, too. And in the big catalogs you can find any size men, women, children, and babies. How do you like this?"

From a pile of little men and women paper dolls, which were braced to stand, she took a go-cart into which she had placed a paper baby. She had done it by slitting the pictured arm nearest on the go-cart and slipped the baby up the right height. Part of it was behind the little top, making it look perfectly natural. She stood it up and behind the go-cart placed a little lady, by her side a little boy and dog, and all standing looked too sweet for anything. I just knew some heart of four or five would be full of thrills over such a family. I told her so, too. Her pretty eyes just shone for I am never stingy of praise.

"Now what are you doing?" I questioned. She had glued the headboard of the bedstead on a piece of cardboard and was drawing from it.

"Making a bedstead. I have the dolls and the animals all finished. But you didn't see this!" she exclaimed.

So the next thing that appeared before my bewildered eyes was a horse on which she put a saddle and then a man. She must have had a dozen saddles and several little ladies in divided skirts, too. Then some were sitting and when placed on a sidesaddle looked perfect. They all seemed so natural.

"I don't see how you can get ideas for such things," I said.

"Used to make them for myself when I was little," she relied. "You see a child's mind is more imaginative and creative than that of a grown person so these dolls act as a suggestion and their little minds do the rest. They imagine them real, see all the wheels on the go-cart, see the horses hitched up even if the traces don't reach the wagons, the saddles on if they are not cinched, and this bedstead will be perfect. I think it is pretty."

It was finished and she stood it up. The headboard was beautifully finished—in the picture—and she had glued on the footboard to match; it was a thing to delight some little girl.

"Tell me how to make it," I demanded.

"Well, you first cut your cardboard, then get your cardboard and lay the former on it, then you draw—but, pshaw, I'll make you a sketch so you won't forget when you get home. I'll make you a chair first. Of course," she explained as she drew, using an envelope for a ruler, "you don't make them all one size. You can tell that by the pictured back and legs you are going to use for your chair and the head and foot-board of the bed. The rest must be in proportion. Same way with your dresser. Here is your chair pattern." She handed me the paper, figure number one. How simple it was. It was so easy to see that the middle was the seat, the longest lines were the back and folded up, the shortest were the legs and folded down.

"It takes you, Zara, to think of such things. How do you figure everything out?" I asked.

"Oh, I just like to plan things. I study and decide such things while I'm washing dishes and helping Mama." She was drawing something else and I watched her eagerly. I wondered what it was going to be.

"This is your dresser," she said at last and handed me figure two. "You see everything doubles away from the front and then the back folds up, making your top. In making a set it's always best to take the picture of the bed where there is a dresser to match. That way you always have perfect proportions between the two. On the back of the dresser you glue the mirror, on the front, the front of the dresser, of course; then when you have cut around the mirror and doubled the back sides you have a dandy piece of furniture.

"And you can make just as many different ones as there are pictures, can't you?"

"Oh, sure."

"But do you leave the top plain?" I continued my questions.

"Oh, no, you pick out a pretty pattern of lace and cut it for a scarf. Sometimes you can find one to fit, but not often. And you use window curtains for the bedspreads. They are just fine. And the carpets and rugs are nearly always shown in colors so you can use them for just what they represent. The couch covers are colored, too, and by slashing the corners they make nice couches. Glue them on cardboard, of course. They are easily made as they are completely covered."

"What are you making now?" I asked, as she went on measuring with envelope and pencil.

"A bed for you. And if you don't like the raw cardboard on the inside of the foot you can find pictured wood that is good for nothing else and glue it on. I always do." She showed me a nicely finished footboard. "A round table is a little more difficult to make but with some studying it can be done. A square one is easy but don't forget to slash the cover you put on it." A slip of paper was placed beneath my inquisitive nose. It was numbered three. Easy to see how it works. The head and footboard up and the legs down. "Now, you want to remember that you make the things the size the picture suggests, or you will lose part of the artistic effect. I will have eleven presents done by night. Don't think I give just one thing. There won't be a gift of less than fifteen pieces. Look at these two."

She handed me two envelopes, both stuffed. From the first I took four pigs, two cows, six chickens, a buggy, a wagon, six workhorses and one trotter, and a family consisting of a man, woman, and three small boys. From the other came a bedstead, commode, dresser, two bedroom chairs, five rugs, a rocking chair, two parlor chairs, one sofa, a stand, and a family of four: husband, wife, son, and daughter. On the bed was a white lace spread.

"And who are these for?" I asked.

Zara laughed. "Don't you dare to tell; but it seems to me that you have a little brother and sister, haven't you?"

"For Johnnie and Gorda!" I exclaimed. "How good of you. I'm going to make a lot of presents, too." Just as I finished speaking I saw something green beneath a large piece of cardboard and before Zara could remonstrate had it out. It was white cardboard about fourteen by twenty-four inches and on it was drawn a large tree. The leaves were colored green. It wasn't half bad and glued all over it were pictures of dolls, a ring, horn, toys of all kinds, little shoes, almost everything to be found in a catalogue. Even candles were there. And she had colored everything.

"Zara! Zara!" I cried, "what can't you think of? Who is it for?"

"Little Ruth Everton. She's fourteen months old, you know, and will like that little Christmas tree because she is crazy over pictures."

"It's just as cute as—"

"May, oh May," shouted Zara's brother Ned, "your father is waiting for you."

And I had to hurry into my sweater and grab my hat long before I wanted to leave Zara and the wonderful things she was making. But I couldn't keep Papa waiting so just said a hundred things in a minute and in another one was in the spring wagon. I didn't forget the figures Zara drew and now I can surely make some presents, too. I've got the dime for the glue and there are lots of old catalogues scattered about.

Make Your Own Christmas Cards
December 1932

Block-print Christmas cards are becoming more popular each year because they have a personal touch that other cards cannot give. They also give an opportunity to work out your own design.

Last year a 4-H club girl from Massachusetts sent her 4-H friends cards with a gold candle burning in front of a green four-leaf clover. Golden rays spread from the candle. Below the candle were printed these words: "How Far the Little Candle Throws Its Light."

Billy, a peppy girl from Montana, had as her design a girl riding a busting bronco, with "Greetings from Montana."

Sometimes the print is made on a piece of colored note paper and the paper folds like an envelope and is held together with a Christmas stamp. The other side is for the address. Oftentimes it is hard to find suitable envelopes for the cards, so this takes the place of them and also lessens the cost.

These for Christmas
December 1937

The carpenter apron which Skippy is wearing is an item every boy who uses tools will enjoy. Use ticking or denim, stitch pockets to hold the various tools, and bind the edges. Then join corner A to B. See sketch below.

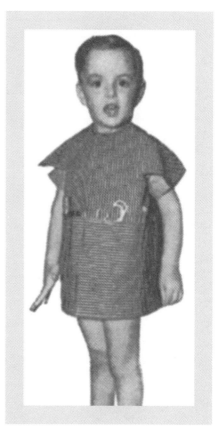

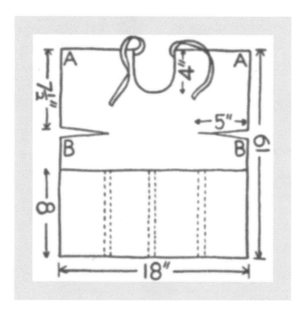

Carol's bib-apron is very simple to make as you can see by the sketch. It was designed, as was the carpenter apron, by the Extension Division, University of California, Berkeley. The apron is made of one-half yard of material, 36 inches wide. Fold it through the center and mark the armholes as indicated on the sketch. Bind them and reinforce the corners. At the top make a half-inch casing and run cotton tape through it for tying.

The smartest idea in many a day is the sock knit without a heel. It fits any size or shape of foot and, what is more, can be turned to distribute the wear. Send a three-cent stamp for directions.

Give him a horse he can ride if you want to please the smallest member on Christmas morning. This toy is one you can make as the pieces come stamped ready to be sewed up. The horse as pictured is about 15 inches high and 12 inches long. We suggest you sew oilcloth on the bottom so he can slide around easily.

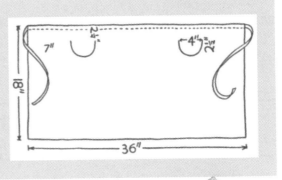

Oiled silk which can be purchased by the yard makes the smart shoe cases illustrated here. They measure 6x15 inches and may be cut without a pattern.

The tea apron is made of 21 inches of figured lawn with a 7-inch band of organdy across the bottom decorated with red, green, and blue bias tape. The double waistband measured 5 inches in the center and tapers to 3 inches at each end.

Up In Polly's Room

December 1937

Nosing Out Interests

Dear Polly: What can I give my boyfriend? He has several billfolds and doesn't care for candy. Would a signet ring be all right? Or a book?—Irene

Half the men I interviewed on the gift question said they'd like a book from "that certain girl." The other half said they definitely would not. And do you know what I think? I think the other half are afraid to trust a girl to choose a book—afraid she'll choose a "gooey" love story. Men just don't like love stories as well as women do.

Detective stories have special appeal to some men, sports and adventure stories to others. Try being a detective and "nose out" the boy friend's interests. Turn the conversation to books some evening and see if he has a "yen" for jungle tales, western romances, history, science, or travel. He may surprise you.

Unless you are engaged to the young man it's better not to give him a ring or anything expensive. You don't want to scare him away. A simple gift of moderate price is in better taste.

Doing Things Your Way

Dear Polly: I don't know what to give my mother for Christmas. She doesn't like little fancy gifts, and I haven't enough money to buy her anything she really wants.—15-year-old, Wisconsin

I think a smart thing to do is to give a hard-working mother a little bit of a lift. I know a 13-year-old boy who gave his mother a month's freedom from washing supper dishes. That was a Christmas gift Mrs. W— appreciated as much as anything she received.

I can hear you saying, "But I've washed all the supper dishes for years." No matter, you can find some other task to do for Mother.

Can you do a bit of extra cleaning or repairing at home—something Mother's been wanting done for a long time? Perhaps the kitchen furniture needs a new coat of paint or the cupboards need cleaning and rearranging. Maybe you'd like to give your mother a month's freedom from planning and cooking suppers. I'll wager she'd be pleased and proud if you'd hand-hem a half-dozen flour sacks she's saved for dish towels.

Dear Polly: What can I do about a gift for my father? Since I have to ask him for the money to buy his gift, I don't feel that I'm really giving him anything.

—Harriet

A girl should save for Christmas out of her regular allowance if she has one. If she hasn't an allowance or another way to earn money, she deserves to be given a little for Christmas buying, it seems to me. And if she's done her share of the work at home, she's earned this money.

You needn't spend much for your father's gift, Harriet. If you can hit on something he really wants, a small gift will look big to him. If he's a hunting or fishing enthusiast, a 50-cent subscription to an outdoor sports magazine, a hunting cap, or a box of shells will be just the thing.

When They're in the Bag

Some gift packages are so pretty you have qualms of conscience in unwrapping them. But then, that's the fun—the floor around the tree piled with exciting looking things for days, and then the growing pile of ribbon, tissue and packing as the family tears the wrappings off. Here's a letter from a girl who knows about clever gift-wrapping:

Dear Polly: My plan for gift-wrapping has grown on me until it has become a hobby. You see, I collect materials all year.

When I go shopping out of town I keep my economical eye open for dainty, cleverly-designed gift papers. Sometimes I find packages of assorted ones, and usually where there are pretty papers there are attractive cords and ribbons, too. When Nan gave a "white elephant" party, I used a green cellophane tie that had a row of white elephants marching down the middle of it. I used the same for Jimmie's circus party and shall use it at Christmas for some little folks' presents. I had had that tie for nearly two months before I used any of it. See how the plan works?

Now I have a grand collection of tie and paper and will have plenty to choose from to make my gifts the brightest and most unusual of all those under our tree.

—Hazel

Things a Girl Can Make
Useful Christmas Gifts for the Home
By Mrs. Mary Underwood • December 1912

With her needle and a little patience a girl can make some very nice presents for the whole family at small expense. Here are a few simple things which she will like to make and which take only a little time.

Boxes for Silver

Any housewife will like to have a box for the extra pieces of small silver spoons, etc., that one is sure to accumulate. Take any small box (a cigar box will be all right), clean it thoroughly, and line with velveteen of any preferred color. The outside may be decorated with burnt work or the word "Silver" painted on. The lining should be glued in.

A Clothespin Bag

Make a bag eighteen inches long by ten inches wide out of denim or bed ticking, cut the upper right-hand corner off so the hand may be easily slipped in, bind it all around with braid; fasten on a band, leaving strings to tie with.

A Magazine Cover

Cut heavy cardboard an inch longer and half an inch wider than the magazine you intend to cover, then take a strip of pretty brown or blue denim and cut it long enough to cover both back and front of the magazine and to extend at least three inches longer on each end; this is the part that the covers of the magazine fit into. Turn each end up so as to make a sort of pocket and stitch it together, then finish the raw edge by turning under and gluing down; when all is dry slip in the pasteboard covers and then either embroider or paint the word "Magazine," and any little flourishes you may want to add, then slip in all the advertising (unless it is too much) and you will have a cover that is very dainty at very little expense. This cover is made on the same principle as a book cover.

Scissors Guards

These are very convenient for either work basket or bag. Cut a hole in the center of a large cork, making it large enough to admit the points of the scissors. Crochet a netting of silk to cover all of it, leaving an opening which may be drawn up around the scissors and tied with baby ribbon.

A Poster Blotter

Cut a showy picture out of some magazine and cut it so only the outline is left, cutting away all the background. Take a piece of cardboard the size of the picture and at least two inches larger all around, fasten pretty ribbon across each corner, gluing the two together, and glue your poster onto that; dry under pressure, and when dry several pieces of blotting paper may be slipped under the ribbons and renewed when necessary.

A piece of crocheted lace will make a nice present, or enough of the hairpin lace for a pair of pillow cases will be appreciated by most anyone. Bits of linen may be utilized in making collars and bows; with the addition of a little colored embroidery they are lovely. Candy boxes are made by cutting out a piece of cardboard the shape of a cross, bend up the arms and the short top piece and let the long piece be cover as well as end; tie a ribbon around.

Christmas Love Tokens That All May Give

Dear Home Club: Here are a few Christmas love tokens that all may give. Letters, brimful of Christmas cheer, containing interesting items of home and neighborhood life, to those who have gone from the home nest or community to a distant state or faraway land.

Christmas postals, bearing appropriate messages of peace and goodwill to the bereaved and unfortunate.

Beautiful potted plants, just bursting into exquisite bloom, to flower-loving friends or to the sick and the shut-in.

A box of pretty pictures, clippings of children, birds, and flowers and other attractive scenes, to the child who is lonely and neglected.

Your favorite recipes and household helps, neatly copied and placed in envelopes, bearing suggestive quotations, to the young bride or inexperienced housekeeper.

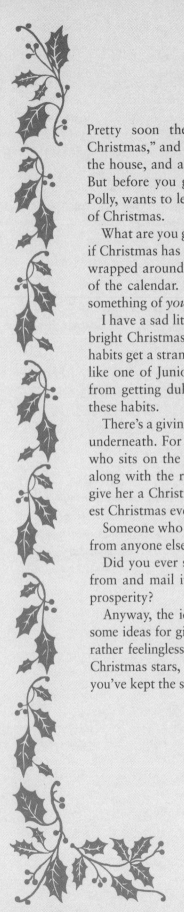

Up in Polly's Room

December 1936

Pretty soon the newspapers will say "only four more days until Christmas," and little brother will start looking for the longest stocking in the house, and an orgy of tinsel stringing and bauble hanging will begin. But before you get completely caught in the Yuletide whirl your friend, Polly, wants to lead you gently aside for a little private talk on the subject of Christmas.

What are you going to give this year besides presents? I'm asking because if Christmas has come to mean only so many yards of ribbon mechanically wrapped around so many packages, it's nothing more than a red number of the calendar. I hate to see you cheated. That's why I hope you'll give something of *yourself* for Christmas.

I have a sad little feeling that buried under the jingle and tinsel is a lot of bright Christmas joy that too many of us miss. All because a lot of stupid habits get a stranglehold on us. We go through the same motions each year, like one of Junior's mechanical toys. If for no other reason than to keep from getting dull and unimaginative I'm all for jerking ourselves out of these habits.

There's a giving that takes a thoughtfulness which comes from way down underneath. For instance, your best chum has a mother. She's the person who sits on the other side of Ann in church, and whom you just accept along with the rest of Ann's background. Wouldn't it be a bright idea to give her a Christmas present, containing a card, maybe: "Wishing the jolliest Christmas ever to a mother who deserves the best."?

Someone who hasn't heard from you in ages, and probably seldom hears from anyone else, either, would like a long letter.

Did you ever slip a dollar in an envelope without saying where it came from and mail it to someone to whom a dollar looks like the arrival of prosperity?

Anyway, the idea is to dig down deep in your imagination and pull up some ideas for giving which spring from warm, friendly impulses, not from rather feelingless habits. And when you go to bed at night and look at the Christmas stars, you'll find that you really haven't given anything at all . . . you've kept the sweetest part yourself.

Decorations

Woods Treasures
At Glad Yuletide We Bring the Lovely
Outdoors Indoors
By Grace Lovell May • December 1918

Growing plants keep a Christmas memory green for many months. Lily-of-the-valley roots or eyes, arranged in a dish of sand about three weeks before Christmas, will make good-sized plants for the Yuletide. Moss should be placed over the sand; the roots should be well watered and kept in a room whose temperature averages about sixty-five degrees during the day and forty-five at night to insure success, but the resulting bowl of sweetness will more than compensate for any care or trouble.

Chinese sand narcissus will flower in from four to six weeks from the time of planting. Early in December procure bulbs with tiny roots and leaf blades, place them in a shallow bowl of water with a few pebbles to steady them in a sunny window, and you will have good-sized plants ready to burst into bloom for Christmas.

Hyacinth bulbs in hyacinth glasses . . . started by the first of December . . . will show well by Christmas time, and freesia and star-of-Bethlehem, brought to the light at the same time, will also be "in" for Christmas.

Garden salvia, if it has not bloomed during the summer, makes a very appropriate Christmas flower, and the scarlet geranium in a pot covered with red tissue paper will be an acceptable addition to the window garden of any flower lover.

Cyclamen is difficult to grow but is a beautiful Christmas plant and the begonia, primrose, Christmas pepper, and poinsettia are always Christmas.

Christmas Table Decorations
Suggestions for Centerpieces and Place Cards
By Lulu G. Parker • December 1912

Centerpieces

Cut holes for windows and a door in a pasteboard box and cover the outside with red paper that has been marked with white crayon to represent bricks. Put a roof on and cover it with cotton snow, drawing it out at the eaves to represent icicles. Make a chimney for the roof and set a tiny Santa Claus doll with his pack in the chimney. The pack may contain bonbons, or tiny gifts attached to a ribbon which runs to each plate. These are to be drawn out at the end of the dinner.

Or make a chimney from a broad, flat box covered with the imitation brick paper, and fill it with fruit or bonbons.

Hang a big bunch of holly, mistletoe, or cedar from the chandelier, and from it run strings of popcorn, or red ribbon to the corners of the table. Have a sprig of the greenery and a small popcorn ball at each place. Red flowers are always in order for the Christmas table, and nothing can be prettier than a pot of red geraniums, peppers, or poinsettias.

Place Cards

Use Christmas postcards, or a plain card to which a spring of evergreen is tied with a bit of narrow ribbon. Cut the small Christmas pictures which are appearing in the newspapers and magazines at this time, and paste them carefully onto blank calling cards, if you have not an amateur artist in the family who can copy them freehand. For making pen and ink sketches use India ink instead of common writing fluid as it is much blacker. One can easily find simple outline pictures in the advertising columns of the papers, which can easily be copied by anyone with the aid of carbon paper.

A very simple place card may be quickly made by cutting a full stocking from colored cardboard using the pattern given. Write in the name of the guest upon it, and hang it on the water glass at each place by means of a little flap which should be bent back. The holly leaf and the Christmas tree should be used the same way but should be cut from green cardboard.

Our Home Club
December 1912

Dear Sisters: As it is coming so near Christmas time, I am sending you some dolls of sheet wadding to please the little ones. Ten cents' worth of wadding would make ten. Get five cents' worth of white sheet wadding for the body and arms and one sheet at five cents of either pink, blue, red, green, or yellow sheet wadding for the cape, cap, and muff. Cut a strip six inches wide, lengthwise of the white sheet wadding; begin at one end and roll this up rather tight and catch it with thread down the back to keep it in place. This is the body. Now one inch from top tie a thread around tight to form neck. Sew on two black beads for eyes, a red stitch for mouth. On forehead pull wadding out to form bangs. Sew up the cap and slip over back of head and sew around the neck. Pleat the cloak and lay it around body and sew in place. Use mercerized silk to overcast the cape all around and also the front of the cap. Make little bows of the same silk over forehead and on top of cap. Now tie cape around doll's neck with the mercerized silk in a bow and long ends to hang down front. Roll up a small piece of white wadding for arms. Put a small piece of colored wadding in center over the arms to represent the muff.

If you make them just right they look just as though they could smile and the little ones go wild over them.

With these directions and the picture I think anyone can make them.

Here are some sheet wadding owls you may like to make. Cut owls of white sheet wadding about six inches square; sew up on the back, gather one inch from top; now stuff with wadding and then gather again from the bottom for the tail; cut two circles of yellow paper and bill of yellow paper. Use shoe buttons in center of paper for pupil of eyes and sew in.

Community Christmas Picnic
By Lucy D. Cordiner • December 1920

Decorations
Each locality has its advantages for decorations. The Arabs who live in rocky deserts, where nature's decorative material is scarce, use rugs and pieces of gay cloth to enliven their surroundings. I once spent half a day in a large community room, cheerfully hung with gay, pieced quilts. Flags are always fascinating and have power to arouse feelings that are fully in accord with Christmas. A Christmas tree, evergreen branches, such as Arbor Vitae, and ground pine are available in many localities. With these, use red berries as abundantly as possible, rose haws, bittersweet, cranberries, holly. Small pumpkins give much color. Apples are always decorative. The Oregon Grape, so abundant in the far west, makes a beautiful decoration. It is really one of the native hollies. Oak branches give a feeling of festivity especially when our flag is used with them. Sheaves of grain are beautiful. These should be used with color to bring out their true beauty. Wild grasses and sumac and the seedpods of many of the roadside weeds add to the beauty of community rooms.

Christmas Decorations
By Mabel K. Ray • December 1930

The mention of Christmas table decorations brings a groan to some and a speculative glint to the eyes of other housewives, but to the children the suggestion always brings interest and enthusiasm. It would be a regular lark for them to make a centerpiece for the table, depicting a miniature Santa Claus land, the first Christmas, or to make that scene as pictured by the lines:

> "When what to my wondering eyes should appear
> But a miniature sleigh and eight tiny reindeer
> With a little old driver so lively and quick
> I knew in a moment it must be Saint Nick."

Santa Claus land is quite easy and inexpensive to make also. Just take a glass serving tray or an old "looking-glass," some cotton, snow sparklets, animal crackers, a miniature Santa, and any other figures that your imagination happens to demand. Make snow-covered hills and dales with the cotton on the tray, a snow hut, Santa in a sleigh made of square crackers and drawn by eight reindeer held upright by sticking toothpicks through their sides, thus harnessing a pair together. Here and there lake peeks through the snow made by allowing part of the mirror or glass to show.

With the light reflected by the lakes and snow from the candles—placed at either end of the centerpiece—a clever decoration is completed. Tiny fir or evergreen trees may be planted here and there in Santa Land; I'm sure the big Christmas tree wouldn't begrudge a few twigs for the dining room.

When it is finished—behold, the above illustration! It is a reproduction of our idea of Santa Land. How does it compare with yours?

If you do not care for a snow scene on your table a bowl full of holly, or evergreen with artificial poinsettias, would give that Christmas atmosphere which we all adore. If your pocketbook isn't as flat as you thought it would be (impossible—what?), a real poinsettia for the table would give a decided touch of beauty. Red candles lighted at mealtime add a true Yuletide glow.

A table decoration favored by many is a toy Christmas tree placed in the center of the table, bedecked in all its usual finery, as well as having little individual gifts for each member of the family. These gifts usually border on the frivolous and add much merriment to the occasion. Take care that the tree is low enough to enable the people at the table to see each other and participate freely in the gay conversation that is the best course the dinner provides. Such is the reaction of us talkative people anyway.

The cake, decorated in season and placed amid a bed of holly on the table, reigns supreme at some occasions. Of course there is always the old stand-by—a bowl of brightly colored fruit. Such a centerpiece adds graciousness, and any extra Christmas atmosphere can be gained by the room decorations.

Besides the table centerpiece, useful decorations are Santa Claus with sacks on their backs—which can be purchased at almost any five-and-dime store. The family will get a real thrill out of passing Santa around and taking nut meats, hard tack, or raisins from his sack.

Next comes the "loot" for each individual—in other words, favors. If you have never before tried having little surprises at mealtime, just try it this Christmas. One surprise that everyone will enjoy is a small candle and candlestick placed before each cover, to be lighted as the family files into the dining room for *the* dinner of the year. These are made by using different-colored gum drops for the candlesticks with a "life-saver" stuck on for the handle, and with a tiny birthday candle placed in the center of the gum drop. The birthday candle in the little rose holder is good for this.

Another favor that is inexpensive but enjoyed by many is the miniature Christmas tree made by taking evergreen twigs and tying about a small lollipop, then forcing the stems into an empty spool or through a small hole in a round piece of wood that will fit an individual nut basket. Around the trunk of the tree may then be placed nut "goodies" or candy. With various colored lollipops peeping out at the top of the trees the table makes a very colorful appearance.

A "Fine Idea" sent in by one of our Pennsylvania readers is for a "Rosy Apple Santa" favor made from a shiny red apple, snowy white surgical cotton, toothpicks, and ink. Make a round head of cotton (size of a walnut) and pin to the apple. Take a toothpick wound with a bit of cotton and ink in the features. For the cap take a three-inch-square piece of cotton. Pin it over the head and to the apple at the back, then twist to a peak at the top. Whickers may be made by fraying out a piece of cotton fluff and pinning under the chin. Cut a narrow strip of cotton and pin around his "middle" for a belt. Wrap four toothpicks with cotton and insert for arms and legs. Use a third toothpick at the back to put the props on Santa.

The Legend of the Bayberry Candle
December 1912

A pretty sentiment clings about the making and burning of Bayberry candles. In olden days the pretty maiden searched the woods for the fragrant berries, and with her own hands, moulded two slender tapers—one for herself and the other for her lover, who might be far away. On an appointed evening the candles were lighted and the incense was supposed to drift together as a symbol of their love.

Bayberry candles are still made by hand, layer on layer, in the quaint old fashion. Whether the ancient virtue of conjuring up memories of absent loved ones still lives in them, each maid must prove for herself—but this slender gray-green grace, soft mellow light, and spicy fragrance they leave in the air (also suggestive of old oak halls and colonial candlesticks) are as charming as in the days long since past.

Recipe for Making Bayberry Candles

Properly speaking the fragrant berries should be gathered in summer, but the dried berries, obtainable at any well-equipped drug store, will do as well. You will need more than with the fresh berries, however.

Boil the berries in the kettle for hours and then set them on the back of the stove to simmer for another hour. Allow the contents of the kettle to cook off slowly and by morning of the next day a cake of clear green wax will have formed.

Skim the wax off and reheat it by placing in a tightly covered pan over steaming water. Add an ounce of paraffin, melt both this and the wax together, and blend them well. Finally, run the liquid wax into candle moulds or better, dip them by tying the round wicking to a long, thin stick. Shape with your fingers.

Good Cheer in the Wrapping
By Ethel M. Arnold • December 1928

Are you a bit tired of wrapping your Christmas gifts in red paper, tying them with green cord, or do you use holly paper and red ribbon? I've been planning some new wrappings—spending thought instead of money, and the outside of my gifts isn't going to be prosaic looking this Christmas [even] if I did have to be very economical on the inside.

A clown doll for a young nephew is hidden in brown wrapping paper as befits the jester's homely self. But pasted hit-and-miss over the package are brilliant polka dots cut from colored pages of magazines. A lacquer advertisement will usually furnish what you need. Toys, building blocks, games, or books would be at home in such wrappings.

For cousin Bob I selected a handkerchief with a plaid border and that very plaid suggested the wrapping. A half sheet of white tissue paper plus a yardstick and the baby's crayons made a striking plaid in the same colors as the border. The thin flat box was wrapped in the plaid paper, the edges fastened carefully with paste. Stickers or seals would be superfluous besides spoiling the simple smartness of the design.

Several packages conveying little remembrances to some of my club friends heed the modernistic trend and are smartly futuristic. Black paper forms a fitting background for the dashing diamonds, triangles, and zigzag patches cut from crimson and gold, or magenta and green figured papers. Sheets of such paper are very expensive, but I used envelope linings, salvaged from old letters and Christmas cards. Arrange the designs with a thought to pattern and an eye for color.

To suggest the atmosphere of Christmas some of my gifts will carry gleaming stars. I am using silver ones, but they may be purchased in gold, blue, and red. Gummed, ready for use with fifty to one hundred in a box for ten cents—you have stars enough for many a package.

For variety I am using a medium and a small star, studding them over the surface of the package which has been first wrapped in plain paper. Silver on midnight blue, on black, on red, or on white are my favorite combinations.

If you live on a farm your family no doubt follows the happy trend of giving farm products for gifts. Black walnuts look attractive in a green burlap bag tied with a perky bow of red. Red apples, fragrant pinecones, and eggs wrapped in yellow tissue paper, all tucked into a rough brown basket make an individual, pleasing gift.

For some of my larger packages I have cut several delightful borders from colored paper just as I used to cut strings of paper dolls. It is so easy to do pine trees in a row or swinging bells or holly leaves. Demanding a bit more skill are fat Santas under huge packs. Magazine pictures will often furnish your patterns. Silhouette-like bands may be used in various ways, pasted around the ends or sides of the packages, or lengthwise of the top.

Mother bakes fruitcakes in angel food pans for Christmas gifts. We carefully wrap the cake in wax paper, then in green tissue paper. In the center we place a little branch of evergreen with paper stuffed around the stem to hold it in place. Cranberries, held to the branches by pins with the points bent back, add gaiety to the package.

Your scraps of colored paper can be turned into very individual seals. Little ships a-sail, wee lighted candles, a green wreath, a simple cathedral window, a decorative tree, or flower are suggestions for these special seals. Or you might use the initials of the receiver. You will find such seals a delightful change from the ordinary ones. An originality in the wrapping brings added pleasure with the gift.

Our Home Circle

Christmas Garlands and Vines Make the Home Walls Gay

Conducted by Mrs. Annis Farnsworth • December 1915

Dear Members of the Circle: There is only one thing better than Christmas in the country and that is Christmas on the farm. Here Santa comes into his own with a jingle. No Christmas setting could be more complete than that of the farm house with the snow sparkling on the white lawn or starring the red chimneys and the green fir trees with frosty crystals.

It is indoors, however, that the Christmas spirit must reign. Instead of using the wonderful decorations of their own outdoors many farm folk imitate the expensive style of city people who, after all, use tinsel and artificial greens just to remind them of the glittering snow and the leafy garlands of the country.

Some of the most effective trimmings for the farmhouse at Christmas are garlands, so easily made and so inexpensive that no room should be without its vivid ropes of green. They are especially good to frame the window and mantel or to wind upon the banister. To make these garlands use any sort of green foliage, vines, or twigs from the woods. Holly is supreme for Christmas decoration but is expensive when used in large quantities. Besides, there is a decided individuality about your own homegrown decorations that makes them far more choice and homey than holly unless it is also a native growth.

Red bittersweet berries are lovely mingled with the dark green of pine branches. The southern woods yield cherry laurel and on the Pacific coast there is the holly cherry. Other evergreens found in various localities are smilax, English ivy, several species of juniper, the evergreen magnolia, and the Christmas fern.

The children can help make these garlands. After you have selected your foliage, plait it together with twine, green or red. Make the garlands only a day or so before Christmas as they dry out quickly. If made earlier, dampen and keep in a cool room. Long strings of cranberries are very effective looped alternately with the garland or lying like a bright red line upon it. One of the most popular uses of this berry is to let it suggest the holly berry by dotting the green wreath.

Christmas wreaths surely belong to the American farmhouse for they were one of the best colonial country decorations. There was a wreath around the turkey and encircling the punch bowl; wreaths hung at the windows, on the walls, and about the knocker on the trimmed doorway. Little children wore them on their heads and many a lass blushed under her crown of holly.

The living room fireplace with its cheery Yule log helps out the Christmas spirit and the mantel above should have its trimming to correspond.

Wreaths in the windows should never be omitted. They are pleasant reminders to neighbors of the cheer within. If the outer curtains fall in straight folds the window garlands should frame the entire oblong, but if the curtain loops back let the greens make graceful loops over the curtain pole and hang half way down the sides. If the color of the curtains admits, sashes of green or red are a pretty change at this season.

Nowhere are garlands more effective than on the staircase where they wind in and out the rail or over the top of the banister. A small tree decorated with cotton balls and popcorn may be securely placed on the newel post, and if there is a new baby at the farmhouse this can be his own tree with his presents and toys upon it.

—CVD, NY

Home Circle Dear: Here is a jolly little game for Christmas. The children stand in a circle. One steps inside holding a holly wreath. The others face out singing to the tune of "My Bonnie":

Heigho for the bright Christmas holly,
For Christmas is coming 'ere long.
Heigho for the bright Christmas holly,
For Christmas is coming with song.
Chorus:
Holly! Holly! Holly with berries so red and bright!
Holly! Holly! Oh hang up the holly tonight!

The child holding the wreath now chooses a child and crowns him with it. They exchange places and the game continues as before.

—*L. R. S., Wisconsin*

Dear Home Circle Comrades: We have great fun devising amusing ways of distributing Christmas gifts. One year we had no tree. The house was gaily decorated with evergreen and holly. We hung our stockings on a clothesline stretched across the living room. Each person slipped in secretly to place the gifts. Father and I waited until everyone was asleep and then took the things from the stocking and hid them in out-of-the-way places, substituting cards with puzzling directions. For instance, "In cold storage" meant in the refrigerator; "In sleepy hollow" meant a large chair; "In the conservatory" sent the searcher to our single shelf of geraniums!

The next year we made a booth from a large dry goods box covering it with white cheesecloth. We trimmed it plentifully with evergreen, red tissue paper, and fluffy cotton, sprinkling the whole with diamond dust. The presents were placed on a shelf underneath the counter and Father as the good saint of the house distributed them with amusing comments.

This year a card will be put under each person's plate at the breakfast table directing him to look in a certain place, but when he reaches that spot he will find another card sending him somewhere else. In this way each member of the family hunts from cellar to garret all the others gaily "tagging," until the last gift is found.

—*I. G. S., New York*

Sisters of the Home Circle: Here is an old-world Christmas custom that is a surprise for a gathering unprepared for it. When the Christmas candles are shedding their glow and the fun of opening the packages is at its height, the door is opened mysteriously and a large box addressed to some member of the company is tossed into the midst of the circle. When unsealed a smaller box is found inside addressed to still another and so on to the last person—and woe to him! His pet failing, his most recent foible, is illustrated by a small present and pointed by a jingle that the entire company must enjoy! Sometimes two members of the circle, each unknown to the other, prepare the Christmas bomb and in that case the fun is increased, each addressee thinking his hour has come. This could be used as a joke at a Christmas party, omitting the "making fun" of anybody and having the last box contain candy for all or a present for the minister.

—*M. L. P., Washington*

Fun With Christmas Parcels

By Paula Nicholson • December 1920

Last year we had much more fun over the Christmas tree than ever before because each parcel was wrapped in such a way that it was impossible to guess what it contained.

To stimulate the children's ingenuity, a prize box of candy was offered to the member of the family who displayed the greatest cleverness in wrapping gifts. This was won by eight-year-old Jack. He hung a string of remarkably lifelike sausages upon the tree, as an offering to his mother. When the strings were untied half-a-dozen hemstitched handkerchiefs tumbled out. Each handkerchief had first been rolled in a small cardboard and then wrapped in brownish mottled paper. The finished sausages were linked realistically together with bits of string.

A close second to Jack's was a fountain pen concealed in a candle made of thick pasteboard wrapped in white tissue paper twisted to a point at the top to represent the wick and blackened with a drop of ink to show that the wick had been lighted. This was stuck into the kitchen candlestick before placing it under the tree where it presented a very realistic appearance.

A wristwatch was hidden in a bouquet of paper flowers. The tiny watch hid itself in the heart of a huge American Beauty that formed the center of the blossom of this masterpiece. A bracelet was concealed among the stems and the wide ribbon which tied them together.

This year, a silk umbrella is to be disguised as a dachshund by first wrapping it in strong paper and then twisting a wire around each end and bending the ends up to form the short legs of "long bowwow." Another bit of paper twisted on the ferrule forms the tail. The crook handle of the umbrella is padded with cotton batting for the head and the whole thing covered with brown crepe paper. Two big pins are used for eyes. The long melancholy ears are easily cut out of paper and attached.

Small gifts are easiest of all to make mysterious. They can be hidden in imitation apples, bananas, oranges, or other kinds of fruit or paper cornucopias or drums. A set of doilies has been made into Old Glory by using crepe paper covered with American Flags. Two of these were cut out, pasted on cardboard, and fastened together on each side of the flat package of doilies and a small stick attached to one end. This will "wave" most effectively from the Christmas tree.

A bottle of cologne is made into a doll. A round cake of soap forms the head which is swathed in a frilly cap of white crepe paper. Eyes, nose, and mouth are lightly traced upon its vacant countenance in watercolors. The head is tied to the top of the bottle, the long dress of white crepe paper put on, and another twist of paper runs crosswise for arms.

Decorate Your Wrapping Paper

December 1933

One of the newest tricks with a block print is to make individual wrapping paper for Christmas packages. The most clever and attractive designs can be worked out and cut on a block and stamped on any kind of plain paper.

Since art gum or erasers have taken the place of linoleum for the block, this craft has become very simple. One 5-cent art gum eraser gives room for a design on each end.

Transfer a design with carbon paper or draw it free hand on the gum. Cut away all of the eraser, except the design, to about ⅛ inch depth. The cutting is no trick if a sharp pointed paring knife is used.

Stars in various sizes, holly leaves and berries, small pine trees, holly wreaths, pinecones, girls on skis, are just a few of the more common designs. No doubt you will have a design in mind that will just suit your personality.

Ink poured in a saucer on several thicknesses of flannel may be used for getting the color on the block evenly. This is transferred to the paper immediately. If oil paints are used, it is economical to use a "dauber," made from a little ball of cotton wrapped in thin muslin. Dip the dauber lightly in the ink and spread evenly on the block.

In case you do not wish to work out an original design, our artist has worked out some very lovely ones which you may want to use. Send a 3-cent stamp to "For Our Girls," *The Farmer's Wife*, St. Paul, Minn., and begin right away planning the outside of your packages as well as the inside. After all, a good-looking package is half the fun of getting a gift, isn't it?

I'm asking Santa to be good to you

Boxes for Your Gifts
December 1927

Decorative boxes, covered with gay papers and prints, not only give an attractive wrapping to the simplest of gifts but make charming gifts in themselves.

Shoe, lingerie, hat, candy, and small odd-shaped boxes of every kind are effectively covered with wallpapers in quaint designs, Japanese and Chinese papers, Italian block papers, and even the fancy papers used for kindergarten work; oilcloth, chintz, and calico can also be used.

Old maps, Godey and flower prints, and colorful prints cut from advertisements add an interesting touch. The boxes are usually lined with a vivid paper which contrasts with the outside covering. If a print is used the background and lining should emphasize some color shown in the print.

A wastebasket can be made from a small hatbox covered with a black paper with a tiny flower design in rose and green. A silhouette print on the front can be outlined with bright green passé partout or pictured binding. The inside of the box can be enameled black and green bindings can be used to trim top and lower edge.

A small wastebasket can be covered with black paper with a gold dot. Print and edges can be trimmed with gold paper bindings. The inside should be enameled black. Both boxes are covered with a coat of white shellac.

An old-world map can be used to cover the top of the square box covered and lined with bright red paper. Black passé partout covers edge of the print. It can be filled with practical gifts from the notion counter which include tiny gold safety pins, a small box of darning cotton, a supply of hairpins, and lingerie tape.

The long, narrow box above makes a nice container for stockings. The shops show many of these attractive stocking boxes with twelve compartments. The one shown here is covered with a chintz paper, lined with a vivid blue paper, and finished with silver paper binding.

The nest of boxes illustrated below are cunning containers for the dresser drawers. Any group of small boxes that fit inside each other can be used. They are covered with a creamy white paper with a lavender, blue, yellow, and green flower design.

They are lined with a bright coral shade, bound with matching bindings, and covered with a coat of white shellac.

They can be sent as a gift or the separate boxes can be filled with some fancy Christmas sweets or used for wrapping useful and inexpensive gifts from the notion counter such as sewing and darning supplies, garters, lingerie tapes, supplies of pins, etc.

There are the loveliest red, green, gold, and silver novelty ribbons, and tulle, fancy stickers, seals, cards, and tags to use for giving them the Christmas-y touch.

The Christmas Season
December 1910

Christmas Fireplace

There was no place to hang the stockings so Father put up a shelf four feet long by one wide at about the height a mantle should be; strips of the brick paper were fastened to the wall to look like brick facing to a grate, and another strip was placed upon the floor in front of it.

The center was covered with black cambric to represent the inside of the grate. The shelf was covered with plain red, and along the edge were screwed as many brass cup hooks as there were to be stockings. The shelf came in handy to place articles upon that were too bulky to go into the stockings.

Out in the West where Christmas greens cannot be had—armfuls of white sage brush are dyed green, with diamond dye for cotton, and peas dyed scarlet are fastened upon the twigs for berries, by using a little strong glue. Lovely wreaths, crosses, and festoons can be made in this way.

—*Mrs. H. L. Miller*

Humpty Dumpty

This is fine for a children's party. Cover a long, narrow box with the brick paper to represent the wall; make an egg-shaped frame out of wire, and cover with white crepe paper, leaving a place at the top to put small gifts, nicely wrapped up. Put a tiny hat upon the egg and draw features upon the upper half. Put a bright paper sash around the middle and glue spindling arms and legs, also made of paper, upon it. Place upon the wall and at a given time tumble it off by means of a concealed string. It will usually burst open and the children can get the gifts.

For Christmas

Now that evergreens are so scarce, numerous ways of distributing gifts have been devised.

A Santa Claus chimney is easy to get up and inexpensive. All that is required is a roll each of Dennison decorated crepe paper No. 916 which represents red brick, blocked off with gilt, and No. 907, that has large-sized heads of the dear old Saint.

Take any wooden box that is about as large as a common chimney, remove one end, and nail on the cover. Now cover the outside with the brick paper, and the inside with the same or wrapping paper.

Paste all of the Santa Claus heads upon heavy pasteboard and place under a weight to dry.

When dry, trim around the outline carefully and fasten to the inside of the box, so that he appears to be just climbing out. The gifts, daintily wrapped, are placed inside of the box.

—H. L. Miller

AFTER-DINNER HOLIDAY ENTERTAINMENT

How to entertain the guests once the meal was through (and bellies stuffed) was a matter of ongoing consternation for the farmer's wife. She solved the problem by devising parlor games that could be played by guests of all ages and telling inspiring stories of Christmases past and present.

A Few Games to Enliven the Party

Will You Come to My Party?
By Myrtle J. Trachsel • December 1935

Do you love to hang holly, put mistletoe where people least expect it, trim trees with gay baubles—really get excited and have some fun out of the holiday season? Then by all means give a Christmas party—and notice how anxious all your friends are to come! If you can invite them with a telephone call, that sometimes provides a unique touch.

It adds interest to ask each guest to bring an inexpensive gift to be distributed by lot later on. Set a price limit of 10 cents and make people stick to it. Gifts are numbered as they are received and stacked under the Christmas tree. Later the numbers are drawn, and the guests asked to show how their gifts are to be used, while the others guess what it is. If there is an institution near, or any children in need of gifts, these may be taken to them.

Season's Greetings
Don't worry about there being any stiffness at your party—even at first. Start by giving each guest a sheet of paper with his name at the top. At a given signal each person is to get as many persons as possible to write "Merry Christmas" on his paper together with his full signature. No initials or abbreviations will be permitted. Since each person is being sought after while on the hunt himself, many funny things will happen.

Christmas Stunts
The guests will now be in a jolly frame of mind and can be trusted to do amazing things. Pass slips calling for the following stunts. Let each one in turn read his stunt and then perform it.

1. Give an imitation of a baby playing with building blocks.
2. Choose a partner and sing the chorus of "Jingle Bells," singing the first note as high as possible, the second as low, the third high, and so on.
3. Tell us what you would like to have for Christmas, and name the things you will probably get.
4. Walk across the room imitating a Mamma doll.
5. Draw a picture of Santa in the air, using your index finger.
6. Imitate the next performer, doing and saying exactly what she does and says.
7. Read the first verse of "'Twas the Night Before Christmas." Then, beginning with the last word, read it backward slowly and with much expression.
8. Sing chorus of a Christmas song, turning completely around after every fourth word; you may need an umpire.

9. Spell "Merry Christmas" backward.
10. Imitate three different Christmas toys.
11. Pantomime a sleigh ride.

Finding Partners

To find partners for a pencil game, let the men draw Christmas seals that have been pasted to small cards. The girls draw sheets of paper decorated with corresponding seals. The papers contain a list of words relating to Christmas which are misspelled. The men find the girls who have the same seals at the top of the list and help correct the words.

1. Natas Ucals: Santa Claus
2. Matrishcs: Christmas
3. Siew Emn: Wise Men
4. Lhyol: Holly
5. Namerg: Manger
6. Erte: Tree
7. Sdehpehrs: Shepherds
8. Tsokcgnis: Stockings
9. Atsr: Star
10. Mihcyen: Chimney
11. Fitsg: Gifts
12. Eteostmil: Mistletoe
13. Eldnacs: Candles
14. Einredre: Reindeer

A Guessing Game

The following questions concerning a Christmas tree may be read and guessed by the entire company, they may be used as a pencil game, or may be the means of finding partners for a later contest.

1. Why is it like the home office? (It has branches.)
2. What part is enjoyed by children when filled? (Cone.)
3. What baggage has it? (Trunk.)
4. What part interests a seamstress? (Needles.)
5. What keeps us warm? (Fur-fir.)
6. Why is it not sophisticated? (It is evergreen.)
7. What act of courtesy does it feature? (Bow-bough.)

A Christmas affair ends naturally in the singing of Christmas carols. For this feature divide the company into groups by allowing each person to draw a line of a familiar carol. They must then seek out the others having lines of the same song and sing it when called upon. Those unfamiliar with the carols may try to insert their lines in the wrong hymns. These humorous situations will be straightened out at the private rehearsals, and all will join lustily in the final performance.

At the Party
By Mary E. Underwood • March 1918

This game will be greatly enjoyed by the young people at their [Christmas] party. The fortune teller is stationed in a corner of the room cut off with curtains and made to represent a den. She is provided with as many pieces of paper as there are guests. On the left side of each sheet are written the numbered questions and to the right of the questions are corresponding numbers:

1. Have you a lover?	1
2. What is his (her) name?	2
3. How old is he?	3
4. How long have you known him?	4
5. Does he know you love him?	5
6. Is your affection returned?	6
7. Have you proposed?	7
8. What color is his hair?	8
9. What color are his eyes?	9
10. Is he handsome?	10
11. Is he conceited?	11
12. What shape is his nose?	12
13. What size is his mouth?	13
14. What is his fortune?	14
15. How much of the fortune will he allow you?	15
16. What is his chief virtue?	16
17. What is his profession?	17

18. Where did you first meet?   18
19. What is the name of your rival?   19
20. Where do you intend to live?   20
21. How many proposals have you made?   21
22. Will the marriage be happy?   22

Write the list on very wide paper so there will be room for the answers on the same sheet. The fortune teller folds over the sheet so as to hide the questions but leaves the second row of figures visible. She then instructs the one seeking information to write "yes" or "no" opposite the figure one. Opposite two she tells the fortune seeker to write a lady's name (or gentleman's, if a lady's fortune is being told). Opposite number three is to be written . . . and so on. The list of directions which the fortune teller gives to the fortune seeker are:

1. write yes or no
2. state name of lady or gentleman
3. give a number
4. length of time
5. yes or no
6. yes or no
7. yes or no
8. a color
9. a color
10. yes or no
11. yes or no
12. a shape
13. a measure
14. a sum of money
15. a sum of money
16. a virtue
17. a profession
18. the name of a place
19. the name of a lady or gentleman
20. the name of a place
21. a number
22. yes or no

When all the answers are written the fortune teller takes the folded paper and reads out the questions and answers. Suppose that opposite the number 9 the player has written "green." When read aloud, question and answer will be: "what color are his eyes? Green."

Another fortune-telling ruse that furnishes fun is to have a number of prophecies written in short sentences. Each sentence is cut into separate words. These are put into envelopes, sealed and handed out to those who come to have their fortunes told. When all the guests have received their envelopes they are opened and the fortune teller states that the words properly arranged will tell something about the player.

Holiday Time—Party Time
December 1931

For an indoor party for either young or old or both, progressive games are surer to give your guests a good time and to give them opportunity to "mix." You should plan for at least one game for every four persons, each game to be played 10 minutes. Some of the games should be table games and others should be of a more active nature.

In playing progressive games, each game is numbered, and the winners of game No. 1 move to game No. 2 and so on. The losers stay at the same game and play it again. Every time a player moves up he gets a score, which may be in the form of a feather in his headband.

The following games work in nicely.

Anagrams—Print three sets of alphabet letters on cards, about one-inch square (one letter on a card), and add to each set about seven additional cards for each vowel. Place these cards face down in the center of the table. Each person in turn draws a letter and tries to make up names of flowers, cities, animals, or birds as told by the person in charge. The two persons completing the most words in a given time progress to the next table.

Cootie—on each side of a one-inch cube print one of the following letters: B, H, L, T, E, A

    B—represents body
    H—represents head
    L—represents legs
    T—represents tail
    E—represents eyes
    A—represents antennae (horns)

Players may be seated on floor or around table, each supplied with a small piece of paper and pencil. Each person in turn rolls the cube. No player can start the game until a B is rolled. When a player rolls something that can be used in the construction of the cootie he has another turn rolling. The cootie is made up of body, head, tail, two eyes, each of which must be rolled separately, six legs, each rolled separately, and two antennae. The head must be rolled before eyes and antennae are counted. The parts are drawn on the paper as they are successfully rolled—the person getting a complete cootie first wins.

Peanut Jab—A bowl of peanuts is placed in the center of table and each player supplied with a hatpin. In turn with a single jab, each one spears for nuts, using the hatpin. The couple getting the most peanuts moves on.

Pitching Quoits—Take a footstool or piano stool and turn it upside down so that the four legs will make pegs. Each player takes three ordinary rope quoits (rings made from ½-inch rope by tying together) and from a distance of seven feet tries to ring the stool legs. Ten points are counted on each "ring."

Jar Ring Toss—A board is prepared by driving into it at a 40-degree angle twenty-three nails (3 inches long driven in ½ inch) or by screwing in the little right-angle hooks that are used to hold curtain rods. Each hook is given a number value. The figures may be painted on or cut from an old calendar and pasted on the board. The board should be 28 inches square and may be hung against the wall or set on a table. The center of the board should be about shoulder high.

The players stand 8 or 10 feet from the board. Each is given twelve rubber jar rings which he tries to hang on the hooks having the largest values. The players throw three times in a play and rotate four times; it is well to mark the rings with crayon or paint so that each may identify his own in scoring.

Christmas Telegrams—This game is for all to play just before refreshments. Give the players a pencil and paper and ask them to write, in ten minutes, a telegram using the letters in "Poinsettia" as the initial letters for the words. The letters must be used in order in which they come. Example: "Percy out in Nebraska selling eggs to the Indian Agency." Read during lunch.

After the program's games are finished the one who has the most feathers in his headband is given a prize and boobie may also be given.

Stories of and for Christmas

A Spot of Ice

In Winter time
It's very nice
To find a slippery
Spot of ice.

I run four steps
And then I slide
With one foot front
And arms thrown wide.

But if I tip
A little bit,
My feet fly out
And down I sit!

The Night Before Christmas

There had been a joke in the Dean family household ever since the twins could remember. It was about being the first one to shout "Merry Christmas" on Christmas morning. The one who was first always had the happiest Christmas, so they said. Benny made up his mind that this year he would be first. He never had been before.

The night before Christmas the whole family sat before the Christmas tree and tried to decide which ornaments they liked best. There were dangling bars of silver, tiny tinsel ropes with bells at the ends, and the old star that had belonged to Grandma Dean at the very top.

Mrs. Dean read the Cratchit Family Dinner out loud and Mr. Dean read the Christmas Bible Story, just as they did every Christmas Eve. They all sang a carol or two and then it was Baby Bud's bedtime.

"Ho-hum!" yawned Benny. "Guess I'll go to bed, too."

"That's funny," said Becky. "You never want to go to bed other Christmas Eves. You just want to get up first tomorrow morning."

"Fine!" said Mr. Dean. "The first fellow up around here gets to build the fire."

"And that's not all," said Benny as he trotted off to bed.

"You'd better go to sleep," said Becky to Benny a little later as Benny kept twisting and turning in his bed. "If you don't you'll be awake when Santa brings the presents in, and you're not supposed to watch Santa."

"I don't care whether Santa brings the presents or the cat drags 'em in, I'm going to be the first to shout Merry Christmas!"

Hours later, or so it seemed to Becky, she heard Benny creep from his bed and steal down the stairs. The third step gave a loud squeak and quick as a wink the stair door popped open and Becky heard Mother's voice say, "Why, Benny! Go back to bed."

"Isn't it morning?" mumbled Benny sleepily.

"Dear me, no. It isn't even midnight. Daddy and I haven't gone to bed yet."

Benny stumbled back to bed and Becky didn't let him know she'd heard a word. In a moment or two he was so sound asleep he was really snoring.

"Now he'll be so tired after having been only half asleep all this time that he'll never hear me when I get up. It will be easy now to stay awake until I hear the clock strike midnight and then *I'll* hop out to the head of the stairs and shout Merry Christmas so everybody can hear me." She shivered a little to think how cold it would be and thought it wouldn't hurt if she dozed off a little.

Suddenly she sat bolt upright in bed. What time was it? She felt like she'd been asleep a long time. It looked rather lightish outdoors. Could that be daylight or was there a moon?

"Well," thought Becky, "I'll just creep downstairs and peek at the clock."

When she felt the doorknob in the dark, she hit it with a bump. Immediately Mother's flashlight came on from her room across the hall.

"What's the matter?"

"M-M-Mer-" Becky wasn't sure—what if it wasn't Christmas yet? "M-M-Mother," she finally said, "d-did you put that red rubber ball in the toe of Baby Bud's stocking?"

"Dear me yes, child. Now skip back to bed or you'll take cold."

Becky curled her icy feet under her and wondered if she'd better not try to stay awake again. "It's on my mind now and I'm a light sleeper. I'll probably hear the clock when it strikes."

But she didn't. She didn't even hear Benny fifteen minutes later when he sat up in bed.

"What's that?" he said to himself. Was it Daddy breaking kindling or the trees in the wind? Was that the stove lids or the telephone wires rattling? He listened a long time. It might be Daddy making the fire. If he went very carefully and stepped over the third step he could peek out the door to be sure before he said anything.

He got to the foot of the stairs without a sound—and then he sneezed.

Mr. Dear's voice came down the stairs. "Benny, what do you want?"

"I-I-what time is it?"

"Oh, about 11:30. Soon be Christmas, won't it?" said Mr. Dean with a chuckle. "Now skip back to bed."

"That's easy," thought Benny. "I can stay awake all right until the clock strikes twelve and then wake everybody up."

But he didn't! The first thing he or Becky knew was that Mother, Daddy, and Baby Bud were standing in their room. The sun was shining in the windows and Daddy was saying, "Now all together! 1, 2, 3!"

"Merry Christmas!" shouted the Dean family.

Up in Polly's Room

December 1930

If this United States wasn't so large, I'd say let's have a glorious Christmas party and invite every single one of "Our Girls."

"But oh my!" you may say, "What in the world would you do with us all?"

That's easy! At dusk we would all gather on the big hill back of our house, with bobsleds galore. And such fun as we would have, racing over the thick-crusted snow clear to the foot of the hill.

On second thought, I'd say that the boys should be invited, too. For it's rather nice to have them ready to pull the sleds to the top of the hill, don't you think?

After an hour or more of swift rides, tumbles in the snow, and "heap big fun" we would go to the house. Of course the fire in the open fireplace, heaped up with hickory sticks, would be roaring and crackling and sending up sparks to the chimney top. Dad always sees to that! The light from the fire is all that is necessary to see the wreaths of holly in the windows, and clumps of mistletoe tied to the chandeliers. In the back of the room a nice, fat Christmas tree stands laden with trimmings and silver tinsel, colored popcorn and cranberries on strings, icicles and snow, candles in tin holders, and a beautiful star on the tiptop, made of tinfoil.

While we would sit on the floor with our toes to the fire, big bowls of steaming soup would come to our rescue, followed by red apples, popcorn balls, and chestnuts.

As we would sit there toasting our toes, I'll bet one of you would start a Christmas story. Others would follow with legends and tales of Christmas in other lands. Then, when the candles of the tree were being lit, we'd sing carols!

But just a minute! Don't go home yet. I have something for you. Red stocking of tarleton, filled with homemade candies, nuts, fruits, and in the toe a tiny present. And more than that! A hearty wish from the bottom of my heart for a MERRY CHRISTMAS.

Farm Women's Letters
"A Gift for the Future"
December 1937

Dear Editor: Yesterday afternoon three neighbor women and myself were making pickles and got to talking about Christmas giving. Two of the women have become mothers-in-law this year, for the first time. Mrs. Brown was unable to decide whether to give the newlyweds a nice radio or a vacuum cleaner. The radio would be more of a joint present, yet her daughter really needed the cleaner.

Mrs. White said she had already decided on her Christmas present. Her daughter and son-in-law were to receive the price of a baby. Shocked amazement followed her statement.

"I don't care," Mrs. White insisted. "Folks can be shocked if they want to. I remember how Helen's own coming was spoiled for us because we couldn't afford her. I don't want her to have the same dread. I don't care when they have a baby, but I want them to know that money is in the bank, waiting to pay the expenses when their first-born does come. They will know the money is not available for any other purpose, and will not worry for fear it has to go for interest or taxes. I am resolved that lack of funds shall not detract from the happy planning of our first grandchild."

Wise mother!

—*Dare, Idaho*

One Page Missing
(A Christmas Advertisement along Wholly Different Lines)
December 1928

Sherlock Holmes was amused—interested. "Never had a case quite like it," he mused as he studied the youth sitting opposite him. "You gave your wife thirty-five dollars to buy gifts, Mr. Wentworth?"

The young man nodded. "That's all I had."

"Go on!"

"I didn't get home till late. The things she bought were on the table. Lots of things, Mr. Holmes—too many of 'em! And all silver—beautiful silver—piece after piece of it. They must have cost twice what I gave her. I tried to figure out how she got them. Doubts kept coming in my mind. I thought I'd go mad! I couldn't stand it any longer so I came to you. Mr. Holmes—*where did she get that extra money?*"

The great detective looked at him through half-closed eyes. "Tell me what she purchased," he asked.

"A serving piece for Aunt Julia—a cold-meat fork for Aunt Louise—six butter spreaders for Cousin Ella—a steak set for her brother's wife—salad forks for my sister—a gravy ladle for a friend—" He paused.

"Anything else?"

"Worst of all—a twenty-six piece set for her sister."

Holmes looked at him quizzically. "That magazine you're carrying has something to do with it. Otherwise you wouldn't have brought it here. What is it?"

"*The Farmer's Wife.* I saw her making notes in it before she went shopping. Tonight I looked to see if I could find them—"

"Yes?"

"Page 29 is missing!"

Holmes picked up his own copy and began to thumb through it.

"The solution is simple," he said. "Mrs. Wentworth bought Wm. Rogers & Son Silverplate. You can buy twice as much of that silver for thirty-five dollars as you imagined possible. Every piece is heavily plated with pure silver and reinforced with extra silverplate where the hardest wear comes. Every piece carries an unlimited time guarantee—if you are ever dissatisfied with the service it gives you (for fifteen, twenty, thirty years, or as long as you have it) the silver will be replaced."

"How do you know all that?" gasped young Wentworth.

"I'm reading it from the Wm. Rogers & Son advertisement," smiled the great detective. "That's the page Mrs. Wentworth hid from you. That is how she got twice as much silver as you thought she could buy. Check up this advertisement and you will see that the things she purchased cost exactly thirty-five dollars and ten cents."

Wentworth smiled sheepishly. "I'm going home to tell her what a fool I've been and apologize."

Again the great detective gave evidence of his master mind. "Don't do it," he advised sagely. "Tell her you've been in conference. Merry Christmas!"

A Real Christmas

By M. Jamison Trachsel • December 1928

Until they moved out West onto the big ranch in the plains, Jerry and Jane had always spent Christmas day at Grandfather's big farmhouse where all the cousins, uncles, and aunts gathered for a happy time together.

"It won't seem like Christmas if we can't go to Grandmother's," sighed Jane. "It was so much fun to hang the big glass ornaments on the tree on Christmas Eve, and play Christmas games before we went to bed."

"I thought we might have a Christmas tree of our own this year," Mother said, hopefully. "I didn't think it wise to have glass ornaments sent through the mail but I ordered several boxes of tinsel ribbons. They came just before the big snow. I am sure that there is nothing prettier than a tree hanging with silver ribbons."

"But where will we get the tree?" Jerry asked.

"I had expected to have one sent out from town, but now the big snow here upset my plans. It really is a problem."

There was a long silence. Presently Jane said, "Well, Lizzie Stone says that she never saw a Christmas tree and never had a celebration." Lizzie was one of several children of the family of the sheepherder, who lived down by the gorge, and all had grown up away from church and Sunday School. "My, how surprised Lizzie was when I told her what good times we had at Christmas."

"Lizzie and Jim and the rest of them would be welcome to come to our tree if only we had one," said Jerry. "We could play some Christmas games if they were here."

Mother sat up very straight. "We will ask them. Mr. Stone will be away, for Father had to send him over to see about the sheep wintering on the west range, but Mrs. Stone will enjoy helping me with dinner. Tree or no tree, we will have a special dinner. Wasn't that why we raised turkeys and wasn't that why we saved back a fine young gobbler when the other went to market? Jerry can go down and ask them as soon as it stops snowing."

Jerry looked out of the window. "It has almost stopped. I think I will put on my snowshoes and go now." He stood a moment looking out of the window then whirled about excitedly.

"Mother! That scrubby tree out there by the road! It's no good, is it? Why can't we have it for a Christmas tree?"

"The very thing!" Mother and Jane ran to look at the tree. It was small—but little better than a shrub—and its branches were of bare leaves.

"There are lots of small branches and twigs to hang the silver ribbons on," said Mother.

"We can whitewash the branches and glue cotton to the tops to look like snow. Then if they do show through it won't matter."

Jane liked Jerry's plan of whitewashing the tree, "I will make some little chains of colored paper and string some popcorn to hang on it," she offered.

Mother spoke up quickly. "You have given me an idea, Jane. We will make some popcorn balls with red vegetable coloring in the sugar. Won't the pink balls look pretty and won't they taste good? And we can use some of our birthday candles."

"Oh!" Jane was jumping up and down in her excitement. "Could we put a cookie doll with a red sugar dress on the tree for everyone?"

"There will be a cookie doll with a red sugar dress for everyone."

Jerry got his snowshoes. "I'll bet we can show Jim Stone and Lizzie and the rest of them what a real Christmas is like. I'll just bet we can!"

School was out of the question when the snow was so deep, so there was time enough, but not any more than enough. The week flew by like an exciting dream. Jerry and Jane were so busy and so happy they no longer sighed about missing the good times at Grandmother's. While Jerry worked on the snowshoes, Jane cut out pretty pictures from the magazines and made a muslin picture book for the littlest one of the Stone children. She also helped Mother make a doll for Lizzie Stone. It was made from a white stocking and stuffed with rags, its nose, mouth, and eyes were outlined with black thread and painted with watercolors, its hair was loops of brown yarn sewed into its head. But when it was dressed in neat gingham rompers it was a very pretty doll indeed.

Then came the making of Christmas pies and puddings and the decorating of the tree. Jerry and Jane were sure they had never seen a prettier tree. They carefully trimmed into the night before Christmas while they listened to the Christmas carols that came over the radio. They did not light the candles. These were not lighted until they saw Mrs. Stone and the children trudging through the snow very early the next morning.

How surprised those children were!

Jerry said it was worth much more than a week's work just to look at Jim's face when he saw the tree. And when he caught sight of his name on the tag tied to the snowshoes—well, no one seemed able to say anything but "Ohs" and "Ahs."

Jim wanted Jerry to show him how to use the snowshoes and when they got back dinner was on the table—a real Christmas dinner with turkey and all the other good things. Then came the Christmas games.

Late in the afternoon Mr. Stone came through the snow, bearing on his shoulder a box that held all the Christmas good things Grandfather, Grandmother, and all the aunts and uncles and cousins could get into it. The postman had succeeded in getting the box as far as the shelter cabin on the west range where Mr. Stone was watching to see that the sheep weathered the storm. As soon as it had stopped snowing he had started home, going out of his way in order that the new people on the ranch might have their Christmas box on time. As he trudged along he was wishing his own children might have a taste of Christmas. And there they were as happy as could be!

They shared in the Christmas nuts and candy in the box and were as excited over the gifts as Jerry and Jane themselves. But Lizzie Stone did not think the beautiful doll that came for Jane was one speck nicer than the one she had found on the tree. Jane, seeing her joy in the homemade doll, went and hid her face in her mother's lap.

"Why, Jane dear," said her mother. "What is there to cry about?"

"I don't know," Jane smiled though her tears. "I feel so good on the inside I want to cry."

Jerry snorted scornfully, "Well, I'll say there's nothing to cry about. This is a real Christmas if there ever was one."

"Yes," echoed Father, Mother, Jane, and the family of the sheepherder. "Yes, this is a real Christmas."

It Is Christmas Where Love Is

By Ada Melville Shaw • December 1925

As we notice the date line December 25 on this copy of *The Farmer's Wife*, someone is heard to exclaim, "Christmas will be here in no time!"

Christmas!

May I tell you what it used to mean to me, when I was still too little to have been drawn into the whirl of grownups' preparations for the Great Day of the Feast? It meant something mysterious in the air, something I could not have put into words. I had been told over and over the story of the Birth of the Child and on Christmas Eve I used to stand by the window and try to melt a little clear place on the frosted pane so I could see the sky. My mind was full of pictures: a queer place called a manger and a baby with a shining something around his soft little head; gentle animals standing quietly about; stars and A Star and strange folk called "wise men" with priceless "offerings" in their hands; a field of sheep and shepherds and angels and a song. I would steal secretly out into the wintry night and listen—would these angels perhaps draw near the earth and sign again? Then back into the warm house which was filled with delicious odors—of piney branches and spiciness from the kitchen. Then there was Santa Claus and a church service, although it was not Sunday, and bursts of happy hymns and burning candles and the incense and candle smoke, laughter and mystery, and being tucked into bed to dream and waking up in the tingling cold of Christmas morning to a bulging stocking hanging from the fireplace, a sparkling tree, smiling dear ones in their best clothes, and always in the back of my mind that lovely mystery of the Star . . . Angels . . . Shepherds . . . Wise Men . . . a Mother and a Child . . . and then, as a crown and conclusion of all else, a secret and firm determination that after this I was "going to be good for ever and ever."

The years have made me a woman and my hair is graying, yet on Christmas Eve if I can get away long enough from the hurry and rush, the tiredness, the shopping, and the confusion, there floats to me across the years some of the sweet old feeling and I lean out of the window and look up at the stars, hush the noise of my breathing and my thoughts. . . . That minute or two snatched out of the crowded hours is my real Christmas and dearer to me than any other part of the best conventional celebration the world can possibly offer.

Children's Page
So Little Girls Play with Dolls?
By Elizabeth C. Wherry • December 1934

The toy store was gay with red and green Christmas decorations. There were toys on shelves, in boxes, under counters, and all over the tables. There was one whole counterful of dolls.

A woman stopped before this counter and said to the clerk, "Dear me! Why all the dolls? Don't you know little girls don't play with dolls anymore? They want roller skates, or books, or games for Christmas but they don't want dolls."

The dolls could hardly believe their china ears. Their lips kept on smiling because they were made that way, but their sawdust hearts sank.

When midnight came of course all the toys came alive and the dolls began to talk.

"Whatever was the matter with that woman?" cried the penny dolls. The baby doll in the highchair burst into tears. The lady doll in the pink silk dress said, "If I hadn't been wired in my box I'd have fallen in a faint."

"Won't anybody want us?" said the little girl dolls.

"Mamma-mamma-mamma," chattered the talking dolls. "Surely somebody will want us. Our voice boxes are bigger and better than the ones last year's dolls had."

"B-but you're not b-broken," stammered the big-as-life baby doll. "I've a crack in the back of my neck. N-nobody will want me."

There wasn't a cheerful doll on the whole counter. If little girls didn't play with dolls anymore what would become of them? It was dreadful to be a Christmas doll and not be wanted.

"Oh, oh," wailed the little boy doll. "And I've always wanted a little girl for a sister. Boo-hoo!"

That set all the dolls to wailing. Such a hubbub! The Teddy bears and gingham dogs trembled on their shelves and the games all pulled their lids down tight. The tool chests shivered until they set the saw's teeth on edge. The fire truck jumped off his shelf and rolled up to see if he could help. The only thing in the whole store that wasn't alarmed was the big red Santa in the center of the store. He blew his nose with such a blast that even the dolls were hushed.

"Now listen here," he said, shaking his finger stiffly. (He was a pasteboard Santa.) "I've been through Christmas ever since the North Pole was no bigger than a stick of candy and I've never seen a doll yet that somebody didn't want. Styles in dolls change, but little girls don't. They've loved to play house and cuddle dolls ever since time begun. A doll's whole duty is to be cheerful, cuddly, and smiling. Of course somebody wants you. Now fix your smiles and go to sleep."

Several days went by. Somebody took the lady doll in blue satin to make into a lampshade. Somebody else bought a little doll to make into a pincushion. And somebody else bought two small dolls for Christmas decorations. But nobody bought dolls for little girls. It looked as though the pasteboard Santa was wrong.

Then something happened.

Dr. Gray came into the store. "I want that big-as-life baby doll for a little girl in the hospital," he said.

"I'm sorry," said the clerk, "but the back of its head is cracked."

"Fine," said Dr. Gray. "The little girl who wants the doll to play with was in an auto accident and her head is broken, too. She'll know just how to take care of such a doll." He whipped out some tape and gauze, bound up the crack and whisked the big baby doll off to the hospital.

The rest of the dolls stared wide-eyed. Hadn't he said "the little girl who *wants* this doll to *play* with?" Now if one little girl wanted a doll, surely other little girls would.

The very next day was Saturday and little girls from all over the country came to town. They brought their fathers and mothers into the store to show them the dolls. Suddenly the dolls began to go so fast that the clerk said, "If Christmas doesn't hurry, I'll have to order more dolls."

The dolls that were left could hardly wait till midnight to giggle about it. Two days before Christmas there wasn't a doll left in the store—not even a penny doll. The big red Santa in the middle of the store never spoke again—not even after midnight.

He didn't need to! For even a pasteboard Santa knows that of course, little girls will always want to play with dolls.

Aunt Sade on Christmas
December 1928

"Christmas certainly makes a lot of work," suggested the Woman Who Lives Up the Road to Aunt Sade, as she stood watching the latter string popcorn to decorate the Christmas tree, which already stood in the corner awaiting its holiday dress of tinsel and crepe and candles.

"Yes," replied Aunt Sade, "It's a lot of work, but it's wuth it. If all th' days in th' year could be made just half as happy as Christmas I'd be glad to do the same amount of work from one year's end to the other. What's a little extra cookin' and dishwashin' and tidyin' up compared to the real faith and trust and happiness that seems to come to everybody on Christmas day?"

"I guess you're right," said the Neighbor Lady, "and it would be nice if we could have Christmas all the year 'round, for then there wouldn't be a bit of meanness left in the world. But you've seen so many Christmases come and go that I thought maybe you would begin to be tired of them. And it surely is a lot different at Christmas time now than when you were a girl, isn't it?"

"No, I never get tired of Christmas," replied Aunt Sade musingly, "and it ain't changed a mite that I can see. Of course there are a lot of newfangled toys for the children and electric lights and aeroplanes and automobiles and store candy and little things like that which we didn't know about when I was young, but underneath it all it's jest th' same now as it was fifty years ago.

"When I was a little girl I always looked forward to Christmas because I generally could count on a new doll. Sometimes it was jest a homemade rag doll and sometimes it would be a store doll with fancy underclothes and a china head. I always expected it and that new doll, no matter how fancy it might or mightn't be, got to be a kind of symbol of Christmas to me. I can still remember, as if it was yesterday, of the Christmas when my uncle in Chicago sent me a real imported doll with arms and legs that moved, and with real hair and eyes that opened and shut. I've still got that doll laid away in a trunk in the attic. I guess I was the happiest girl in seven counties that Christmas morning long, long ago.

"And to this day I still kinda reckon Christmas in terms of new dolls, and I guess every girl or woman is the same if you could peek into their heart. The older I git the more I appreciate 'em and it's just the same today as it was in 1870."

"But," put in the Lady Who Lives Up the Road, "you surely don't expect to get a new doll every Christmas now, do you?"

"Don't I?" smiled Aunt Sade. "With six sons and daughters grown up and married, and all of them home each Christmas, I look forward to a real live new doll every year—and it ain't often I'm disappointed. Yes ma'am, Santy Claus still remembers me."

The White House Makes Merry

By Evelyn Crane • December 1935

"It was always said of him, that he knew how to keep Christmas well, if any man alive possessed the knowledge. May that be truly said of us—all of us! And so, as Tiny Tim observed, 'God Bless Us, Every One!'"

The time is Christmas Eve, 1934, the place is the oval study of the White House, the famous voice reading the beloved lines is that of the President of the United States, his audience is his family.

The custom dates from the first year of the President's marriage . . . this gathering of the family around him every Christmas Eve as he reads Dickens' Christmas Carol. They are all there . . . from three-year-old Grandchild Sara Roosevelt to eighty-year-old Sara Delano Roosevelt, the President's mother.

Christmas is the great family celebration of the Roosevelts. And all the good old American customs have been added to the traditions that Jacobus, founder of the American branch of the family, brought over from Holland.

Mrs. Roosevelt extends Christmas the year 'round in that thrilling way of women . . . Shopping! She buys tempting things and puts them away. By the time Christmas rolls around, she has accumulated enough merchandise to fill an entire third-floor room. Last year, her gifts to the president included a half-dozen ties. Don't you dare laugh! "The Misses," as Mr. Roosevelt calls her, stoutly maintains that the ties were "the kind he likes." The President himself refuses to be quoted.

The White House 1935 Christmas will probably duplicate in many ways the previous year's. Let's go back to Christmas, 1934.

At five o'clock Christmas Eve, the President presses the button that lights the community tree in Lafayette Park. It is the signal that ushers in the Christmas festival for all Washington. Later in the evening, the White House is serenaded by carolers in red and green costumes such as might have been in vogue in Dickens' time. Spruces and poinsettias flank the White House portico, pine-coned wreaths bloom in the windows, and the great satin-tied wreath on the gleaming white door welcomes the visitor. All like a scene on a picture postcard . . . a lovely and fitting prelude to the time-honored custom of reading the Christmas Carol.

It is long past midnight before the President retires. The last sight his drowsy eyes take in is the row of children's stockings hanging by the fireplace in his bedroom.

Mr. Roosevelt is usually a late riser. But gracious, not on Christmas morning! He had been but a few hours in the land of dreams . . . it is 6 a.m. to be exact . . . when he is aroused by what must seem like bombs dropping on his bed. His grandchildren have raced from their beds just a few doors away to catapult themselves into his bed. They are anxious to see what Santa Claus has brought them.

Soon above their shouts of childish rapture echoes the President's gleeful guffaws, that laughter for which Mrs. Roosevelt once scolded him as "rude, crude, and vulgar, thank heaven!" Now it draws to Grandfather's room the entire Roosevelt clan. Gifts are brought to Grandfather's bed, opened, inspected, oh'd and ah'd about.

Presently, Mr. Roosevelt must shoo them all out to give him a chance to dress. He joins them later at the family Christmas tree erected in the spacious second-floor hallway. Here other gifts assembled at the foot of the tree are distributed. It's a breathtaking tree, a-glitter with icicles and shiny baubles, an enormous silver star on top, and dozens of candles.

Downstairs in the historic East Room, the 25-foot spruce for the public has electric lights. But nothing but honest-to-goodness wax candles of horse-and-buggy days will do for this private tree. Mr. Roosevelt denied to a joshing Congressman that his campaign against the power utilities is responsible for his insistence on wax candles. The President likes the smell of burning wax which recalls other Christmas nights at his Hyde Park estate on the Hudson.

After breakfast, the President and his entire family drive through Washington's tree-lined avenues to St. Thomas Church. A formal dinner is served at night in the state dining room. The huge turkey is one of the thousands of gifts and cards that pour into the White House at this season.

So ends another Roosevelt Christmas night. The dying candles cast a gentle glow over the portraits of past occupants of the White House. Their spirits people the stately rooms and carry one back to other Christmases . . .

Celebrating the Yule
How We Gladdened Our Home
with the Christmas Spirit of Merrie England
By a Western Farmer's Wife • December 1915

My boys were still little fellows when they got hold of the idea of writing down "what we want for Christmas." There was nothing radically wrong with this but there was a better way of doing. While still in the impressionable years they were mine to lead into the better way of making Christmas the occasion for giving joy to others.

In my childhood it had been my privilege to enjoy the British yuletide festival which covers something over a month and combines merriment in the family and of one's friends and neighbors, with the Christmas spirit of remembrance for those who are under stress of sickness or sorrow. There were so many things to be planned for and by the children in this annual season as old England observed it, that I longed to introduce the festival into my own home.

It would take one a long time to read just how and why and how the different holidays and customs came to be woven into the English celebration of yuletide. What I wanted to do, however, was to glean the loveliest, best part of them that our Christmas season might be alive with its original purpose of happy thought for others.

We were living in California where, oddly enough, there are to be found a very few of the old customs. The mid-winter vacation begins early in December and permits five weeks' merrymaking. When we live in other parts of the country, we can enjoy yuletide only at weekends, but when we are on the ranch we observe, just as far as you can, a genuine yule such as our ancestors enjoyed.

The word *yule* carries two meanings, standing for a winter month and also for the idea of jollity. So it became linked up with our fest of Christmas. Open fireplaces were in every house and the log for the Christmas fore was to be bigger and make a brighter blaze than any other log of the years' burning. So it came to be called the yule log. It was cut and hauled home with shouting and joy and rolled into place on Christmas Eve with all sorts of jolly ceremonies that made the poor forget their troubles, cheered up the sad, and set generosity a-stir in everybody's heart.

With much glee and delighted recalling of my English childhood I planned for our first yuletide ceremony—a merry frolic for young and old. I remembered the Yule Swain who came on December sixth, sent as we youngsters were told, by good Saint Nicholas—you can find out who he was in your encyclopedias and dictionaries!—to find out who among the children are "being good" and whether they are preparing to give joy to those less fortunate than they. Our American Santa Claus has some similarity to St. Nicholas.

I prepared my children by telling them about the Yule Swain and his mission. They responded gloriously and I could tell you many touching tales of their dear plans for "being good" and doing good to others.

Just before bedtime on the appointed day, in strode our mysterious visitor. He said he had come on a goat which waited for him outdoors! Our Yule Swain was as tall as the ceiling, dressed in flowing garb not unlike the costumes Santa wears, with big red beard and wig. He discoursed not about what he should bring to us but about what we should do for others, promised to report truly to St. Nicholas, and disappeared into the night followed by cheers and laughter and generous impulses.

The makeup of the merry Swain is not in the least difficult. A boy sits astride the shoulders of a tall man and the double figure is covered with the full, floor-length parti-colored gown which makes him look like a giant. Red, green, and white are the Christmas colors. The sleeves are enormously long and full with slits through which the tall man's hands appear, the lad's hands hidden underneath helping to make the gestures all the more ridiculous.

In England the Yule Swain used to make his call beginning December sixth, every night until Christmas Eve. This may not be convenient nor desirable. Why not do as we once did—induce him to be a neighborhood saint giving his service for every night of the ten days before Christmas but appearing at a different home each night? The children will be wild to know where he will turn up next. He fits into any and all plans for others' joy. He never helps any child think about "Number One."

December sixth is also Pantomime Night in "merrie England" and is made very elaborate in town and theatre celebrations. We brought it down to our own "made in America" plans by helping the children get up a single play requiring little costume but plenty of spirit. Mother Goose rhymes reproduce splendidly. Charades are always enjoyed. Yule Swain stumbles on to the scenes at the close of the play and proceeds with his investigations.

During the ten days leading up to Christmas Eve, the family's spare time was devoted to making gifts, finding out where the choicest greens grew, gathering and preparing them, planning always for someone who needed us, and watching for the Swain who kept his witching tab on all.

During this getting-ready time great interest gathered about the preparation of a little stable, manger, tiny doll dressed as a baby, and large doll made to represent a mother. These were to be put at the base of the Christmas tree as a simple object lesson to keep childish minds directed to the heart of the Christmas thought and doing.

We made a stable out of cardboard—a cracker box will do. The manger was a box standing in the middle of the stable floor, filled with hay or straw and covered with a small cloth over the rear end. On this cloth lies the tiny doll. The mother-doll bends over the manger. She is dressed in a loose robe, light blue or white, gathered at the neck. Tiny toy animals stand near. English children have the stable and manger completed before December seventeenth and it is laid away till the twenty-second but as we do not closely follow the traditional stories, it is sufficient to have it ready for the foot of the Christmas tree.

Beginning December seventeen five days compose the Feast of Misrule. During this time the young folk have nightly charades and masquerades. We planned to have the five parties at five different homes thus adding to the neighborhood sociability, keeping them very simple and never forgetting the spirit of Christmas. A chosen leader, called the Abbott of Misrule, dressed something like Santa Claus but not masked, presides over these jollifications. On the first day of Misrule a gaily decorated box is placed where no one can possibly ignore it. In this small gifts are dropped for the carol singers or "waits" who later in this program of Christmas events will besiege the doors with their music.

All this brought us jubilantly up to December twenty-first. "To mump" meant to beg, and the poor had special license then to go door to door begging for food, cast-off garments, and other practical help. Our home celebration of Mumping Day was that we then distributed to needy ones whatever we could spare, not for their Christmas gift, mind you, but just for a help-along that, given at Yuletide, is all the more in the spirit of the days.

From Mumping Day—and how the Swain did quiz us about that!—till Christmas Eve, we used spare moments (sparing all we possibly could by eating simple meals, everybody helping to get work out of the way) in getting garlands, greens, other decorations, holly, and mistletoe into place. The mistletoe fable was originally very lovely: the plant seems to have done something naughty and was placed in the care of a sky-goddess who promised it should never again do evil until it touched the ground. Since then the beautiful parasite has grown on trees and when two people met under the smile of the waxen berries they greeted each other with a kiss of love and peace. Of course lovers always slyly watch the mistletoe!

On Christmas Eve come the waits or carol singers. The waits were the watchmen who told off the flying hours and proclaimed to Old England's king that

> "A child this day was born
> A child of high renown
> Most worthy of a sceptre,
> A sceptre and a crown."

How the children loved the carol singing! I have faith to believe that when they lifted their sweet shrill voices under the Christmas stars something unspeakably lovely took root in their young hearts.

When Santa Got Stuck

By Myrtle Jamison Trachsel • December 1926

"Great lollipops and gumdrops!" cried Santa.

Mrs. Santa on the other side of the fireplace looked up at him over her spectacles. "What in the world is the matter?"

Santa reached for a chocolate drop before replying. "I have an idea," he said.

"Now, Santa," scolded his lady. "I am sure that is nothing to get excited about. You have had ideas before. And besides you really must not eat so much candy. Sweets make you take on flesh and if you get much fatter you will stick tight in some chimney."

Santa had often been scolded for eating so much candy but how could he help it with a candy factory right there in his own house? However, he did want to tell about the idea so he sat down again in the fat chair. He was about to reach for a pink mint when he saw Mrs. Santa's eye upon him. He tried to look innocent.

*Light a Christmas Candle, Neighbor,
In your window let it shine,
It may help to tell the story
Of the Christ Child's love divine*

"Every year," he said, "I send my little elves out to get the names and addresses of the children who are good enough to deserve presents. But now there are so many children I need all my elves to help make the presents. This is the splendid idea: I will build a big wireless station and listen to what the children say. I may even find out what they want without waiting for the letters that often come too late."

"That is a splendid idea," Mrs. Santa agreed.

Hour after hour Santa sat before his fire with his radio tuned in, listening to what the boys and girls all over the world were saying. Beside his easy chair was a long roll of paper upon which he wrote the children's names and the things he had discovered about them.

Often he would leave the comfortable chair by the radio to go through the shops and inspect the newly finished toys. At such times he would stop at the candy factory and fill his pockets with peppermints. Then he would listen in as long as the peppermints lasted.

"Here, here," he said to Mrs. Santa one day, as she sat knitting by the fireside. "I must order a special little bicycle made for Sarah Smith. She loaned her tricycle to her playmates and never scolded the least bit when they broke it."

Santa hurried away although he had emptied only one pocket of peppermints and Mrs. Santa laid down her knitting to take his place by the radio.

"Such a strange thing happened," she told Santa when he returned, the empty pocket filled with red hots. "A boy named Clarence says he didn't believe there is a Santa because he has never seen you."

"He won't be expecting any presents if he doesn't believe in me," said Santa, "but I should like to ask him if he saw the wind that blew off his cap the other morning."

When it came time to deliver the presents, Santa was sure he had just the thing each boy and girl deserved. That was because of the splendid idea. Santa loaded up his sleigh and hitched his reindeers to it. He might have had a big airplane. Yes indeed! All the little elves who helped him deliver presents in other parts of the world had them. But the reindeer would have been disappointed if they had been left behind.

"Now, Santa, please don't try to go down the chimneys. You know you have grown much too fat," warned Mrs. Santa as he was starting.

Santa knew his good lady was right and he meant to take her advice. Presently he came to a house with a wide old-fashioned chimney.

"It would seem just like old times to go down that chimney with my pack," he told his reindeers. "Sneaking in at the windows is no fun."

He climbed up on the chimney and began to let himself down inside. At first all was well, then the first thing he knew he was stuck tight, his arms and his pack still above the chimney top. He pushed and pushed but could not lower himself another inch. Then he tried to pull himself out but with no better success. Poor Santa could neither go up nor down! What should he do? "It will never do for the children to find me here in the morning," he thought.

Then he remembered the splendid idea. He knew each little elf has made himself a radio just as soon as Santa had finished his. Perhaps he could wireless a call for help. He could. So all over the world went his call and, discovering that he had not crushed the pocket where he carried his gumdrops, he munched away while he waited. Presently the air was full of little elfin airplanes. Each one threw Santa a rope, then they all rose in the air in fine formation like an orderly flock of birds and easily pulled Santa out of the much-too-tight chimney.

"Ah," chuckled the jolly fellow, "wasn't that radio a splendid idea?"

Rural Recreation
Christmas That Brings Joy to the Entire Neighborhood
By Constance D'Arcy Mackay • December 1915

They have a fine old way of celebrating Christmas in Boston. On Christmas Eve a huge, gaily decorated Christmas tree is set on the common. When darkness sets in the people gather about it and sing the good old songs and carols. While this is going on bands of youngsters with lighted candles in their hands march through the streets of the city singing carols at the top of their fresh young voices. In every house thus visited, candles are set in the windows and wreaths are hung.

At least part of such a celebration is possible in the country. If you live in a village, the tree may be set up at some central point and everyone contribute to it. Some will give popcorn, others the simple ornaments and candles. The children can make strings of light-colored tissue paper rings that will show well at night. Large lumps of suet are sometimes hung on the tree so that the birds also have Merry Christmas.

You have no idea what delight and interest such a tree will create. Practice the carols long enough beforehand so that every one will be fully prepared. Have people present with pitch pipes to lead off. Each singer should be provided with the written words so that all may have a share in the singing. You have no idea how lovely this scene looks to bystanders nor how wonderfully sweet and clear the voices sound on the crisp air.

After the singing around the tree is over, let the little carol singers, with some grown persons to lead them, march through the village street and sing beneath the windows of those who for some reason may not have been to the general celebration; in these windows let candles shine and wreaths be hung. In old England long ago the singers were rewarded with something to eat and if hot gingerbread and cocoa greet some of the youngsters, it will be more Christmas-y than ever.

If your town is large enough to have a mayor, appoint a committee to present the plan to him that he may appoint a Christmas committee to help carry the celebration through.

Sometimes excellent results are obtained by having different organizations responsible for several different details. The Boy Scouts and the girls' clubs can sing and other organizations see about buying the music and the tree. The plan should be nonsectarian, everyone having a part in it.

The following carols are delightful: "Lordings, Listen to Our Lay"; "Oh, Come with a Noise, My Merry, Merry Boys"; "God Rest You Merry Gentlemen." For hymns select such as "Oh, Little Town of Bethlehem!" and "Holy Night, Silent Night." Perhaps you may have foreigners in your community who will be willing to sing a Christmas hymn in their own tongue. This will greatly add to the interest.

If you live where farms are very far apart you can scarcely have the tree and the carols. But you can have a merry group of young folk bundled into sleighs or onto a big wagon filled with straw to drive from farm to farm to sing their carols.

Then there is the Christmas celebration in the town hall with a tree and music. If you wish to be more elaborate, show lantern slides of pictures on religious subjects appropriate to the occasion. Perhaps one or two phonographs could be borrowed. For most phonographs there are good Christmas carols records such as "It Came Upon a Midnight Clear," "While Shepherds Watched Their Flocks by Night," "The

First Noel," and so forth. The entertainment comes to a climax by the whole audience singing carols and choruses.

Some of you may live on prairie or plain far from growing trees and for other reasons find it difficult to provide an evergreen. Then have a Christmas ladder topped by a huge silver star as one farm community did. They wound the ladder with dark green tissue paper, festooned it with green and holly, red and gold and silver till it looked like a magic thing. On the top they put the huge star of cardboard covered with silver paper. The presents were hung from the rungs of the ladder, those whose names began with A or B finding theirs on the first rung and so on.

Following is a program that may be substituted for the lantern slide and phonograph plan. It is also used to advantage in country schools.

Recitations: "The Three Kings" and "Christmas Bells"—Longfellow.
Carols: "A Set of Carols"—Kate Douglas Wiggin. *A Set of Old-Time Carols.*
A Christmas Shadowgraph, Play, or Tableaux.

For decorations there are red and green garlands already mentioned that can be bought by the yard. Wide and inexpensive crepe paper borders, a yard or two in each, come in the piece. On these borders are represented Santa Claus and his galloping reindeer with a snowy landscape behind them, or Santa Claus climbing down a chimney with his pack of toys on his back. They are invaluable for decorating schoolroom or church parlor or for a border for the platform in the auditorium where your grange or farmers' club meets. The gay tissue paper for these decorations is carried by nearly all general stores, drug, and jewelry stores—in fact any that handle stationery.

For children's songs, "Santa Claus"; "Snow"; "Twinkle, Twinkle Little Star" are appropriate. They are in the *First Reader of the New Educational Music Course* published by Ginn and Company, Boston, Massachusetts. "Santa Claus" is an especially attractive song.

The best and most reliable shadowgraph is given in the *St. Nicholas Book of Plays and Operettas*, the Century Company, New York City.

As there are very few Christmas plays published for adults, perhaps a short farce is as merry an entertainment as one could give to wind up the evening. Harper and Brothers publish quite a list of these in cheap paper-covered editions.

The Birds' Christmas Carol, by Kate Douglas Wiggin, affords delightful pictures for a Christmas tableaux.

Christmas Tree

By Marie Mitchell • December 1936

Throughout the year there were just two really important social events in our town. One was the Fourth of July. The other was Christmas Eve, when each of the three Sunday schools held its annual Christmas tree and entertainment.

The Methodists usually had the best program because of the Harris family being Methodists. Each Harris, from ten-year-old Flossie up to Albert, leader of the town band, could sing, and play at least one musical instrument. I blush to record that envious Baptists and Presbyterians sometimes resorted to most un-Christian wiles in a desperate effort to convert the Harrises and thus improve the quality of their own programs. But the Harris family stood firm, assisting other churches only in revival and Union meetings.

We Baptists did pretty well though. We had the Barton sisters, Ada and Alma, whose spinster souls found emotional outlet in an overwhelming devotion to church work. And what the Barton girls lacked in musical ability, they made up for with a stern determination that caused the most unruly small boy to give time and thought to his part.

We older girls spent endless hours in discussion of the new dresses we were to have for the program. These were of greatest importance because in most cases they would be our Sunday dresses until spring. Usually they were of serviceable brown or blue woolens, stitched with care by tired fingers that must sandwich the task in between intervals of baking and washing and churning. But there was always some special dress-up touch, gold buttons or lace collars or bright colored silk piping. The year Stella Long had a changeable blue and green taffeta with an accordion pleated skirt, it almost caused a scandal in the church. "Outlandish, decking a child out like that," was the adult verdict. But we all envied Stella.

"What do you s'pose you'll get off the tree?' was another favorite topic of conversation. It was important to have your name called at least twice. Some lucky children received seven or eight presents. And there were always the forlorn few who gazed wide-eyed at the program and the tree and were thankful for the "treat," a red-and-green-striped paper sack of hard, mixed candy distributed to young and old alike.

Chores were done up early on Christmas Eve so that the important business of getting ready could begin. Father shaved, even though it was the middle of the week. Mother hurried around, laying out clean underwear and stockings, with special attention to the appearance of those members of the family who were on the program. Her own toilet, affected at the last minute, was usually made by running a dampened comb through her long hair, twisting it into a smooth coil, and buttoning herself into her good black silk with the lace collar and bar pin that Father had brought from Kansas City one time when the cattle sold well. As a last touch she might rub her face vigorously with a chamois skin dipped into the box of pink powder that stood on the dresser.

We all walked the half mile from our house to the edge of town to the church, since it would never have occurred to anyone to hitch up Dexter and Kate for that short distance. We children watched closely for any bulges in Father's overcoat pocket, or Mother's handbag, that might indicate presents. We were somewhat depressed by the absence of any signs thereof, although we knew from past experience that parents almost always took the things to the church in the afternoon.

And then we were at the church with its brightly lighted windows and the dark fringe of horses and buggies and wagons bordering the hitchracks around the churchyard. People were coming from all directions, some with lanterns if the night was dark, although it seems that most Christmas Eves of long ago were clear and starlit.

Inside there was the scent of cedar and pine and steaming overshoes and coal oil lamps turned too high, mingled with the faint, pervasive odor of mothballs from old Mrs. Minott's fur neckpiece. The green and red tissue paper bells that decorated the aisles were somewhat lopsided from being in the Sunday school room since last Christmas, but nobody noticed. All were looking at the tree. Jim Brown had cut the biggest cedar from the patch of timber on his south forty. Even trimmed down, its green tip brushed the ceiling. Glittering with tinsel and festoons of popcorn, hung with handkerchiefs and toys, it was a sight to gladden any youngster's eyes.

At the Christmas program, as at any other church gathering, the audience was divided imperceptibly, but none the less definitely. Two rows of pews in front were reserved for the young performers. Next came a phalanx of proud parents, the mothers wearing slightly worried expressions that would vanish only when May or Georgie had successfully passed through the ordeal of Speaking a Piece.

Behind this section sat the young couples who were "going together." And no matter how casual their relations heretofore, if a young man asked a girl to go to the Christmas tree, things were getting serious. It meant, too, that he would buy her a good present. A comb and brush set, a bottle of perfume. Even a locket and chain, or a set of furs ordered from the mail-order catalog at $9.98, if he were a free-spending young man and very much in love. A hazy aura of romance and Sen-Sen, of white rose perfume, and hair on which the curling iron had lingered a second too long, hung over this part of the church.

Sitting in the last row of seats or leaning against the walls were the unattached males of the community, and around the big stoves huddled the old men. On a level with the rostrum and a little to one side was the choir, its collective ankles modestly concealed from view by a short green curtain hung on rungs from the low brass rails that divided the musical from the non-musical.

Promptly on the stroke of seven-thirty, the minister rose to his feet and the buzz of conversation subsided. There was a prayer. And then Mr. Whirsett, the Sunday school superintendent, stepped to the front and announced in stentorian tones that "First on the program will be a song by the school!" Pretty Alice Montgomery, who was marrying the high school principal in the spring, adjusted the organ stool, pulled out all the loud stops, and swung into the march. The program had begun.

When the last agonized small boy had stuck hopelessly in the middle of "The Night Before Christmas" and the last four-year-old had been stricken with stage fright and been borne screaming from the platform, there came the dramatic silence that preceded the entrance of Santa Claus. Even though you were eleven years old and knew that it was only Clyde Hudson, the town barber, you couldn't help feeling that thrill of half-fearful excitement that had been yours as a mere child of six or seven. And then he arrived with a jingling of sleigh bells and much talk of reindeer and the perils of the trip from the North Pole. After that the evening was a jumble of laughter and talk, of names being called and presents distributed to the rustle of tissue paper and the crunching of hard candy.

It was ten o'clock when we started home, the younger children stumbling along half drugged with sleep. Brother Joey was voluble over a new pair of skates, and I hugged the bulky package that was my new comb and brush set and pictured the beautiful pink and gold of it lying on my bureau.

Trudging along in the chill, starlit silence behind Mother and Father, the excitement of the Christmas tree faded and something of the real spirit of the night seeped vaguely into our careless minds.

Mother was humming softly the refrain of one of the songs the choir had sung, "Oh, little town of Bethlehem, how still we see thee lie . . ." We wondered, Joey and I, if our own little town that lay so quietly against the dark earth, wasn't something like Bethlehem. Looking up into the cold blue winter sky, we speculated as to which of those big, glittering stars had been the STAR. The hills south of town, we decided, might have been the ones where the shepherds watched their flocks. And so real was the fancy, that I was almost sure I could hear music—strange and clear, and sounding a long way off.

The Gardener at Christmas

By the Gardener • December 1938

In the nigh onto fifty years that I've sojourned hereabouts, many a Christmas has come and gone. I've been thinking back, trying to figure out which was the happiest of all. I believe it must have been the year my brother and I got the monkey for a present. That was the same year we had our first Christmas tree, too, for Christmas morning we found the monkey at the top of the tree.

It was just a little woolen monkey, dark gray, not more than three or four inches long. There it was, on the tree. Somehow it set that Christmas apart from others of my boyhood. I would be surprised if mother doesn't have it yet, stored away somewhere with the things that mothers keep for long years after the children have gone away.

We were living on the Valley farm in those days. Usually we had no Christmas tree but instead, we children would "set our plates." We'd put a plate on the dining room table. Next morning it would be filled with candy and an orange or two. Country folks had oranges but seldom in those days. Beside or behind the plate would be whatever presents Santa Claus had brought. It was never much we found. Money was scarce forty years ago on a little rented farm. But we never knew it wasn't much. To us, it was immense.

In those days, too, when we had a Christmas tree, my brother and I would take a sled and go up a little along the river, where we'd cut a little cedar tree—correctly, a juniper. But nowadays I like to have a live Christmas tree for the children, which I buy at the nursery, already planted in a candy bucket painted green. This stands erect without any trouble and holds its needles. After the holidays are over we plant it out somewhere.

A Christmas Editorial
December 1916

My childish Christmases on the farm were exceedingly meager, compared with what most children of the present generation consider a proper holiday. My earliest memory is that of hanging up my stocking to the awesome thrill of a vivid visualization of prancing reindeer and a red, rotund form. Realization brought only a doughnut man, a beautifully polished apple, a new dress of suspicious likeness to one my mother had worn, and a fascinating Dinah doll made from a black stocking, gowned in Turkey red, and turbaned in yellow. I had no slightest feeling of disappointment. I was happy in the excitement of surprise and in the air of festivity my mother had managed to impart with a few sprigs of evergreen and a partially savory smell coming from the oven.

I am telling you these homely incidents to show you how little, after all, it takes to make a small child happy and to give pleasant and lasting memories as long as his life is kept simple and sweet.

I know how every normal mother longs to bestow upon her child such fascinating toys as the Christmas shops thrust under her covetous nose and I know that it takes a leveler head than most of us can boast to withstand their temptation. I know how difficult it is to deny ourselves the pleasure of buying carts and barrows and engines and tracks but I know, too, that a bushel basket full of blocks of all sizes and descriptions gathered up at a carpenter's shop or sawed from two-by-fours and colored with Easter egg dyes, will give greater and more lasting entertainment than any number of smashable toys bought at the ten-cent stores.

Of course if the child is taken to the stores while the Christmas orgy is on, he will hold out both hands and bellow lustily for everything in sight. Equally of course because he is a child, his disappointment at not getting everything in sight will be short-lived and if desire is not abnormally aroused, he will be very happy with what he gets.

The child's tastes and wants are simple. It is we who covet for him and so arouse his own thirst for useless and burdensome possessions. If we consider the child absolutely, his immediate happiness and his ultimate good, we would try harder to make his hours happy through constructive play and his memories sweet by harmonious and peaceful surroundings.

We do not take the Christmas holiday simply enough. We make it a burden instead of a pleasure. Above all things and aside from all gifts, we want to make it a beautiful day, a day from which the early anticipatory rising of the first eager child, to the last hour of retiring, is full of sweet associations, unhurried and lingering delights, tender communications; a day of love and peace and forgiveness; a day of good will and generosity; a day to be eagerly awaited and long looked back upon.

—*Della Thompson Lutes*

Christmas Night
KATHERINE EDELMAN

There's a teddy bear upon the stair
And a sleepy clown in the big arm chair;
There's a soldier of war upon his back
And a fast mail train that's off the track;
There's a woolly dog with an awful bark
And a motor car, with a place to park;
There's a man of war, with a mast and sail
And an auto truck of U. S. mail;
There's noise and confusion every place
But a boy of six wears a shining face.

Christmas in the Red Flannel Decade

By Alta Booth Dunn • December 1930

I

As we open the big white gate and jingle up the driveway this Christmas morning so glittering and blue, you will see that my grandfather's farm is one of many acres of field and woodland—all well kept and prosperous. Some of the guests for the day's festivities dash up in smart, red-painted cutters; but we are in the roomy old bobsled of home carpentry, the youngsters snuggled cosily in the bright straw at the back, under the gay log-cabin quilt.

Grandfather's house, which is large, painted white with green shutters, wears an air of comfort and permanence in its setting of shrubs and evergreens which, diamond-dusted with snow, gleam like "the plane tree the Persian adorned."

Below a little knoll stands a big red barn with a bull's head painted above the sliding doors; grouped conveniently about are carpenter and blacksmith shops, cribs and granaries, poultry and hog houses. These bespeak the diversity of farming operations and the self-sufficiency of this small rural kingdom. Nor must I omit mention of woodshed and "summer" kitchen—arenas of interesting seasonal and rainy-day activities, such as the repairing of implements, oiling of harnesses, and mending of fly-net; the making of lard and sausages and other butchering-time arts; the curing of the autumn crop of hickory, hazel, and walnuts, and their subsequent delectable cracking and eating; corn popping and doughnut frying.

The driver pulls the team, Dandy and Pet, up sharply at the old oak stepping block, and throws back the buffalo robe to let us women and children out. Bundled up in seal plush cloaks and red yarn mittens, azure, rose, and cardinal beaded nubias, and high arctics, we jump out awkwardly, like seals flopping off a cake of ice into the sea.

Now meet Grandfather, who calls out a hearty, "Howdy—a happy Christmas to you all!" as in fashion truly rural he comes out to help put up the horses for the day.

Grandpa is a tall man, gaunt and slightly stooped. His hair and chin whiskers are iron grey. He is wearing his Sunday blacks and a mangy fur cap (on which he dotes), jauntily cocked. This rakish headgear somehow gives an accent of jocular profanity to his otherwise ministerial aspect. He is indeed a deacon in the church and son-in-law of a circuit-rider of the famous Peter Cartwright school. But Grandpa's quizzical blue eyes belie a sober, almost stern countenance. He dry wit and caustic comment proclaim him but one generation removed from the "ould sod." His relish in telling a doubtful yarn at times causes Grandmother to exclaim reprovingly, "Why John—before the children!"

II

But come, hurry up the path to the warm house! How the snow creaks and scrunches underfoot—zero-ishly! Enter the kitchen. For where but in the kitchen would you find an old-fashioned country housewife of a Christmas morning?

As the door swings in we are simultaneously assailed by a wonderful smell—a composite of roasting fowl and savory stuffing, fresh-baked mince pies, steaming plum pudding, hickory smoke—and Grandma's cordial "Christmas Gift!" for she is from Virginia and still clings to [that] phrase. And the warmth and geniality of your true southerner are always marked in her hospitality. Amply proportioned, she is symbolic of the largeness that obtains over the whole farm.

Here there is always bounteous food for the household and welcome for the chance guest or the wayfarer at the back door, and lendings unaccounted to improvident neighbors. Smallness, the petty and the niggardly, are alien here. And here, in addition to a plenitude of substantials, the cooky jar and doughnut crock are everbearing and the pie perennial. Truly a food paradise to the child . . .

And now, if you please, meet me—a wiry, leggy, plain-faced, tow-headed girl-child of eight or so. Indeed if you had (though who but the minister or the book agent ever did?) formally lifted the knocker at the front door opening into the long hall, with its marvelous tessellated flooring of green-and-red oilcloth, you probably would literally have met me whizzing down the steep black walnut banisters, shamelessly showing my red flannel "combinations"—no short and simple flannels of the poor. Not that I can recall actually wearing such hectic underthings, but I vaguely remember that once this flamboyant fabric was all the rage. And *rage* must have been right! But doubtless a peeping wrist or neck band of scarlet on this occasion lent an appropriate and decorative Yultide touch to the costume—sort of a personal hanging of garlands, as it were . . .

III

. . . So the great house is warm and cheery, although the windows are all painted with glistening frost scenes. The Christmas party is scattered throughout; the women are hurrying back and forth between kitchen and dining room, preparing the holiday feast, and visiting over church and neighborhood affairs, recipes, fancywork, and that never-obsolete topic—babies. The men are off to themselves smoking and (I regret to report) some of them chewing. The children scamper hilariously all over the house . . .

IV

But how loud our childish voices sound as we exclaim over the Christmas tree that reaches clear up to the ceiling in the bay window! O, it's splendid with festoons of popcorn, cranberries, and rose haws; its golden balls that really are oranges and crimson ones that are "Jonathans;" red taffy-on-a-stick; molasses popcorn balls; "snow" of cotton wool and candles all ready to light. How spicy the pine smells in the heat of the room! Sniff! Sniff! and see how the sunlight makes rainbows in the glass prisms of the hanging lamp—beautiful!

At last the grown folks are all seated at the great, bountiful table!

Someone hisses "S-h-h!" Abruptly a hush falls. Grandpa is going to ask the blessing. He utters a few simple phrases earnestly, reverently, as if he meant them. He is a plain man and outspoken, and generally *does* say exactly what he means, both to God and man; now heads are lifted and napkins unfolded.

My, how good things smell! Suddenly I am aware of an awful hungriness. Grandma is a famous cook. But as it the custom, children must wait for the second table. But by standing well back from the door in the back parlor I may politely feast my *eyes* on the table, which of course will not *look* so nice by the time we get there.

The moss rose china is in use, pieced out with the tea set with the fat brown robins on it. Both are so pretty that it is a double delight to have them on the table at once. They, too, are reserved for company events. Then there are the "coin silver" teaspoons, spade-shaped, delicate, and thin. With only a monogram on the handle they are austerely beautiful.

But my dears, let us see what there is to *eat*: Roast turkey, corn bread stuffing, and giblet gravy; cold sliced fresh ham; celery sticking up in a tall glass suggesting a bouquet; mashed white potatoes and browned sweet ones; ruby cranberries in little green glass dishes like baskets; odiferous onions which we young ones spurn; spiced peaches in a brown glass log cabin; amber honey in a fluted clear glass dish; three colors of jelly on a glass plate, and a lot more goodies. But what can be in that darling funny dish shaped like a hen sitting on her nest? Cold slaw, maybe, or pickled beets richly colored as American Beauties. Gracious but that big fruitcake looks good with its fancy white icing and Merry Christmas outlined in red hots!

One of the boy cousins jerks my long yellow braids and says, "C'mon, play hide-and-seek—there's dandy places to hide in *this* house." And I say "all right" and scoot away upstairs and whis-s-sh down the banisters again in sheer exuberance. After we have exhausted the mysterious hiding places, we play drop-the-handkerchief and authors and other games in one of the big rooms upstairs.

Pretty soon the noise gets so fierce that Cousin Hetty calls, "Children–children–*chil*-dren!" warningly. Whereupon ensues audible silence for a few moments. Then we commence to play again so as not to think about our appetites.

Presently Grandma comes to the foot of the stairs and calls "Come to dinner, my dears; I know you-all must be sta-arved!" And I feel proud that she is Grandma to me only; and just Aunt Mary to the others.

The minute her back is turned I make for the banisters and the rest follow the leader or troop down the stairway. Next we sit down to the table and find that dear thoughtful Grandma has saved some of the white meat and other choice goodies for us children. Then we attack our heaped-up plates and—there just aren't words to tell how good everything tastes! "Yes, thank you—some more, please!"

V

By the time the best china and glassware and silver have been carefully washed and put away, and the delectable leftovers set in the pantry, it is almost dusk. The relatives are beginning to leave. It is pleasant to think that Papa and Mamma and I, Cousin Karl, Great-uncle Robert and Great-great-aunt Susan are to remain overnight . . .

When the chores are done we gather in the back parlor to light the candles on the tree. It is the happiest time of the day for me. I sit by the fire on the little stool with the dog done in shaded crewels, dreaming and holding my big wax doll that Santa left on the tree.

"Mercy, child!" Grandma startles me by exclaiming from her rocker near me. "Look at your pretty dolly—get back from the stove—quick!"

I look and wail a long "o-o-oh . . . oh, oh, oh!"

It is the tragedy of an otherwise perfect day. For my pink-and-white waxen beauty's face has sagged horribly and no amount of lifting can ever fix these poor distorted features.

"It's too bad," consoles Grandma, "but never mind, childie; we can get her a new head, but you must remember that wax dolls are delicate creatures . . . "

Presently I realize that I am afraid to go upstairs to bed alone; so Mamma says that I may take a nap on the sitting room lounge. I like this, for it has a cornhusk mattress and a gorgeous red-flowered calico cover and the oddest turned spindles at head and foot, reminding me of Medusa's hair of twisted snakes.

After a long time I wake up, as Grandpa gives a loud yawn that sounds like the "Ow-ooo" of a coyote. Then he declares, "It's ten o'clock and time for prayers and bed."

Then he stretches his long arms and gets down the big shabby family Bible and reads about Mary and Joseph and the Child in the Manger; the shepherds tending their flocks by night; the star in the east; the wise men bringing gifts of frankincense and myrrh to the Child in swaddling clothes.

As I take Mamma's hand and stumble drowsily upstairs to bed, I wonder what swaddling clothes are—and frankincense and myrrh. What funny people the Mary-and-Josephs were—sleeping in the stable with the stock—but nice though, and interesting. I'd like to know them better. Sleepily getting into the trundle bed that slid out from under the big bed, I think as my tired body begins to feel like it is floating in air, that my grandfather's farm is the nicest place in all this world to have a Christmas party.

The Boy Who Makes Trapping a Hobby Prepares for Santa Claus

The Little Clay Man

December 1930

Among the things on Jerry's Christmas tree was a box of modeling clay. One piece was red, one was yellow, one was green, and the fourth was brown.

Jerry liked to play with the clay because it did what he wanted it to. He liked to roll it and punch it and press it. He liked to make things of it.

He made a Little Clay Man. He made the head of red clay, the coat and shoes of brown, the trousers of green, and on the top of the head he put a wide yellow clay hat.

Jerry played with the Little Clay Man until he was tired. He climbed up on the couch to rest. The couch was in front of the window so he put the Little Clay Man on the windowsill.

No sooner did Jerry's tired little head touch the big sofa pillow until he was sound asleep. But the Little Clay Man didn't fall asleep. He felt very lonely.

"I've never been a man before," he said. "I believe I'll take a walk." He tried to look out of the window behind him, but his clay neck was too short and sticky. He couldn't twist himself around, for his brown coat was too thick and stiff. So he lifted one foot. "T-s," it said as it pulled away from the windowsill. Slowly he turned around on the other one.

Outside the window he saw a bird on the feeding shelf. He started to walk toward it. "T-s, t-s," his sticky brown feet said as he walked across the windowsill. He had never seen a windowpane before. He didn't even know it was there. He was much surprised when walked smack up against it.

It flattened his nose down between his cheeks and the little round buttons on his brown coat were smashed out like tiny flat pancakes. He was stuck rather tight, but he pushed until he got away. Then he walked slowly up and down the windowsill.

He stickily lifted one foot up and forward. "T-s," it said. Then he leaned over and fell stiffly onto it, for of course he hadn't any knees to bend. And that was the way he had to walk. First on one foot, "T-s," and then on the other "T-s." Up and down the window sill he walked—"T-s, t-s, t-s." But there was no way to get out to the shelf where the bird was eating sunflower seeds. There was always that pane of glass that he could see through, but couldn't walk through.

He turned himself toward the living room. There was a dog sleeping on the rug near the fireplace. "I'll go play with him," thought the Little Clay Man.

He tried to jump from the windowsill to the couch, but his right foot stuck and tripped him and he fell down the crack behind the couch with a sticky thud. It was quite a bump, for it smashed one of his brown coat sleeves so tightly against his brown coat that he couldn't get loose. The brim of his yellow hat was bent down over one eye and there it stuck.

But the Little Clay Man got bravely up and stickily marched out from under the couch. "T-s, t-s, t-s," said his funny, chunky feet.

The dog was awake. It stood up and stretched its legs. It looked ever so much bigger to the Little Clay Man than it did when he was up on the windowsill and the dog was lying down. The dog stretched its neck and opened its mouth with a wide yawn.

"Goodness," thought the Little Clay Man as he saw the dog's sharp teeth. He was terribly frightened and tried to turn and run, but in his excitement, he forgot how.

All he could do was pull up one foot, "T-s," and then the other "T-s." He had quite forgotten how to lean forward and fall over onto his feet. He tried to push his yellow hat brim away from his eyes with his loose brown arm. He thought he might see something to hide behind. But his arm wouldn't reach to his hat. Jerry hadn't made it long enough. He tried to put his arm back down but it stuck to his chin.

"Dear me! Dear me! What a pickle I am in!" thought the Little Clay Man.

All this time he was lifting his feet, "T-s, t-s, t-s," trying to remember how to walk.

Then the dog saw him and growled a deep "Gr-rr-rr." The Little Clay Man was so frightened that even his feet forgot to go up and down anymore. The dog's growls wakened Jerry. He picked the Little Clay Man from the floor and said to the dog, "Bouncer, did you knock my Little Clay Man off the windowsill?"

Bouncer came over, wagged his tail in a most friendly manner, and sniffed the Little Clay Man. The Little Clay Man was very still but he was no longer afraid. He and Bouncer became the best of friends but the next day Jerry made the Little Clay Man into a clay basket, so they never went walking again.

Russell Sambrook

A Briarville Christmas
Santa Claus Entertains the Children
By Maude Meredith • December 1910

We had never had a public Christmas tree in Briarville. And as Christmas Eve fell on one of our regular singing school nights, I suggested that we have a tree.

"Now, ladies," I said as we discussed it, "this will not be to show off gifts, but just for the sociability of it. Those who wish to, bring any presents for their families and friends of course, but the real object is a good time."

Singing schools were held on Saturday nights, the men seeming to select that day. So, of course, we had time to sweep the schoolhouse and set the tree before dark.

We arranged it in the one big corner where the classes recited, and I stretched sheets across the front, to hide the tree from the children. We made great numbers of little candles, and Petie, in a burst of enthusiasm, had bought us little wire fasteners to hold them on. We strung the tree with red apples, many of them shining crab apples, and from a prearranged little fund we had bought oranges enough to give one to each child in town. And then here was our one innovation. We had little paper bags, enough for one apiece all round filled with fresh popcorn. On the stove stood melted butter.

I had sprinkled a filmy tuft of cotton along each limb of the green tree, being very, oh, very careful, to put none near a candle. The illusion was good. It looked like a tree loaded with snow. In behind the tree crept John, before the first child came in, and cautiously hung his string of sleigh bells where he could make them tinkle, as Santa Claus' reindeers drove up.

Over the very opposite corner some of the young people sang a Christmas carol and all faces were turned to them. As they sang we girls hurriedly lighted the candles, and just as the singing closed, I cut the string that held the shielding sheets, and let them fall.

Well! Well! I shall never forget the faces of those children. For a long moment they gazed with open mouths, speechless, then one little tot caught his breath and cried: "Oh, Mama, what is it?" Every one clapped then, and the children let loose in squeals and giggles of delight. That one minute paid me for all the work I had done, a dozen times over.

When we had quieted down, Santa appeared, from his corner, and took down, and called off presents, in the usual way but so very unusual was it to these home-staying children, that many of them had to be led out by their embarrassed mothers to get their presents. They were afraid of Santa.

That great snowy Christmas tree, with its twinkling candles, its fruit, its gifts, and bags of homemade candy, certainly marked an epoch in the lives of every little child in Briarville.

As Santa passed out the presents, the girls and I filled the little paper bags with the fresh popcorn, sifted in salt, and poured over a dash of butter. They were all filled and placed in baskets by the time the gifts were distributed and, with the red-cheeked apples in baskets, we passed them around for our evening refreshments.

People gathered in little groups, some sitting, some standing, and ate popcorn and apples.

The farmers talked of their crops and cattle, and the best seed for next spring's sowing; the women talked of their babies, and housework, and the young people—

well, young people can always find enough to joke and laugh about, and the tots hugged their presents, and raced each other up and down the aisles.

When the popcorn was finished we had music. Violin, with songs; violin and organ; and both with more songs.

Yes, I know "Grand Opera" would have been convulsed. But, remember, "Grand Opera" never visited Briarville, and I venture to say that in all human probability there were many of the older people there who had never heard better music. Certainly they enjoyed it.

Now this first Christmas tree of Briarville had not cost us a penny, except a few candles, an armful of wood, and the oranges, and it was talked of and referred to until the next Christmas came around.

On cold and stormy nights, all winter, the elderly people and the tots stayed at home, as was best, and we had a full attendance on all pleasant nights.

I suppose I should explain that the horses did not stand out in the wind, as the neighbor nearest the schoolhouse offered his big barns for hitching them inside, so that they were quite as comfortable as if at home.

We had "straw rides" on many pleasant nights. Some of the young men packed their wagon boxes with straw, and stopped from house to house until they had a load packed in snugly under the robes. These rides were the most fun of all, I believe, as usually they were composed of young people.

Beside this we had a nursery. There were five young couples in town, each having a little one, and no one at home to leave them with. Now any well-balanced baby will sleep like a bear cub after a ride in the pure cold air, but to sit an entire evening on a hard school seat, and hold a sleeping child, that was not so easy, especially at the end of a day's work. So a crib was improvised. Two boards sixteen-feet long, one the very widest to be had, one about twelve inches wide, were nailed together in a V. two holes bored in the ends of the narrow board, with rope run through ending in a loop. Two spikes driven high to loop the ropes on. Now the wide board was laid on a bench running along the wall, the ropes fastened, and nice little beds made in behind the board that stood upright, for the safe bestowal of the babies. Here they slept like cherubs through all the song and laughter.

At the end of the evening this improvised crib was shoved up through the little trap—out in the cloakroom, into the garret, to be pulled down the next time the babies came.

Now to those who have had parents or friends living with them when they began life, this may seem silly, but to the young couple starting life alone, who feel that they can almost never go out of an evening because of the baby, a little plan like this is admirable. I never did feel that it was right for the young father to leave the wife alone to tend the baby; that is an added hardship for the girl-wife, and yet what kid-boy of, say, twenty-two or three, is really fitted to give up all social companionship? Anything that will make it easier for the young couple to go about a little together, makes for happiness in the home.

When the "festivities" were over, and I was helping wrap up the babies, Ollie Haskins, tying the hood under the chin of her sleeping two-year-old, said to me: "Rosie Hudson, I just bet you thought up this; and don't you know what a good time I have had."

Then came the hullabaloo of "good nights" and "Merry Christmas," shouted uproariously to each team as it drove away from the front door.

The boys removed the big tree, I gathered up my mussed sheets, we shut the stove secure and tight, went out and locked the door, and drove gaily away home.

The Little Lost Cranberry
December 1930

Eileen helped with the preparations for the Christmas dinner by washing the cranberries. Somehow she let a little red cranberry slip through her fingers. It fell unnoticed to the floor and rolled under the edge of the kitchen cabinet.

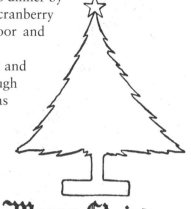

Merry Christmas

The little cranberry thought it quite a joke at first and laughed till his rosy sides shook. But he didn't laugh when he saw the beautiful red cranberry jelly that was turned into the mold. "Oh now I can't be set upon the Christmas table tomorrow," said the Little Lost Cranberry. Then Eileen took a cupful of cranberries that was left and strung them on a long thread to hang upon the Christmas tree among all the toys.

As Little Lost Cranberry saw her carry the shining string away he said, "Oh, I wish I were in that cranberry chain. I do so want to see the Christmas tree."

Poor Little Lost Cranberry! It wasn't really his fault that he was lost and he did so want to have a part in the Christmas fun! He knew it would do no good to shout, for Eileen didn't understand Cranberry-ese and would think it was just the fire crackling.

Night came, everyone went to bed and there was scarcely a sound until the clock struck midnight. "Merry Christmas," sung out the Angel Food Cake. "Merry Christmas," answered the Pumpkin Pies. Then everything began shouting, "Merry Christmas," and when Little Lost Cranberry shouted his "Merry Christmas" in rather sad, muffled tones from under the cabinet everybody asked in surprise, "Where are you?"

Little Lost Cranberry explained his sad plight and everyone was so sorry for him. They knew Eileen hadn't meant to drop him, but what a dreadful thing not to be part of the Christmas dinner.

"Maybe they'll find you when they sweep in the morning," said the pickled peaches.

"They might use you to decorate the top of the salad," said the turkey.

"No," said the maraschino cherries. "We're to do that."

"So you are," said the turkey hopelessly.

Now Mrs. Penny Bun Dough in her crock on the warming oven had been raising slowly, slowly to the top of her bowl. She lifted the lid ever so little and cast one doughy eye about the moonlight kitchen. "Why don't you get to work for yourself, Little Lost Cranberry? I'd never raise if I didn't work. You can't raise but you can roll."

Just then the cellarway mouse came along hunting for Christmas crumbs for his family. "The very thing," said the Angel Food Cake. "I'll give you some crumbs, Mr. Mouse, if you'll start Little Lost Cranberry rolling out to get into the Christmas fun."

So the cellarway mouse gave Little Lost Cranberry a bit of a boost and away he went. He rolled out from under the edge of the cabinet, across the patch of moonlight on the floor, and in through the dining room door.

But there didn't seem to be any way of getting into the Christmas fun in the dining room . . . so he rolled on into the living room. There on the floor in the firelight sat the loveliest thing Little Lost Cranberry had ever seen. It was shining and sparkling like the silver casserole, white and frosty like the Angel Food Cake. It looked up and said in a tinkling voice, "Merry Christmas, Little Cranberry."

"Oh," gasped Little Lost Cranberry, "You look like a fairy."

"I am a fairy. I'm the Christmas Fairy. I go about on Christmas Eve to visit happy homes. Everything was so pleasant here that I sat down to rest a minute. The children are having happy dreams, the Christmas dinner things are looking forward happily to being eaten, the toys are happy, even the tree is happy." And she pointed to the corner where the tree twinkled and shone in the firelight.

"My word," gasped the astonished Little Lost Cranberry. You see he had never seen a Christmas tree before. There on the branches hung the shining string of cranberries calling out, "Merry Christmas, Brother!"

"Why aren't you up there, Little Cranberry?" asked the Fairy.

"Oh," said Little Lost Cranberry, "I fell out of Eileen's hand when she was washing us and I rolled under the cabinet where no one saw me, and now I can't be part of the Christmas fun." And he burst into juicy red tears.

"Dear me," said the Fairy. "This will never do." Flitting over to the tree she looked everything over very carefully. Suddenly she clapped her hands and said, "Roll over here, Little Lost Cranberry. Here is a Gingerbread Santa Claus who has lost his raisin nose. I'll paste you in the dent where his nose used to be."

Little Lost Cranberry was so excited that he got redder and redder and when he was pasted into place all the toys set up a shout of laughter for he looked ever so much more like a Santa Claus nose than a purple raisin did.

"Good night," said the Fairy as she rode away on a moonbeam.

"Merry Christmas!" everything shouted back. And the gayest farewell of all came from the Gingerbread Santa Claus' nose, for the Little Lost Cranberry was now a part of the Christmas fun.

Clubs Carry Christmas Cheer
December 1932

The clubroom was all a-stir with high-school girls who were filling the rows of baskets on the table with food and toys for some of the needy families living in the neighborhood.

"Isn't it fun playing Santa Claus?" said Judy as she picked up a basket to be filled with good things.

"I'm going to pack the basket for the Beards," said Mary. "I'd love to see all those youngsters when they find the candy dogs and canes that are in this box."

"Oh, say! I have an idea!" Ruth's face was all aglow. "Instead of just packing these things in, let's fix them up like we do our own Christmas presents, with bright paper on every package, yet each one different. That would make the basket much more exciting."

"Let's do, and put little surprises in each package."

With twice as much enthusiasm the girls started to work. They shared paper and wrapping cord so that each basket would have a variety of wrappings.

Mary slipped a pink hair ribbon in one of the sacks that went to the Beards. The jointed giraffe, when wrapped, looked like a round soft bundle, and the plum pudding that was baked in the coffee can was the most elegant package of all after the sprig of holly was slipped under the ribbon on top.

At dusk the girls started delivering the baskets, which had lost their "market" look. And the girls themselves now looked like Santa himself, so round and red were they.

Judy went with Mary to the Beards because she wanted to see "all the little Beards" when they saw the basket.

After setting it on the doorstep they knocked on the door and then disappeared in the dusk. Luckily for them the lamps were lighted in the Beard kitchen so they could see the little fellows through the back window. Almost breathless, they stood there watching the mother take out the packages, then they walked gaily home.

"Isn't it fun, Judy," whispered Mary, "to give Christmas cheer."

Althea Ann's Christmas Spirit

By Elizabeth C. Wherry • December 1932

There were two dolls on the West Prairie Christmas Tree. One wore a pink silk dress and had a cream lace hat on its long yellow curls. It was a very stylish doll,

The other wore a blue print dress with a homemade cap on its straight black bon. It was an everyday sort of doll, but its clothes looked as though they might come off and on.

The pink silk doll's clothes had a sewed-on look. Althea Ann thought a little girl could have lots of fun with the everyday doll, but she loved pink silk and cream lace. She'd never had a stylish doll before and she did hope this one would be hers.

There was only one other little girl at the West Prairie Christmas party. That was Sally Blake and she was looking at the pink silk doll, too. But there was such a big family and such a small house at Sally's that surely a pink silk doll would be out of place there.

Suddenly, Mr. Garner, in his red Santa Claus suit, came jumping through the window. His glasses gleamed behind his pug-nosed Santa Claus mask and he said, "Ho-ho-ho," and "Ha-ha-ha," so hard he almost blew the mask off.

Althea Ann and Sally squeezed each other and giggled. Althea Ann felt all rosy and shaky inside like a bowl of jelly salad. She felt quick and prickly as though she had stepped on a thistle—a pleasant thistle—if there was such a thing. And she giggled at the very idea.

Presents began to come off the tree. New paints, hankies, a game, a cunning tub and washboard, some red mittens, and a storybook were piled in Althea Ann's lap. But Althea Ann was watching the pink silk doll. When Mr. Garner took it down, she shut her eyes and held her breath. What if it belonged to Sally Blake!

"For Althea Ann," said Mr. Garner in a very loud voice.

Althea Ann opened her eyes and breathed again. There lay the pink silk doll in her arms. She touched its hair, smoothed its silk shirt, and stroked its tiny shoes. She was so busy looking at it that she didn't hear Mr. Garner say, "This is for Althea Ann, too."

And he laid the everyday doll in Althea Ann's lap.

The rosy jelly and pleasant thistle feeling grew and grew. Two dolls! A pink silk one and an everyday one!

But what about Sally Blake? Sally was looking very sober. She had a lapful of mittens and shoes and hankies—but no doll. All of a sudden the rosy jelly and nice thistle feeling inside Althea Ann went away. Instead there came a feeling like the cake that she had baked all by herself—flat and lumpy and a little soggy.

She looked at the pink silk doll. She looked at the everyday doll. She looked at Sally. She remembered how Sally had looked at the pink silk doll. Althea Ann's cheeks burned and her eyes stung. She walked straight to Sally Blake.

"There's been a mistake," she said. "The pink silk doll is yours."

She laid it in Sally's arms and the very second she did the lovely rosy jelly and pleasant thistle feeling came back. When she saw Sally's eyes, silver bells began to tingle in her head. She felt like an angel food cake beside a crystal candlestick. She felt like a spice cooky with a raisin in it. She felt like a kitten purring on the hearth.

"Whatever is the matter with me?" she giggled to the everyday doll. She touched her hot cheeks. "I must have something.

"I do have something," she said to the everyday doll. "It's the Christmas spirit."

Letters from Our Farm Women
Christmas Every Day
December 1933

Dear Editor: It seems to me that farm people in this country have Christmas every day compared to what we were used to in my native Norway.

About clothes for instance. There are not many farmwomen or girls here who haven't at least one best dress of silk. Well, that was something I never saw on one single farmwoman all those years I lived on a farm in Norway. Silk underwear and stockings were also unheard of there.

I am talking about farm folks, not city folks. The latter lived quite the same as they do here. But on the farm when someone was going to have a new suit or a new dress, we had to spin and weave. Stockings for the whole family were knit from yarn we had spun ourselves. Of course we bought a few yards of cotton goods for blouses and summer dresses, but that was just about all.

And as for food, that was as simple as possible: Meat, potatoes, salted-and-smoked herring and flatbrod (something like rye crust only thinner and made of oat flour). For dessert—when we had any—there was some kind of sweet soup, either of milk or of berry juice made from berries. Sometimes in summer we would pick berries and make a pudding for Sunday. When one thinks of all the pies and puddings, ice creams, and cakes that are consumed during the year on the farms in this country, why it does seem that we ought to be satisfied.

We think we have hard times on the farms in this country, but if our sisters in the Old Country had half of what we have here, they would consider themselves very fortunate.

—Norwegian-American, North Dakota

Letters from Our Farm Women
Christmas Chimes
December 1934

Dear Editor: I suppose everyone has a memory of a childhood day that is outstanding and unforgettable. Such a memory is the Christmas Day when I was eleven years old.

The rule was, no one up until Mother and Dad had the fires going. But Mother and Dad knew how anxious we were to be up and investigating, and the fires were made early.

It was six o'clock Christmas morning, dark outside and dark in the front bedroom. Five huddled bundles of bedclothes in upright positions were conversing in gusty whispers. We could hear the kitchen stove lids clattering, and presently a fire roaring in the living room heater.

Then, while we waited for the call that would give us permission to get out of bed, through a sudden silence there came sweetly and clearly soft music. It was magical in the cold, dark room—those warm, bell-like tones chiming slowly over and over. They were the Christmas Spirit incarnate, living, breathing, uplifting. I think even the younger children felt the spell, for their wriggling little bodies were quiet and tongues ceased impatient whispering. For a long moment the charm held, and then small feet hit the floor, and the door was flung wide, flooding the room with light.

Of course, it wasn't magic. Just three tin angels holding three small bells and so arranged that the whole thing fitted over the top of the heater, where the warm air revolved it, ringing each chime in turn. With a slow fire the chimes were slow and sweet, but when we built up a hot, quick fire, they played a merry, dancing tune.

I have been thinking how that simple little melody has enriched my life. Since I found them, I have often improvised, in my small way, simple melodies and sonorous chords around those notes.

I think you will agree with me that such little things as these—or are they little?—are happiness.

—Happy, Iowa

Answers to Your Letters
December 1920

N. B.—Good for you! We might start a society for the abolishing of kissing games. You and your little group of friends can be the charter members. I wonder who else wants to come in? Just to prove to you that I am heart and soul in this movement, I am going to tell you about some games and contests that can take their place for the holiday parties to which we are all looking forward.

First there is the Lobster Race for boys. The contestants stand on all fours and move backward as quickly as possible. The one reaching a designated line first wins.

Then there is the Cracker Relay Race. Twelve or sixteen may play. They stand in rows, each one supplied with a cracker. At the signal, the first one in each row begins to eat his cracker and as soon as he can whistle after eating his cracker, the next one begins. The row which finishes first wins.

In a Newspaper Race, each contestant is given two newspapers, one for each foot. He places one forward and steps on it with his right foot. Then he picks up the other for his left foot and so on, being allowed to step only on newspaper, racing to a given mark and back.

A Feather Blow is fun, each guest being given a feather which he blows at a signal; the game is to see who can keep his feather in the air the longest.

Of course you know the old game of Gossip? The players form in a circle. The first player whispers a sentence or little story into the ear of the second, who repeats it and so on, until the story comes back to the first who told it. This one then repeats aloud what was originally said and how it became changed in the telling. No one changes it on purpose but if you work fast the changes creep in—amazing ones.

Have you ever had a Silence Party at which taxes were levied for superfluous laughing and talking? They are lots of fun.

But do not forget the Candle Stunt at your Holiday or Christmas party. Get a long, fat candle; light it; choose someone to be candle bearer and another to be blower. Blindfold latter, turn her around three times, and give orders to blow out the candles. A prize may be given for the successful blower.

Above all let us not forget that:

"Cheerful looks and words are very
Sure to make Christmas merry."

And that it is our business: to be merry!

The Christmas Wish

By Myrtle Jamison Trachsel • *December 1927*

The great forest lay still and white under a blanket of snow. The pine trees looked like giant tents reaching their tips up to the sky. In the midst of them stood an orphan boy. He was a small boy but in his heart there was a very great wish—a very great wish indeed. In fact his wish was so great that he had to speak it aloud there in the silent forest.

"I wish," he said, "I wish everyone in this beautiful forest could have a joyous Christmas."

That was a very great wish, for there were many little hamlets or towns dotted here and there through the forest. Many of the people in them were poor and needy. What could a little orphan boy do to bring them all a joyous Christmas?

The little fellow sighed. Well he knew that he could do little for so many. He had nothing himself so how could he make all the people happy? But he determined to go on wishing it just the same.

As he walked along through the beautiful forest, he passed a cottage where an old lady lived alone. He noticed there was no smoke coming from her chimney.

"Perhaps she can find no fagots to burn, with this great snow covering them," he thought. "But I am strong. I can find wood for her."

He kicked around in the snow until he found wood and this he piled at her door, running away before she could thank him.

"Heigh ho!" exclaimed the little old lady hobbling to the door. "Someone with a kind heart has brought me wood just as my fire dies away. Now I can build it up and fry a cake."

She was so happy when she had eaten and warmed herself that she said, "I will fry up another cake and take it to the woman who is sick."

Quickly she fried another cake and left it on the woman's doorstep, hurrying away before she was discovered.

Now it happened that this woman's oldest son had snared a rabbit and broiled it over the fire. But there was no cake to eat with it. So the woman and her children were glad to have the cake to finish out the meal.

Said the oldest son, "I will snare another rabbit and take it to the good doctor who is making you well."

That day the doctor had driven a great distance through the snow to see a sick child. His good wife knew he would come in hungry and cold and she wished very much to have a good dinner ready for him. But the snow was so deep she had not been able to get to the village to buy meat.

"What shall I do?" she asked herself, over and over again.

Presently she heard a knock on her door. No one was in sight when she hastened to open it, but there on her doorstep was a nice, plump rabbit, freshly dressed.

"Someone has a kind heart, and I, too, would like to do someone a kindness," she said. "I will put this meat on to cook and then I will take some books over to the miller's son who loves to read. It is not far and someday, it may be, the boy will be a good doctor like my husband."

When the miller saw the glad look in his son's eyes at the sight of the books he loved to read, he thought of the wood cutter who had not been to the mill for many a day.

"Perhaps he has no money to buy flour. I will take him a sack."

The woodcutter came in from loading his wagon ready for the trip to the Baron's castle. Neither he nor his son had eaten that day. There on the doorstep lay the sack of flour.

"It is the day before Christmas," said the woodcutter. "Someone has a kind heart."

They mixed their cakes and ate them. Then they cut down a large pine tree and loaded it upon the wagon.

"A Christmas tree for the Baron, my son," said the woodcutter. "We cannot do much, but what we can, that we will do."

It was a beautiful tree, shapely and tall when it stood in the Baron's great hall; its topmost branch reached the ceiling.

"A wonderful tree," said the Baron. "Everyone should be allowed to enjoy it. Send out messengers through the forest and bid all the people come to the frolic. Let there be feasting and joyousness in honor of the Christmas season."

And so from far and near they came. Among that great company was the woodcutter and his son, the miller and his sons, the good doctor and his wife, the sons of the woman who was sick but none the less happy at the good luck that had befallen them; there was the old lady and the little orphan boy. Among all the throng that feasted and danced and sang, there was none happier than the little orphan boy. His great Christmas wish had come true.

THE
FARMER'S WIFE
A Magazine for Farm Women

DECEMBER 1921

INDEX

A

Allspice Cookies,
  Swedish, 109
Amy's Caramels, 99
Anagrams game, 172
appetizers. *See*
  hors d'oeuvres
apples
    Apple Salad, 38
    Candied Apple Slices, 87
    Scalloped Sweet Potato
      and Apple, 47
    Taffy Apples, 91
Apricot Whip, 62
aprons, 145
asparagus
    Asparagus-Barley Soup, 21
    Asparagus Tips with
      Carrots, 43

B

baby gifts
    knitted sweater, 131–132
    toy, 139
balls, homemade toy,
  136–137
Bayberry candles, 156
beauty box, 141
Beets, Harvard, 42
Belle's Cabbage Salad, 38
beverages
    Cranberry Cocktail, 11
    Cranberry Gingerale
      Cocktail, 12
    Egg Nog, 12
    Fruit Punch, 11

Mrs. Hey's Cocoa, 12
    Mulled Grape Juice, 11
Black Pudding, 65
Blanc Mange, Chocolate, 58
blocks, toy, 135
blotter, desk, 149
bookcover, 120
Breadcrumbs, Buttered, 53
breads
    Delicate Rolls, 55
    Fancy Norwegian Breads,
      55
    Hot Cross Buns, 54
    Rolls and Fancy Breads, 54
Brownies, Christmas, 104
Brussels Sprouts, 43
Burnt Sugar Candy, 96
Butter Scotch, 87

C

cabbage
    Belle's Cabbage Salad, 38
    Cabbage and Chestnuts,
      44
    Cabbage with Bacon
      Sauce, 44
cakes
    gift boxes for, 105
    Kringler, 114
    "Lady Webb" Cake, 79
    Plain Foundation Cake,
      113
    Raleigh Special Layer
      Cake, 78
    Spice Cake, 75
    Sponge Cake, 74
    See also frostings and

fillings; fruitcake
Candied Nuts, 13
Candied Sweet Potatoes, 48
candles, 156
candy and sweets
    American Toffee, 89
    Amy's Caramels, 99
    for boyfriends, 99
    Burnt Sugar Candy, 96
    Butter Scotch, 87
    Butter Taffy, 90
    Candied Apple Slices, 87
    Candied Citrus Peel, 87
    chemistry of making,
      84–85
    Chocolate Caramels, 83
    Chocolate Flakes, 99
    Christmas traditions, 88,
      90
    Cocoanut Balls, 95
    Cocoanut Drops, 83
    Cream Candy, 89
    Creamed Dipped Orange
      Slices, 102
    Creamed Walnuts, 89
    fondant, 92, 95
    French Loaf, 98
    Fruit Sweets, 100
    fudge, 93
    gift boxes for, 105, 150
    Glacéd Fruit and Nut
      Balls, 100
    kinds of, 85–86
    Maple Sugar Candy, 94
    Parisian Sweets, 96
    Peanut Brittle, 91
    Peanut Butter Creams, 92
    Peppermint Candy, 90

Pinochi, 83
popcorn balls, 101, 102
Pralines, 95
Raisin Clusters, 96
Sea Foam, 88
Soft Nut Candy, 89
Spiced Nut Meats, 100
Taffy Apples, 91
Taffy Candy, 91
Caramel Filling, 74
Caramels, Amy's, 99
carrots
    Asparagus Tips with
        Carrots, 43
    Carrot Cutlets, 44
    Carrot Soufflé, 45
    Glazed Carrots, 45
    Raw Carrot Salad, 38
Celery Stuffing, 27
centerpieces, 152, 154–155
Chair Rest, 132
Cheese and Cracker Tray, 13
Cheese Biscuits, Pinwheel, 15
Cheese Puff, 15
chicken. See poultry
Chicken Broth with Rice, 21
children. See toys and gifts
    for children
Chocolate Blanc Mange, 58
Chocolate Caramels, 83
Chocolate Cookies, 104
Chocolate Flakes, 99
Chocolate Honey
    Rounds, 111
Chocolate Mousse, 58
Christmas cards,
    137–138, 145
Christmas Stunts game,
    168–169
Christmas Sweet Tooth
    cookies, 103
Christmas Telegrams
    game, 173
Christmas Vegetable
    Salad, 40
Chrysanthemum Salad, 39
Citrus Peel, Candied, 87
clothespin bag, 148
Cockie Leekie Soup, 18
Cocoa, Mrs. Hey's, 12
Cocoanut Balls, 95

Cocoanut Drops, 83
Coffee Fruit Cake, 115
community picnics, 153
cookies
    Chocolate Cookies, 104
    Chocolate Honey
        Rounds, 111
    Christmas Brownies, 104
    The Christmas Sweet
        Tooth, 103
    Drop Cakes for Holiday
        Baskets, 111
    Dutch Christmas Cakes,
        106
    German Springerle, 106
    gift boxes for, 105
    Half-Bushel Snaps, 110
    Holiday Crullers, 112
    Honey Cakes, 105
    Love Krandse, 110
    Molasses Cookies, 107
    Norwegian Krumkake,
        108
    Old English Gingernuts,
        107
    Rolled Honey Wafers, 112
    Sandbakels, 109
    Sand Tarts, 104
    Swedish Allspice
        Cookies, 109
    Swedish Spritsbakelser,
        109
    Swedish Spritz Cookies,
        108
Cootie game, 172
Corn Custard Pudding, 47
cranberries
    Cranberry Cocktail, 11
    Cranberry Gingerale
        Cocktail, 12
    Cranberry Molasses Pie,
        72
    Cranberry Pudding, 63
    Cranberry Salad, 39
    Cranberry Steamed
        Pudding, 65
    Cranberry Water Ice, 62
    Spiced Cranberries, 42
Cream Candy, 89
Creamed Dipped Orange
    Slices, 102

Crème de Menthe Pears, 62
Crown Roast of Lamb, 32
Crullers, Holiday, 112

D

Danish recipes. See
    Scandinavian recipes
Dark Christmas Fruit Cake, 67
Dark Fruit Cake, 77
Date Tort, 64
decorations
    Bayberry candles, 156
    for community picnics,
        153
    ideas for, 127–128
    plants, 151
    for table, 152, 154–155
    wreaths and garlands,
        158–159
desserts
    Apricot Whip, 62
    Cheese Torte, 64
    Chocolate Blanc Mange, 58
    Chocolate Mousse, 58
    Cranberry Water Ice, 62
    Crème de Menthe Pears,
        62
    Date Tort, 64
    Lemon Floating Island, 59
    Maple Nut Loaf, 63
    Prune Soufflé, 60
    Römme Gröt, 61
    Sour Cream Gingerbread,
        69
    See also cakes; candy and
        sweets; cookies; pies;
        puddings
doll cradle, 135
dollhouses, 121–123
dolls, homemade, 133, 153
dressing. See stuffing
dressings. See salad dressings
Drop Cakes for Holiday
    Baskets, 111
Dutch Christmas traditions,
    129–130
Dutch recipes
    Christmas Cakes, 106
    String Beans, 47

E

easel, 135–136
Eggless Fruit Cake, 69
Egg Nog, 12
embroidered accessories, 139
English Fruit Cake, 70
entertainment
    games, 168–173
    stories, 174–216

F

Fig Pudding, 65
fillings. *See* frostings
    and fillings
Finding Partners game, 169
fireplace, faux, 163
fondant
    For the Christmas Candy
        Box, 92
    Maple Fondant, 95
Fortune Teller game,
    170–171
French Dressing for
    Lettuce, 37
French Loaf, 98
French Lyonnaise
    Potatoes, 53
frostings and fillings
    Caramel Filling, 74
    Chocolate Frosting, 75
    Frosting and Filling for
        Christmas Layer Cakes,
        73
    Lemon Filling, 74
    Marshmallow Filling, 74
    mincemeat fillings, 71
    Soft White Frosting, 74
    Uncooked Icing, 75
fruit
    Fruit Punch, 11
    Fruit Sweets, 100
    Glacéd Fruit and Nut
        Balls, 100
    See also salads; *specific
        fruit*
fruitcake
    Coffee Fruit Cake, 115
    Dark Christmas Fruit
        Cake, 67

Dark Fruit Cake, 77
Eggless Fruit Cake, 69
English Fruit Cake, 70
Fruit Cake, 115
Sallie White Cake, 78
Very Best Fruitcake, 75
White Christmas Fruit
    Cake, 67
fudge
    Fudge (basic), 93
    Fudge Chocolates, 93
    Fudge Variations, 93

G

games
    Anagrams, 172
    Christmas Stunts,
        168–169
    Christmas Telegrams, 173
    Cootie, 172
    Finding Partners, 169
    Fortune Teller, 170–171
    Guessing Game, 170
    Humpty Dumpty, 163
    Jar Ring Toss, 172–173
    Peanut Jab, 172
    Pitching Quoits, 172
    Season's Greetings, 168
    wreath circle, 159
gardening gifts, 138
Garden Salad, Fresh, 38
garlands and wreaths,
    158–159
German Christmas
    traditions, 124
German Springerle, 106
Giblet Gravy, 31
gift boxes and wrap,
    147–148, 156–157,
    160–163
gifts
    baby's knitted sweater,
        131–132
    beauty box, 141
    bookcover, 120
    book ends, 137
    Chair Rest, 132
    clothespin bag, 148
    distribution of, 159,
        163–164

embroidered accessories,
    139
embroidered pincushion,
    134
from the farm, 118–119
for gardeners, 138
gentlemen's four-in-hand
    tie, 134
hairpin case, 133
ideas for, 138, 140–141,
    147–149, 150
Jolly Jenny doll, 133
ladies' necktie, 134
letter file, 137
low-cost options, 125–
    127
lunch cloths, 139
magazine cover, 149
manicure kit, 140
match scratcher, 133
paper dolls, 142–144
pillow, 120
poster blotter, 149
pot holders, 138–139
recipe file, 128–129
scissors guards, 149
sewing book, 132
shoe cases, 145
shopping bag, 120
silver boxes, 148
slipper spool case, 133
sunbonnet work bag, 133
table runner, 120
washcloths, 138
    See also toys and gifts
        for children
Gingerbread, Sour Cream,
    69
Gingernuts, Old English, 107
Ginger Pudding, Steamed,
    69, 116
ginger snaps, Half-Bushel
    Snaps, 110
Glacéd Fruit and Nut
    Balls, 100
Golden Yam Casserole, 49
goose
    accompaniments, 25
    carving, 24
    Roast Goose, 23
Grape Juice, Mulled, 11

Gravy, Giblet, 31
Guessing Game, 170
guinea hen,
  accompaniments, 25

H

hairpin case, 133
ham
  Baked Ham, 33
  Baked Slice of Ham with
    Grape Juice Sauce, 34
  Baked Spiced Ham, 33
  Relish for Ham, 34
Holiday Soup, 19
Honey Cakes, 105
Honey Wafers, Rolled, 112
hors d'oeuvres
  Baked Mushrooms, 13
  Candied Nuts, 13
  Cheese and Cracker Tray,
    13
  Cheese Puff, 15
  Fried Oysters, 16
  ideas for, 14
  Oysters Scalloped with
    Corn, 16
  Pigs in Blankets, 15
  Pinwheel Cheese Biscuits,
    15
  Relish Plate, 13
  Scalloped Oysters, 16
horse toy, 145
hot chocolate, 12
Hot Cross Buns, 54
Humpty Dumpty game,
  163

I

Indian Pudding, Baked, 61

J

Jar Ring Toss game, 172–173
Jellied Veal-Kalve Dans, 34
Jolly Jenny doll, 133
Julienne Soup, 20

K

Kringler, 114
Krumkake, Norwegian, 108

L

"Lady Webb" Cake, 79
lamb
  Crown Roast of Lamb, 32
  Ragout of Lamb and
    Vegetables, 32
Lemon Filling, 74
Lemon Floating Island, 59
letter file, 137
Lobster Salad, 41
Love Krandse, 110
lunch cloths, 139

M

Macedoine of Peas, 46
magazine cover, 149
main dishes
  Jellied Veal-Kalve Dans,
    34
  Meat Balls, 36
  Rabbit Curry, 32
  See also ham; lamb;
    poultry
manicure kit, 140
Maple Nut Loaf, 63
Maple Sugar Candy, 94
Marshmallow Filling, 74
match scratcher, 133
Mayonnaise Dressing, 41
Meat Balls, 36
menus, for Christmas dinner,
  10, 23
mincemeat fillings
  Favorite Mincemeat, 71
  Simple Mincemeat, 71
  Spicy Mincemeat, 71
  uses, 72
Molasses Cookies, 107
Mrs. Hey's Cocoa, 12
Mulled Grape Juice, 11
Mushrooms, Baked, 13

N

necktie, ladies', 134
"The Night Before
  Christmas," 175–176
Norwegian recipes. See
  Scandinavian recipes
Nut Balls, Glacéd Fruit
  and, 100
Nut Meats, Spiced, 100

O

Onion Stuffing, 27
Orange Baskets, 40
Orange Slices, Creamed
  Dipped, 102
owl toys, from sheet
  wadding, 153
oysters
  Fried Oysters, 16
  Oysters Scalloped with
    Corn, 16
  Pigs in Blankets, 15
  Scalloped Oysters, 16

P

paper dolls, 142–144
Parisian Sweets, 96
Parsnips with Cheese, 46
party favors, 155
Peanut Brittle, 91
Peanut Butter Creams, 92
Peanut Jab game, 172
pears
  Crème de Menthe Pears,
    62
  Pear Salad with Honey
    Dressing, 40
peas
  Macedoine of Peas, 46
  Peas in Turnip Cups, 46
Peppermint Candy, 90
pies
  Cranberry Molasses Pie,
    72
  mincemeat fillings, 71
  Plain Pie Pastry, 73
Pigs in Blankets, 15

pillow, 120
pincushion,
    embroidered, 134
Pinochi, 83
Pinwheel Cheese Biscuits, 15
Pitching Quoits game, 172
place cards, 152
Plain Foundation Cake, 113
plants, 151
play house, 136
plum pudding
    Old Fashioned Plum
        Pudding, 116
    Plain Plum Pudding, 68
popcorn balls
    Candied Popcorn, 102
    making, 101
    syrup, 101
pork
    Meat Balls, 36
    Salt Pork Stuffing, 30
potatoes
    French Lyonnaise
        Potatoes, 53
    Potato Croquettes, 52
    Potato Stuffing for Roast
        Turkey, 31
    Scalloped Potatoes, 52
    St. Nicholas Potatoes, 51
    Stuffed Baked Potatoes,
        52
pot holders, 138–139
poultry
    accompaniments, 24–25
    carving, 24
    See also goose;
        stuffing; turkey
Pralines, 95
prunes
    Black Pudding, 65
    Norwegian Prune
        Pudding, 61
    Prune and Raisin Pudding,
        60
    Prune Soufflé, 60
puddings
    Baked Indian Pudding, 61
    Black Pudding, 65
    Cranberry Pudding, 63
    Cranberry Steamed
        Pudding, 65

Fig Pudding, 65
Norwegian Prune
    Pudding, 61
Old Fashioned Plum
    Pudding, 116
Plain Plum Pudding, 68
Prune and Raisin
    Pudding, 60
Steamed Ginger Pudding,
    69, 116

R

Rabbit Curry, 32
Ragout of Lamb and
    Vegetables, 32
Raisin Clusters, 96
Raleigh Special Layer
    Cake, 78
recipe file, 128–129
Red Dressing for Head
    Lettuce, 37
Relish for Ham, 34
Relish Plate, 13
Rice, Chicken Broth with, 21
Rolled Honey Wafers, 112
rolls and buns
    Delicate Rolls, 55
    Hot Cross Buns, 54
    Rolls and Fancy Breads,
        54
Römme Gröt, 61

S

Sage Stuffing, 27
salad dressings
    French Dressing for
        Lettuce, 37
    Mayonnaise Dressing, 41
    Red Dressing for Head
        Lettuce, 37
    Sweet Cream Dressing for
        Salad, 37
salads
    Apple Salad, 38
    Belle's Cabbage Salad, 38
    Christmas Vegetable
        Salad, 40
    Chrysanthemum Salad,
        39

Cranberry Salad, 39
Fresh Garden Salad, 38
inspirations for, 36
Lobster Salad, 41
Orange Baskets, 40
Pear Salad with Honey
    Dressing, 40
Raw Carrot Salad, 38
Salt Pork Stuffing, 30
Sandbakels, 109
Sand Tarts, 104
Santa Clause chimney,
    163–164
Sauce, White, 53
Sausage Stuffing, 31
Savory Dressing, 29
Scalloped Oysters, 16
Scalloped Potatoes, 52
Scalloped Sweet Potato and
    Apple, 47
Scandinavian recipes
    Danish Kringler, 114
    Danish Love Krandse, 110
    Fancy Norwegian Breads,
        55
    Norwegian Krumkake,
        108
    Norwegian Prune
        Pudding, 61
    Swedish Allspice
        Cookies, 109
    Swedish Spritsbakelser, 109
    Swedish Spritz Cookies,
        108
    See also Smorgasbord
        dishes
scissors guards, 149
Sea Foam, 88
Season's Greetings game, 168
sewing book, 132
shaving set, 141
shoe cases, 145
shopping bag, 120
silver boxes, 148
slipper spool case, 133
Smorgasbord dishes
    about, 35
    Fancy Norwegian Breads,
        55
    Jellied Veal-Kalve Dans,
        34

Meat Balls, 36
Römme Gröt, 61
snacks. *See* hors d'oeuvres
snow modeling, 124
Soft Nut Candy, 89
soufflés
  Carrot Soufflé, 45
  Prune Soufflé, 60
  Squash Cheese Soufflé, 49
soups
  Asparagus-Barley Soup, 21
  Chicken Broth with Rice, 21
  Cockie Leekie Soup, 18
  Holiday Soup, 19
  inexpensive recipes, 17
  Julienne Soup, 20
  "Soup," 20
  Spinach Soup, 21
  Tomato Bisque, 18
  White Soup, 21
Sour Cream Gingerbread, 69
Spice Cake, 75
Spiced Nut Meats, 100
spinach
  Creamed Spinach, 45
  Spinach Loaf, 45
  Spinach Soup, 21
Sponge Cake, 74
Springerle, German, 106
Spritsbakelser, Swedish, 109
Spritz Cookies, Swedish, 108
squab/pigeon, accompaniments, 25
squash
  Baked Squash, 49
  Mashed Winter Squash with Pineapple, 51
  Squash Cheese Soufflé, 49
  Zucchini Custard, 51
St. Nicholas Potatoes, 51
store play house, 136
stories, 174–216
String Beans, Dutch, 47
stuffing
  Celery Stuffing, 27
  Onion Stuffing, 27
  Potato Stuffing for Roast

Turkey, 31
  Sage Stuffing, 27
  Salt Pork Stuffing, 30
  Sausage Stuffing, 31
  Savory Dressing, 29
  Sweet Stuffing, 30
  Wild Rice Dressing, 28
sunbonnet work bag, 133
sweater, baby's knitted, 131–132
Swedish recipes. *See* Scandinavian recipes
Sweet Cream Dressing for Salad, 37
sweet potatoes
  Candied Sweet Potatoes, 48
  Scalloped Sweet Potato and Apple, 47
  Sweet Potato Croquettes, 48
  Sweet Potato Puff, 48
sweets. *See* candy and sweets
Sweet Stuffing, 30

table decorations, 152, 154–155
table runner, 120
taffy
  Butter Taffy, 90
  Taffy Candy, 91
tie, gentlemen's four-in-hand, 134
Toffee, American, 89
Tomato Bisque, 18
tortes
  Cheese Torte, 64
  Date Tort, 64
toys and gifts for children
  aprons, 145
  for babies, 139
  balls, 136–137
  blocks, 135
  doll cradle, 135
  dollhouses, 121–123
  dolls, 153
  easel, 135–136

horse, 145
  play house/store, 136
  train, 135
turkey
  accompaniments, 24, 25
  carving, 24
  Giblet Gravy, 31
  leftover ideas, 29
  Roast Stuffed Turkey, 26
  See also stuffing
Turnips with Sour Sauce, 47

veal, Jellied Veal-Kalve Dans, 34
vegetables
  Buttered Breadcrumbs for, 53
  cooking rules, 42
  Vegetable Platter Royal, 43
  White Sauce for, 53
  See also salads;
    specific vegetables
Very Best Fruitcake, 75

W

Walnuts, Creamed, 89
washcloths, 138
White Christmas Fruit Cake, 67
White Soup, 21
Wild Rice Dressing, 28
wreaths and garlands, 158–159

Y

Yam Casserole, Golden, 49

Z

Zucchini Custard, 51